PEARSON

Literature

Student Companion All-in-One Workbook

GRADE 8

PEARSON

NEW YORK, NEW YORK • BOSTON, MASSACHUSETTS
CHANDLER, ARIZONA • GLENVIEW, ILLINOIS

PEARSON

ISBN-13: 978-0-13-327117-1
ISBN-10: 0-13-327117-X
10 11 12 13 14 15 16 17 18 19 19 18 17 16

CONTENTS

UNIT 1 • PART 1 Setting Expectations

Big Question Vocabulary 1 1
Big Question Vocabulary 2 2
Big Question Vocabulary 3 3
Applying the Big Question 4

UNIT 1 • PART 2 Guided Exploration

"Raymond's Run" by Toni Cade Bambara

Writing About the Big Question 5
Reading: Make Predictions and Support Them 6
Literary Analysis: Plot 7
Vocabulary Builder 8
Conventions: Nouns 9
Support for Writing to Sources: New Ending 10
Support for Speaking and Listening: Radio Broadcast 11

"The Tell-Tale Heart" by Edgar Allan Poe

Writing About the Big Question 12
Reading: Compare and Contrast 13
Literary Analysis: Character Traits 14
Vocabulary Builder 15
Conventions: Pronouns 16
Support for Writing to Sources: Character Profile 17
Support for Speaking and Listening: Oral Response 18

"Flowers for Algernon" by Daniel Keyes

Writing About the Big Question 19
Reading: Notice Details to Make Inferences 20
Literary Analysis: Point of View 21
Vocabulary Builder 22
Conventions: Adjectives and Adverbs 23
Support for Writing to Sources: Dialogue 24
Support for Research and Technology: Summary of an Article 25

"The Story-Teller" by Saki (H. H. Munro)

Writing About the Big Question 26
Reading: Identify Connections to Make Inferences 27
Literary Analysis: Theme 28
Vocabulary Builder 29

Conventions: Principal Parts of Verbs 30
Support for Writing to Sources: Comparison of Works 31
Support for Speaking and Listening: Panel Discussion 32

Comparing Texts: "The Finish of Patsy Barnes" by Paul Laurence Dunbar and "The Drummer Boy of Shiloh" by Ray Bradbury

Writing about the Big Question 33
Comparing Characters of Different Eras 34
Vocabulary Builder 35
Support for Writing to Compare Characters 36

Writing Process 37
Writer's Toolbox: Conventions 38

UNIT 1 • PART 3 Developing Insights

"Who Can Replace a Man?" by Brian Aldiss

Vocabulary Builder 39
Take Notes for Discussion 40
Take Notes for Writing to Sources 41
Take Notes for Research 42

"John Henry" Traditional

Vocabulary Builder 43
Take Notes for Discussion 44
Take Notes for Research 45
Take Notes for Writing to Sources 46

"Julie and the Turing Test" by Linda Formichelli

Vocabulary Builder 47
Take Notes for Discussion 48
Take Notes for Research 49
Take Notes for Writing to Sources 50

"The Good News, Dave, is that the computer's passed the Turing test. the bad news is that you've failed." by Chris Madden

Vocabulary Builder and Take Notes for Writing to Sources 51

"Robots Get a Feel for the World at USC Viterbi" by USC Viterbi School of Engineering

Vocabulary Builder 52
Take Notes for Discussion 53
Take Notes for Research 54
Take Notes for Writing to Sources 55

from *Star Trek: The Next Generation*—"The Measure of a Man"
by Melinda M. Snodgrass
Vocabulary Builder 56
Take Notes for Discussion 57
Take Notes for Research 58
Take Notes for Writing to Sources 59

UNIT 2 • PART 1 Setting Expectations
Big Question Vocabulary 1 60
Big Question Vocabulary 2 61
Big Question Vocabulary 3 62
Applying the Big Question 63

UNIT 2 • PART 2 Guided Exploration
***from* "Harriet Tubman: Conductor on the Underground Railroad"**
by Ann Petry
Writing About the Big Question 64
Reading: Use Details to Identify the Main Idea 65
Literary Analysis: Narrative Essay 66
Vocabulary Builder 67
Conventions: Simple Tenses of Verbs 68
Support for Writing to Sources: Biographical Sketch 69
Support for Speaking and Listening: Skit 70

"Always to Remember: The Vision of Maya Ying Lin"
by Brent Ashabranner
Writing About the Big Question 71
Reading: Make Connections Between Supporting Paragraphs and the Main Idea 72
Literary Analysis: Biography and Autobiography 73
Vocabulary Builder 74
Conventions: The Perfect Tenses 75
Support for Writing to Sources: Reflective Essay 76
Support for Research and Technology: Multimedia Presentation 77

"The Trouble With Television" by Robert MacNeil
Writing About the Big Question 78
Reading: Use Clue Words to Distinguish Fact From Opinion 79
Literary Analysis: Persuasive Techniques 80
Vocabulary Builder 81

Conventions: Verb Mood—The Subjunctive 82
Support for Writing to Sources: Evaluation 83
Support for Research and Technology: Snapshot 84

"Science and the Sense of Wonder" by Isaac Asimov
Writing About the Big Question 85
Reading: Use Support for Fact and Opinion 86
Literary Analysis: Use Word Choice to Convey Ideas 87
Vocabulary Builder 88
Conventions: Active and Passive Voice 89
Support for Writing to Sources: Response to Literature 90
Support for Speaking and Listening: Speech 91

Comparing Texts: "Forest Fire" by Anaïs Nin, "Why Leaves Turn Color in the Fall" by Diane Ackerman, and "The Season's Curmudgeon Sees the Light" by Mary C. Curtis
Writing About the Big Question 92
Literary Analysis: Comparing Types of Organization 93
Vocabulary Builder 94
Support for Writing to Compare Types of Organization 95

Writing Process 96
Writer's Toolbox: Conventions 97

UNIT 2 • PART 3 Developing Insights
from *Travels with Charley* by John Steinbeck
Vocabulary Builder 98
Take Notes for Discussion 99
Take Notes for Writing to Sources 100
Take Notes for Research 101

"Gentleman of Río en Medio" by Juan A. A. Sedillo
Vocabulary Builder 102
Take Notes for Discussion 103
Take Notes for Research 104
Take Notes for Writing to Sources 105

"Choice: A Tribute to Martin Luther King, Jr." by Alice Walker
Vocabulary Builder 106
Take Notes for Discussion 107
Take Notes for Research 108
Take Notes for Writing to Sources 109

"Tears of Autumn" by Yoshiko Uchida
Vocabulary Builder 110
Take Notes for Discussion 111
Take Notes for Research 112
Take Notes for Writing to Sources 113

from *I Know Why the Caged Bird Sings* by Maya Angelou
Vocabulary Builder 114
Take Notes for Discussion 115
Take Notes for Research 116
Take Notes for Writing to Sources 117

"Study Finds Americans Increasingly Rooted" by Cindy Weiss
Vocabulary Builder 118
Take Notes for Discussion 119
Take Notes for Research 120
Take Notes for Writing to Sources 121

Media: "Relationships to Place" by Jennifer E. Cross
Vocabulary Builder and Take Notes for Discussion 122

UNIT 3 • PART 1 Setting Expectations
Big Question Vocabulary 1 123
Big Question Vocabulary 2 124
Big Question Vocabulary 3 125
Applying the Big Question 126

UNIT 3 • PART 2 Guided Exploration
Poetry Collection: Walter de la Mare; Alfred, Lord Tennyson; Eleanor Farjeon; Eve Merriam
Writing About the Big Question 127
Reading: Using Context 128
Literary Analysis: Sound Devices 129
Vocabulary Builder 130
Conventions: Types of Sentences 131
Support for Writing to Sources: Poem That Uses Sound Devices 132
Support for Speaking and Listening: Poetry Recitation 133

Poetry Collection: Emily Dickinson, Patricia Hubbell, Langston Hughes, Richard García
Writing About the Big Question . . . 134
Reading: Context Clues . . . 135
Literary Analysis: Figurative Language . . . 136
Vocabulary Builder . . . 137
Conventions: Subject Complements . . . 138
Support for Writing to Sources: Study for a Poem . . . 139
Support for Research and Technology: Mini-Anthology . . . 140

Poetry Collection: Emma Lazarus, William Shakespeare, Henry Wadsworth Longfellow
Writing About the Big Question . . . 141
Reading: Paraphrase . . . 142
Literary Analysis: Lyric and Narrative Poetry . . . 143
Vocabulary Builder . . . 144
Conventions: Direct and Indirect Objects . . . 145
Support for Writing to Sources: Lyric or Narrative Poetry . . . 146
Support for Speaking and Listening: Evaluation Form . . . 147

Poetry Collection: Amy Ling, E. E. Cummings, John Updike, N. Scott Momaday
Writing About the Big Question . . . 148
Reading: Paraphrase . . . 149
Literary Analysis: Imagery . . . 150
Vocabulary Builder . . . 151
Conventions: Pronoun Case . . . 152
Support for Writing to Sources: Review of Poetry . . . 153
Support for Research and Technology: Profile . . . 154

Comparing Texts: "The Road Not Taken" by Robert Frost and **"O Captain! My Captain!"** by Walt Whitman
Writing About the Big Question . . . 155
Literary Analysis: Comparing Types of Description . . . 156
Vocabulary Builder . . . 157
Support for Writing to Compare Description in Literary Works . . . 158

Writing Process . . . 159
Writer's Toolbox: Conventions . . . 160

UNIT 3 • PART 3 Developing Insights

"Old Man" by Ricardo Sánchez and "For My Sister Molly Who in the Fifties" by Alice Walker

Vocabulary Builder 161
Take Notes for Discussion 162
Take Notes for Writing to Sources 163
Take Notes for Research 164

"The Medicine Bag" by Virginia Driving Hawk Sneve

Vocabulary Builder 165
Take Notes for Discussion 166
Take Notes for Research 167
Take Notes for Writing to Sources 168

"Cub Pilot on the Mississippi" by Mark Twain

Vocabulary Builder 169
Take Notes for Discussion 170
Take Notes for Research 171
Take Notes for Writing to Sources 172

"Thank You, M'am" by Langston Hughes

Vocabulary Builder 173
Take Notes for Discussion 174
Take Notes for Research 175
Take Notes for Writing to Sources 176

"Tutoring Benefits Seniors' Health, Students' Skills" by David Crary

Vocabulary Builder 177
Take Notes for Discussion 178
Take Notes for Research 179
Take Notes for Writing to Sources 180

"The Return of the Multi-Generational Family Household" by Pew Research Center

Vocabulary Builder 181
Take Notes for Discussion 182
Take Notes for Research 183
Take Notes for Writing to Sources 184

UNIT 4 • PART 1 Setting Expectations

Big Question Vocabulary 1 185
Big Question Vocabulary 2 186
Big Question Vocabulary 3 187
Applying the Big Question 188

UNIT 4 • PART 2 Guided Exploration

The Diary of Anne Frank, **Act I, by Frances Goodrich and Albert Hackett**
- Writing About the Big Question 189
- Reading: Use Background Information to Link Historical Causes With Effects 190
- Literary Analysis: Dialogue 191
- Vocabulary Builder 192
- Conventions: Prepositions and Prepositional Phrases 193
- Support for Writing to Sources: Diary Entries 194
- Support for Speaking and Listening: Guided Tour 195

The Diary of Anne Frank, **Act II, by Frances Goodrich and Albert Hackett**
- Writing About the Big Question 196
- Reading: Ask Questions to Analyze Cause-and-Effect Relationships 197
- Literary Analysis: Character Motivation 198
- Vocabulary Builder 199
- Conventions: Participial and Infinitive Phrases 200
- Support for Writing to Sources: Film Review 201
- Support for Research and Technology: Bulletin Board Display 202

The Governess **by Neil Simon**
- Writing About the Big Question 203
- Reading: Draw Conclusions 204
- Literary Analysis: Setting and Character 205
- Vocabulary Builder 206
- Conventions: Clauses 207
- Support for Writing to Sources: Public Service Announcement 208
- Support for Speaking and Listening: Debate 209

Comparing Texts: *The Governess* **by Neil Simon and**
The Ninny **by Anton Chekhov**
- Writing About the Big Question 210
- Literary Analysis: Compare Adaptations With Originals 211
- Vocabulary Builder 212
- Support for Writing to Compare Adaptations With Originals 213

Writing Process 214
Writer's Toolbox: Conventions 215

UNIT 4 • PART 3 Developing Insights

from **Kindertransport, Act II** by Diane Samuels
Vocabulary Builder 216
Take Notes for Discussion 217
Take Notes for Writing to Sources 218
Take Notes for Research 219

from **Anne Frank: Diary of a Young Girl** by Anne Frank
Vocabulary Builder 220
Take Notes for Discussion 221
Take Notes for Research 222
Take Notes for Writing to Sources 223

from **Anne Frank Remembered** by Miep Gies
Vocabulary Builder 224
Take Notes for Discussion 225
Take Notes for Research 226
Take Notes for Writing to Sources 227

from **Night** by Elie Wiesel
Vocabulary Builder 228
Take Notes for Discussion 229
Take Notes for Research 230
Take Notes for Writing to Sources 231

"Remarks on a Visit to Buchenwald" by Elie Wiesel
Vocabulary Builder 232
Take Notes for Discussion 233
Take Notes for Research 234
Take Notes for Writing to Sources 235

"Local Holocaust Survivors and Liberators Attend Opening Event for Exhibition" from the Florida Holocaust Museum
Vocabulary Builder 236
Take Notes for Discussion 237
Take Notes for Research 238
Take Notes for Writing to Sources 239

UNIT 5 • PART 1 Setting Expectations

Big Question Vocabulary 1 240
Big Question Vocabulary 2 241
Big Question Vocabulary 3 242
Applying the Big Question 243

UNIT 5 • PART 2 Guided Exploration

"Coyote Steals the Sun and Moon," retold by Richard Erdoes and Alfonso Ortiz

Writing About the Big Question 244
Reading: Create a Summary 245
Literary Analysis: Myth 246
Vocabulary Builder 247
Conventions: Basic Sentence Structures 248
Support for Writing to Sources: Myth 249
Support for Speaking and Listening: Oral Presentation 250

"Chicoria" retold by José Griego y Maestas and Rudolfo A. Anaya and from *The People, Yes* by Carl Sandburg

Writing About the Big Question 251
Reading: Use a Graphic to Summarize Literature 252
Literary Analysis: Oral Tradition 253
Vocabulary Builder 254
Conventions: Commas and Semicolons 255
Support for Writing to Sources: Critical Analysis 256
Support for Speaking and Listening: Storytelling Workshop 257

from *Out of the Dust* by Karen Hesse

Writing About the Big Question 258
Reading: Ask Questions to Set a Purpose for Reading 259
Literary Analysis: Cultural Context 260
Vocabulary Builder 261
Conventions: Ellipses and Dashes 262
Support for Writing to Sources: Research Proposal 263
Support for Research and Technology: Letter 264

"An Episode of War" by Stephen Crane

Writing About the Big Question 265
Reading: Set a Purpose for Reading and Adjust Your Reading Rate 266
Literary Analysis: Author's Influences 267
Vocabulary Builder 268

Conventions: Capitalization . . . 269
Support for Writing to Sources: Persuasive Speech . . . 270
Support for Research and Technology: Research Article . . . 271

Comparing Texts: "Davy Crockett's Dream" by Davy Crockett, **"Paul Bunyan of the North Woods"** by Carl Sandburg, and **"Invocation"** ***from*** **John Brown's Body** by Stephen Vincent Benét
Writing About the Big Question . . . 272
Literary Analysis: Comparing Heroic Characters . . . 273
Vocabulary Builder . . . 274
Writing to Sources: Compare-and-Contrast Essay . . . 275

Writing Process . . . 276
Writer's Toolbox: Conventions . . . 277

UNIT 5 • PART 3 Developing Insights

"The American Dream" by Martin Luther King, Jr.
Vocabulary Builder . . . 278
Take Notes for Discussion . . . 279
Take Notes for Writing to Sources . . . 280
Take Notes for Research . . . 281

"Runagate Runagate" by Robert Hayden
Vocabulary Builder . . . 282
Take Notes for Discussion . . . 283
Take Notes for Research . . . 284
Take Notes for Writing to Sources . . . 285

"Emancipation" from ***Lincoln: A Photobiography*** by Russell Freedman
Vocabulary Builder . . . 286
Take Notes for Discussion . . . 287
Take Notes for Research . . . 288
Take Notes for Writing to Sources . . . 289

"Harriet Beecher Stowe" by Paul Laurence Dunbar
Vocabulary Builder . . . 290
Take Notes for Writing to Sources . . . 291

"Brown vs. Board of Education" by Walter Dean Myers
Vocabulary Builder . . . 292
Take Notes for Discussion . . . 293
Take Notes for Research . . . 294
Take Notes for Writing to Sources . . . 295

"On Woman's Right to Suffrage" by Susan B. Anthony

Vocabulary Builder 296

Take Notes for Discussion 297

Take Notes for Research 298

Take Notes for Writing to Sources 299

***from* Address to the Commonwealth Club of San Francisco by Cesar Chavez**

Vocabulary Builder 300

Take Notes for Discussion 301

Take Notes for Research 302

Take Notes for Writing to Sources 303

Media: Nonviolence Tree

Vocabulary Builder and Take Notes for Research 304

Name ______________________________ Date ______________

Unit 1: Short Stories
Big Question Vocabulary—1

The Big Question: Can all conflicts be resolved?

Thematic Vocabulary

argument: *n.* a disagreement, often involving anger; other forms: *argue, arguing, argumentative*

compromise: *n.* a solution in which people agree to accept less than what they originally wanted; other forms: *compromised, compromising*

irritate: *v.* to make someone feel annoyed or impatient; other forms: *irritation, irritated, irritating*

oppose: *v.* to be against or to disagree; other forms: *opposition, opposing, opponent*

viewpoint: *n.* a person's way of thinking about a subject or an issue

DIRECTIONS: *Answer the questions using the number of vocabulary words specified. You can use words more than once, but you must use all five Thematic Vocabulary words. You might use the "other forms" of the words, as shown above.*

Rosa and Ellen shared a bedroom at home. Their mother suggested that they repaint the walls, make new curtains, and rearrange the furniture. At first, the sisters were excited about the project. However, their differences of opinion soon brought a conflict.

"I hate the color pink!" Rosa stormed. "Why do we *always* have to do what *you* want?"

1. How might Ellen have responded? Use at least 2 vocabulary words in your answer.

____

____

Their older sister Paula heard them speaking angrily to each other. She tried to help.

2. What might Paula have said? Use at least 1 vocabulary word in your answer.

____

____

Paula got out a pencil and paper. She took notes as Rosa and Ellen each spoke about how she would like their room to look. Then, she made a suggestion.

3. What did she suggest? Use at least 2 vocabulary words in your answer.

____

____

Rosa wasn't totally satisfied, but at least Ellen had listened to some of her ideas.

4. How did the girls resolve their conflict? Use at least 1 vocabulary word in your answer.

____

____

Name ______________________________ Date ______________

Unit 1: Short Stories
Big Question Vocabulary—2

The Big Question: Can all conflicts be resolved?

Thematic Vocabulary

injury: *n.* damage caused by an accident or attack; other forms: *injured, injuring, injuries*
insecurity: *n.* the feeling of being unconfident or unsafe; other forms: *insecure, insecurities*
interact: *v.* to talk or work together; other forms: *interaction, interacting, interacted*
mislead: *v.* to lead in the wrong direction or give false information; other forms: *misled, misleading*
solution: *n.* a way of solving a problem or dealing with a difficult situation; other form: *solve*

A. Directions: *On each line, write the Thematic Vocabulary word that best completes the sentence.*

1. Jane's ______________ and nervousness before the play caused her to forget her lines.
2. Will the suspect tell the truth, or will he attempt to ______________ the detective?
3. The football player had to leave the game due to an unfortunate ______________.
4. At the press conference, the president will ______________ with members of the news media.
5. A fair compromise is often the best ______________ to a conflict.

B. Directions: *Write the Thematic Vocabulary word that best completes each group of related words.*

1. communicate, cooperate, ______________
2. pain, wound, ______________
3. anxiousness, uncertainty, ______________
4. answer, resolution, ______________
5. deceive, trick, ______________

Name _______________ Date _______________

Unit 1: Short Stories
Big Question Vocabulary—3

The Big Question: Can all conflicts be resolved?

Thematic Vocabulary

negotiate: *v.* to discuss, with the goal of settling a conflict; other form: *negotiation*

reaction: *n.* a response to a statement, event, or situation; other forms: *react, reacting*

stalemate: *n.* a standstill in a conflict, in which neither side can get an advantage

victorious: *adj.* triumphant; on the winning side; other forms: *victor, victory*

violence: *n.* behavior that is intended to cause someone physical harm; other form: *violent*

A. DIRECTIONS: *Respond to each item.*

1. Why is *violence* a poor way to try to solve a conflict? _______________

2. What would you do if you reached a *stalemate* while trying to solve a disagreement? _______________

3. Give an example of a situation in which someone might feel *victorious*. _______________

4. What skills are important for someone to have in order to *negotiate* successfully? _______________

5. Someone disagrees with you. Give an example of a constructive *reaction* you might express. _______________

B. DIRECTIONS: *Imagine that you are a police officer. On your way home, you see two young boys having a fist fight. You try to help them solve their conflict peacefully. Write a dialogue that takes place between you and the two boys. Use all five Thematic Vocabulary words.*

____

Name ______________________________ Date ________________

Unit 1: Short Stories
Applying the Big Question

Can all conflicts be resolved?

DIRECTIONS: *Complete the chart below to apply what you have learned about how and if conflicts are resolved. One row has been completed for you.*

Example	Type of Conflict	Opposing forces	Aids/ obstacles to resolution	Outcome	What I learned
From Literature	Charlie's struggle to be normal in "Flowers for Algernon"	Mental disability vs. science	Aid: surgery increases intelligence Obstacle: limits of science and technology	Charlie is still mentally disabled.	Some conflicts cannot be resolved.
From Literature					
From Science					
From Social Studies					
From Real Life					

Name ________________________________ Date ________________

"**Raymond's Run**" by Toni Cade Bambara

Writing About the Big Question

THE BIG ?

Can all conflicts be resolved?

Big Question Vocabulary

argument	compromise	injury	insecurity	interact
irritate	mislead	negotiate	oppose	reaction
solution	stalemate	victorious	viewpoint	violence

A. *Use a word from the list above to complete each sentence.*

1. Just before a race, a nervous runner is bound to feel ________________ about winning.
2. In a very close race, judges might be uncertain about which runner was ________________.
3. If you make the ________________ that running is healthful, then you should run yourself.
4. Diane's personal ________________ about running is that it's more boring than golf, but I disagree.

B. *Follow the directions in responding to each of the items below. Answer in complete sentences.*

1. Describe two different times when a contest presented a conflict that was hard to resolve.

____

____

2. Write two sentences explaining how each conflict you described was resolved or why it was not resolved. Use at least two of the Big Question vocabulary words.

____

____

____

C. *In "Raymond's Run," the narrator discovers that a conflict is not always resolved in the expected way. Complete the sentence below. Then, write a short paragraph in which you elaborate on your statement and connect it to the Big Question.*

Sometimes, winning or losing turns out to be less important than ________

____

____

____

____

Name ______________________________ Date ____________________

"Raymond's Run" by Toni Cade Bambara

Reading: Make Predictions and Support Them

When you **make predictions** about a story, you make informed guesses about what will happen next based on story details and your own experience. You can **support your predictions** by finding clues in the story that hint at what will happen next.

As you read, try to **predict,** or make reasonable guesses, about what is going to happen. Keep track of your predictions and your support for them. Notice when the story includes details that could support predictions of more than one outcome. Some stories keep you guessing in order to hold your interest and build suspense.

These questions may help you predict what might happen next in a story:

- How would you describe the main character's personality?
- What is important to the main character?
- Does the main character think or speak about the future?
- Do other characters do or say things that hint at the future?

Have you had experiences with people, places, or events that remind you of the ones in the story?

DIRECTIONS: *The following chart lists details from "Raymond's Run." Use the questions above to make predictions based on those details as you read the story. Then, in the third column, write down what actually happens.*

Details From Story	Prediction	Actual Outcome (If Known)
1. Squeaky and Gretchen are good runners, and each girl is sure she is the one who will win the race.		
2. Mr. Pearson hints to Squeaky that she should let Gretchen win the race.		
3. Raymond climbs the fence to meet Squeaky after the race.		
4. After the race, Gretchen and Squeaky smile at each other.		

Name ______________________________ Date ______________

"Raymond's Run" by Toni Cade Bambara

Literary Analysis: Plot

Plot is the sequence of related events in a short story. As you read, identify the following parts of the story's plot:

- **Exposition:** the basic information about the characters and the situation
- **Conflict:** a struggle between two opposing forces in the story
- **Rising action:** the events in the story that increase the tension that readers feel
- **Climax:** the high point of the story, usually the point at which the eventual outcome is revealed
- **Falling action:** the events that follow the climax
- **Resolution:** the final outcome

A. DIRECTIONS: *The following six sentences describe the plot of "Raymond's Run," but they are out of order. Write a number on the line before each part to indicate the order in which the event takes place in the story. Then, write the name of the plot part that the event represents. The parts of the plot are* exposition, conflict, rising action, climax, falling action, *and* resolution.

___ 1. ____________________ Squeaky and Gretchen congratulate each other.

___ 2. ____________________ Squeaky looks after her older brother, and she anticipates a race.

___ 3. ____________________ Squeaky stands up for her brother and defends her reputation as the fastest runner in the neighborhood.

___ 4. ____________________ The race ends, and Raymond begins to climb the fence that separates him from the runners.

___ 5. ____________________ Squeaky meets a group of girls from the neighborhood while practicing for the race.

___ 6. ____________________ Squeaky realizes that Raymond could be a good runner and thinks about coaching him.

B. DIRECTIONS: *Look at the sentences you labeled "rising action" and "falling action." On the lines below, write two details that describe the rising action of "Raymond's Run" and two details that describe the falling action. The details might describe events, actions, a conversation, or a character's thoughts.*

Rising action:

1. ____

2. ____

Falling action:

1. ____

2. ____

Name ______________________________ Date ______________________

"**Raymond's Run**" by Toni Cade Bambara

Vocabulary Builder

Word List

gesture liable pageant periscope prodigy reputation

A. Directions: *Follow the instructions for writing a sentence using each Word List word. Be sure to make the meaning of the vocabulary word clear.*

Example: Use *prodigy* in a sentence about a music student.

Sentence: Soon the prodigy Kayla was playing the violin better than her teacher.

1. Use *prodigy* in a sentence about a child who solves math problems.

   ____

2. Use *reputation* in a sentence about the behavior of an animal.

   ____

3. Use *liable* in a sentence about a fast runner.

   ____

4. Use *pageant* in a sentence about a springtime event.

   ____

5. Use *gesture* in a sentence about welcoming a new neighbor.

   ____

6. Use *periscope* in a sentence about a submarine.

   ____

B. Word Study: *The Greek root* -scope- *means "look at" or "watch." It appears in the names of many scientific instruments that are used for seeing or observing. Revise each sentence so that the underlined word containing the root* -scope- *is used logically. Be sure not to change the underlined word. Consult a dictionary if necessary.*

1. The scientist used a microscope to study the moon.

   ____

2. Jessica looked through her telescope to study a strand of her own hair.

   ____

3. The doctor used her stethoscope to examine the patient's eyes.

   ____

Name ______________________________ Date ______________

"Raymond's Run" by Toni Cade Bambara

Conventions: Nouns

Nouns may be classified as common or proper. A **common noun** names any person, animal, place, thing, or idea. It is not capitalized unless it is the first word in a sentence or is part of a title.

The girl met another girl on a street and talked about a race they would run the next day.

A **proper noun** names a particular person, animal, place, thing, or idea. A proper noun is always capitalized.

Squeaky met Gretchen on Broadway and talked about the race they would run on May Day.

Possessive nouns show ownership or belonging. Both common and proper nouns can be turned into possessive nouns by using an apostrophe ('). To form most possessive nouns, add an apostrophe and *s*.

Did Squeaky's brother watch his sister's race from the children's section?

If a plural noun already ends in *s*, form the possessive by adding just an apostrophe.

The girls' rivalry soured their friendship.

A. Directions: *In the following paragraph, underline the common nouns once and the proper nouns twice. Circle the possessive nouns.*

It was Sunday, the day of the Chicago Marathon. The weather was crisp and clear, a perfect day for a long race. Sara's confidence was high. She had trained for six months on Chicago's streets and along the paths in Lincoln Park Zoo. She had run all over the city's neighborhoods. Now Sara felt anticipation, sure that she was ready for the race.

B. Writing Application: *Write sentences following the directions in each item. In your sentences, underline the common nouns once and the proper nouns twice. Circle the possessive nouns.*

1. Use a proper noun in a question you might ask your teacher.

____

2. Use a possessive noun in a sentence about an activity you enjoy.

____

3. Use a common noun and a proper noun in a sentence about your town or city.

____

4. Use a common noun and a possessive noun in a question about a race.

____

Name ______________________________ Date ______________________

"Raymond's Run" by Toni Cade Bambara

Support for Writing to Sources: New Ending

Plan a **new ending** to "Raymond's Run." For example, Squeaky might lose the race to Gretchen, or Raymond might run on the track beside the racers. Use the following chart to come up with narration and dialogue you can use for your ending. In the second column, write your ideas about the characters' thoughts, feelings, actions, or dialogue. Base your responses on the personality traits described in the first column. As you write your new ending, remember the experiences that the characters share. Look for places in the story that indicate each person's thoughts and feelings about the other.

Characters' Personality Traits	Thoughts That Characters Might Have, Actions They Might Take, Things They Might Say

In your new ending, use dialogue that matches each character's voice to his or her personality. Remember to correctly capitalize characters' names and all other proper nouns.

Name ______________________________ Date ______________

"Raymond's Run" by Toni Cade Bambara

Support for Speaking and Listening: Radio Broadcast

Answer the following questions in preparation for a **radio broadcast** of Squeaky's race in "Raymond's Run." You will be writing and giving the broadcast. Remember to use vivid sensory details and action verbs so that listeners will feel the rising tension and excitement of the close race between Squeaky and Gretchen.

1. How does Squeaky look? ______________________________

2. How does Gretchen look? ______________________________

3. How does Squeaky act—what does she do? ______________________________

4. How does Gretchen act—what does she do? ______________________________

5. What happens as Squeaky and Gretchen approach the finish line? How close are they?

Name ______________________ Date ______________

"The Tell-Tale Heart" by Edgar Allan Poe

Writing About the Big Question

Can all conflicts be resolved?

Big Question Vocabulary

argument	compromise	injury	insecurity	interact
irritate	mislead	negotiate	oppose	reaction
solution	stalemate	victorious	viewpoint	violence

A. *Use a word from the list above to complete each sentence.*

1. Sometimes, another person's bad habits can really ______________ someone else.
2. Someone's bad habit might cause a serious ______________ with a roommate.
3. From my ______________, you should try to control bad habits that annoy others.
4. Some bad habits, like nail-biting, suggest that a person suffers from ______________.

B. *Follow the directions in responding to each of the items below. Answer in complete sentences.*

1. Describe two things other people do that you find really irritating.

____

____

2. In two sentences, explain how you handle one of those situations when it occurs. Use at least two of the Big Question vocabulary words.

____

____

C. *Complete the sentence below. Then, write a short paragraph in which you give advice to a person torn between doing right and wrong.*

When torn between doing right and wrong, a person may ______________

____

____

____

Name ______________________________ Date ______________

"The Tell-Tale Heart" by Edgar Allan Poe

Reading: Compare and Contrast

When you **compare and contrast characters,** you look for similarities and differences among the people in a story. One strategy for comparing is to **identify each character's perspective**—that is, to consider the way a person understands the world.

- As you read, note details about the main character.
- To compare, consider whether the main character's actions, emotions, and ideas are similar to or different from those of other characters.
- Finally, decide whether you can trust what the character says and does.

One of the main ways readers understand the characters' perspectives in "The Tell-Tale Heart" is by looking closely at the characters' reactions to the same person, topic, or event. In this story, readers get most of their information about the old man's reactions from the narrator's point of view. Notice the different reactions to the story's events in the following passages.

The old man (from the narrator's point of view): "Presently I heard a slight groan, and I knew it was the groan of mortal terror. It was not a groan of pain or of grief—oh, no!—it was the low stifled sound that arises from the bottom of the soul when overcharged with awe."

The narrator: "I knew what the old man felt, and pitied him, although I chuckled at heart."

DIRECTIONS: *Answer the following questions. Think about each character's perspective on the events of the night.*

1. How does the narrator describe his feelings and actions as he looks in on the old man sleeping each night?

 ____

2. How does the old man react on the eighth night when he hears a noise at the door?

 ____

3. How does the narrator feel when he sees the old man's eye in the ray of light? What does the narrator hear?

 ____

 ____

4. What has the old man been doing and feeling during the hour after hearing the noise?

 ____

 ____

5. How does the old man react when the narrator leaps into his room?

 ____

6. How does the narrator describe his feelings after killing the old man?

 ____

Name ____________________________ Date ________________

"The Tell-Tale Heart" by Edgar Allan Poe

Literary Analysis: Character Traits

Character traits are the personal qualities, attitudes, and values that make a character unique. For example, one character may be joyless, while another finds pleasure in everything.

- *Round characters* are complex, showing many different character traits.
- In contrast, *flat characters* are one-dimensional, showing just a single trait.

Writers sometimes state character traits directly, but more often they reveal them through details such as a character's actions, thoughts, appearance, speech, and the reactions of others to the character. In "The Tell-Tale Heart," readers learn about the narrator through his own description of his thoughts and feelings. For example, this passage from the story reveals that the narrator sees himself as both nervous and calm. He defends his health and sanity, yet refers to things that suggest insanity.

> True!—nervous—very, very dreadfully nervous I had been and am; but why *will* you say that I am mad? The disease had sharpened my senses—not destroyed—not dulled them. Above all was the sense of hearing acute. I heard all things in the heaven and in the earth. I heard many things in hell. How, then, am I mad? Hearken! and observe how healthily—how calmly I can tell you the whole story.

A. Directions: *On the chart below, list at least three details the author gives about the narrator and what trait each detail reveals.*

Detail	Trait Revealed

B. Directions: *Choose two of the details you recorded about the narrator. Write a few sentences describing him.*

____

____

____

____

Name ________________________ Date ____________

"The Tell-Tale Heart" by Edgar Allan Poe

Vocabulary Builder

Word List

audacity   cunningly   derision   resolved   stealthily   vex

A. Directions: *Revise each sentence so that the underlined vocabulary word is used logically. Be sure to keep the vocabulary word in your revision.*

1. When the basketball player on the visiting team made the difficult shot look easy, the crowd shouted with <u>derision</u>.

2. Simon's good behavior continued to <u>vex</u> his mother.

3. Becca never tried to complete anything she had <u>resolved</u> to do.

4. Because Armando had acted so <u>cunningly</u>, everyone knew what he was up to.

5. Cindy moved very <u>stealthily</u>, banging on a drum as she went along.

6. Sheila's <u>audacity</u> showed in the way she shyly held back.

B. Word Study: *The suffix* -ity *means "state or quality of being." It is used to form nouns. Answer the following questions in a way that demonstrates your understanding of* -ity *in each of the italicized words.*

1. Is there a *possibility* that you could travel back in time to before you were born?

2. What kind of experience would give you a feeling of *tranquillity?*

3. Why is drinking water a *necessity* when you are taking a long hike?

Name ______________________________ Date ______________

"The Tell-Tale Heart" by Edgar Allan Poe

Conventions: Pronouns

Pronouns are words that replace or refer back to nouns. **First-person pronouns** refer to the person(s) speaking; **second-person pronouns,** to the person(s) spoken to; **third-person pronouns,** to the person(s), place(s), or thing(s) spoken about.

	Personal Pronouns	Possessive Pronouns	Reflexive or Intensive Pronouns
First Person	singular: I, me plural: we, us	singular: my, mine plural: our, ours	singular: myself plural: ourselves
Second Person	singular or plural: you	singular or plural: your, yours	singular: yourself plural: yourselves
Third Person	singular: he, him, she, her, it plural: they, them	singular: his, her, hers, its plural: their, theirs	singular: himself, herself, itself plural: themselves

Personal pronouns may refer to people, places, or things.

He had tickets for the zoo but gave them to us so that we could visit it.

Possessive pronouns show ownership.

Cara has her book, but Mia does not have hers.

Reflexive and **intensive pronouns** have the same forms but function differently. A **reflexive pronoun** indicates that something or someone does something to, for, or upon itself. An **intensive pronoun** adds emphasis to a noun or pronoun used elsewhere, often just before it.

Reflexive: Al performed by himself. **Intensive:** Al himself loves to play the guitar.

A. Practice: *Circle each pronoun and write whether it is* personal, possessive, reflexive, *or* intensive.

1. Yesterday, Luisa raced her sailboat across the lake. ______________
2. Eli and Carly studied for their math test. ______________
3. The rain itself was not too bad, but the wind was terrible. ______________
4. Alec told himself not to worry. ______________

B. Writing Application: *Answer each question in a sentence using one or more examples of the type of pronoun in parentheses. Circle the example or examples you use.*

1. Were you scared by Poe's story? (personal) ______________
____
2. Why did the narrator kill the old man? (possessive) ______________
____
3. Was the narrator sane? (intensive) ______________
____
4. Why was the narrator caught? (reflexive) ______________
____

Name ____ Date ________________

"The Tell-Tale Heart" by Edgar Allan Poe

Support for Writing to Sources: Character Profile

To prepare for writing a **character profile** of the narrator in "The Tell-Tale Heart," use the chart to gather specific details about his personality. Think about how the narrator describes his relationship with the old man and his reasons for deciding to kill him. Then, think about the various emotions the narrator experiences and describes—nervousness, anxiety, happiness, anger—as he carries out his plan and, finally, confronts the police officers.

Character Trait	How the Trait Affects Plot and Resolution

Name ______________________________ Date ____________________

"**The Tell-Tale Heart**" by Edgar Allan Poe

Support for Speaking and Listening: Oral Response

To prepare for your **oral response,** write down the ideas and details called for on the lines below. When necessary, refer back to the story or film version to refresh your memory.

Similarities between the story and the film version: ____________________

____

____

____

____

____

____

Differences between the story and the film version: ____________________

____

____

____

____

____

____

Techniques used by Poe and by the filmmaker: ____________________

____

____

____

____

____

____

Evaluation of the filmmaker's choices: ____________________

____

____

____

____

____

____

Name ______________________________ Date ______________

"Flowers for Algernon" by Daniel Keyes

Writing About the Big Question

Can all conflicts be resolved?

Big Question Vocabulary

argument	compromise	injury	insecurity	interact
irritate	mislead	negotiate	oppose	reaction
solution	stalemate	victorious	viewpoint	violence

A. *Use a word from the list above to complete each sentence.*

1. Some people interested in animal rights ______________ experiments that harm animals.
2. Results of animal experiments can ______________ us into thinking the same results would occur in humans.
3. Some experiments can cause a serious ______________ to an animal.
4. The conflict between animal-rights activists and some scientists seems to have no good ______________.

B. *Follow the directions in responding to each of the items below. Answer in complete sentences.*

1. What are two uses of animals that cause conflict in our society?

____

____

2. What is your reaction to one of these conflicts? Use at least two of the Big Question vocabulary words.

____

____

C. *Complete the sentence below. Then, write a short paragraph in which you comment on the conflicts you might feel about a friend who changes.*

When someone I know changes, it is ______________________

____

____

____

____

Name ______________________________ Date ______________

"Flowers for Algernon" by Daniel Keyes

Reading: Notice Details to Make Inferences

Making inferences means **noticing details** that an author provides and using them to make logical assumptions about the events, settings, themes, and other story elements that the author leaves unstated. Consider these details that author Daniel Keyes has Charlie tell us:

> I had a test today. I think I faled it. and I think that maybe now they wont use me. What happind is a nice young man was in the room and he had some white cards with ink spilled all over them. He sed Charlie what do you see on this card. I was very skared even tho I had my rabits foot in my pockit because when I was a kid I always faled tests in school and I spilled ink to.

From these details, you might make the following inferences:

- Charlie is no longer of school age.
- Charlie has a learning disability, so he had a hard time when he was in school.
- Charlie is superstitious.
- Charlie very much wants to pass a test and be used in an experiment.

Directions: *In the chart below, the left column gives quotations from the story. Each quotation provides several details. From each group of details, make at least one inference, and list it on the right.*

Details	Inferences
1. They said how come you went to the adult nite scool all by yourself Charlie. How did you find it. I said I askd pepul and sumbody told me where I shud go to lern to read and spell good.	
2. Their really my friends and they like me. Sometimes somebody will say hey look at Joe or Frank or George he really pulled a Charlie Gordon. I dont know why they say that but they always laff.	
3. Dr. Nemur wanted to publish the results of the experiment at the end of this month. Dr. Strauss wanted to wait a while longer to be sure. Dr. Strauss said that Dr. Nemur was more interested in the Chair of Psychology at Princeton than he was in the experiment.	

Name ________________________________ Date ______________

"Flowers for Algernon" by Daniel Keyes

Literary Analysis: Point of View

Point of view is the perspective from which a story is told. In a story told from the **first-person point of view,** the narrator is a character in the story and refers to himself or herself with first-person pronouns like *I* and *me.* In a story told from the **third-person point of view,** the narrator stands outside the story and refers to all the characters with third-person pronouns like *he, she,* and *they.* A first-person narrator can tell only what he or she sees, hears, knows, thinks, or feels. "Flowers for Algernon" is told from the first-person point of view of its main character, Charlie Gordon, who gives his account in a series of progress reports.

A. DIRECTIONS: *On the lines provided, answer these questions about the story.*

1. Briefly explain the narrator's situation at the start of "Flowers for Algernon" by telling how old he is and how he is different from other people his age.

____

____

____

2. What role do vocabulary and spelling have in showing the changes that take place in the narrator as the story unfolds?

____

____

____

3. Why do you think the author, Keyes, has the narrator, Charlie, tell his story in spaced-out progress reports instead of telling the whole story on a single day in May or in July?

____

____

____

B. DIRECTIONS: *Choose a short progress report or a dated section of a longer report, and then rewrite it from the first-person point of view of Dr. Strauss, Miss Kinnian, or another character. Use a separate sheet of paper, if necessary.*

____

____

____

____

____

Name ______________________ Date ______________

"**Flowers for Algernon**" by Daniel Keyes

Vocabulary Builder

Word List

deceive deterioration intellectual introspective naïveté refute

A. Directions: *Answer each question with a sentence that uses one of the Word List words. Each answer must correctly reflect the details in "Flowers for Algernon."*

1. Do Dr. Strauss's experiments prove that an operation can permanently improve intelligence?

 ____

2. As the experiment begins showing positive results, does Charlie stop examining his own thoughts and feelings?

 ____

 ____

3. Are the doctors trying to fool Charlie by lying about the purpose of the operation?

 ____

 ____

4. In what way do Charlie's co-workers take advantage of his simplicity?

 ____

 ____

5. What is one example proving that Charlie's level of mental awareness has exceeded those of his doctors?

 ____

 ____

6. What is the first sign that Algernon's condition is becoming worse?

 ____

 ____

B. Word Study The Latin root *-spec-* means "to look." Answer the following questions using one of these words containing *-spec-*: *spectator, inspect, respect.*

1. What might you see in a person that would make you *respect* him or her?

 ____

2. Why might a detective use a magnifying glass to *inspect* a crime scene?

 ____

3. When might a *spectator* use binoculars at a sporting event?

 ____

Name ______________________________ Date ______________

"Flowers for Algernon" by Daniel Keyes

Conventions: Adjectives and Adverbs

An **adjective** is a word that modifies or describes a noun or a pronoun. Adjectives answer questions such as *what kind? which one? how many?* and *how much?*

what kind? lovely sunset **which one?** this dog **how many?** two pages

An **adverb** is a word that modifies or describes a verb, an adjective, or another adverb. Adverbs often end in *-ly* and answer questions such as *in what way? where? when?* and *to what extent?*

in what way? walked slowly **where?** went outside **to what extent?** too old

A. Practice: *Underline each adjective or adverb. Draw an arrow to the word it modifies. On the line after each sentence, write whether each underlined word is an* adjective *or an* adverb.

1. We always played many games after school. ______________________
2. Sometimes we invented special rules. ______________________
3. These rules were complex. ______________________
4. We played one unique version of Hide and Seek. ______________________
5. In this game, we all hid nearby. ______________________

B. Writing Application: *Make these sentences more vivid and precise by adding adjectives and adverbs that answer the questions in parentheses. Write each word on the line after the question.*

1. The *(what kind?)* ______________ cat ran *(where?)* ______________.
2. We kicked our feet *(how?)* ______________ as we swam.
3. My sister downloaded *(how many?)* ______________ albums to listen to in the car.
4. The *(what kind)* ______________ practice was boring because it was *(to what extent)* ______________ long.

Name ______________________________ Date ______________

"Flowers for Algernon" by Daniel Keyes

Support for Writing to Sources: Dialogue

The dialogue for a movie scene adapted from "Flowers for Algernon" can start with actual dialogue given in the story. On the blank lines, write notes for expanding this after-dinner conversation with dialogue that you can imagine. Alternatively, on another sheet of paper, prepare notes for expanding a script that starts with a conversation from elsewhere in the story.

[*Scene: after-dinner conversation between Miss Kinnian and Charlie*]

MISS KINNIAN: I won't go much higher than I am now, but you'll keep climbing up and up, and see more and more, and each step will open new worlds that you never even knew existed. I hope . . . I just hope to God—

CHARLIE: What?

MISS KINNIAN: Never mind, Charles. I just hope I wasn't wrong to advise you to go into this in the first place.

CHARLIE: How could that be? It worked, didn't it? Even Algernon is still smart.

____

____

____

____

____

____

On the next set of lines, list each character who will appear in your scene and write a sentence describing him or her.

____

____

____

____

____

____

____

____

____

____

____

Now, on a separate sheet of paper, convert your notes into actual dialogue.

Name ______________________________ Date ____________________

"Flowers for Algernon" by Daniel Keyes

Support for Research and Technology: Summary of an Article

Use the chart below to record the information from the article you use.

Source	
Main Idea	
Significant Details (at least two)	
Quotation	

Name ______________________ Date ______________

"The Storyteller" by Saki (H. H. Munro)

Writing About the Big Question

Can all conflicts be resolved?

Big Question Vocabulary

argument	compromise	injury	insecurity	interact
irritate	mislead	negotiate	oppose	reaction
solution	stalemate	victorious	viewpoint	violence

A. *Use one or more words from the list above to complete each sentence.*

1. In most children's stories, good is ______________ over evil.
2. The audience's ______________ to the shocking story was a loud gasp.
3. There is little ______________ over the idea that ______________ in children's stories is best avoided.
4. In some children's stories, human characters ______________ with talking animals.

B. *Follow the directions in responding to each of the items below. Answer in complete sentences.*

1. Describe a conflict in one of your favorite children's stories.

____

____

2. Why might a parent have inner conflict about allowing a child to view violence on TV? Use at least two of the Big Question vocabulary words.

____

____

C. *Complete the sentence below. Then, write a short paragraph in which you comment on the types of conflict commonly found in fairy tales.*

The endings of fairy tales are ______________________

____

____

____

____

Name ______________________________ Date ______________

"The Story-Teller" by Saki (H. H. Munro)

Reading: Identify Connections to Make Inferences

An **inference** is a logical assumption that you make about something the writer suggests but does not directly state. You often make inferences by **identifying the connections** between story events and outcomes or between characters' behavior and backgrounds, personalities, or other reasons for the behavior. For example, "The Story-Teller" opens with three children cooped up in a hot railway carriage along with their aunt and a bachelor who is a stranger to them. A few sentences later, you read that most of the aunt's remarks seem to begin with "Don't." By connecting these details, you can infer that the children are restless and that the aunt is having trouble controlling them.

Three children are cooped up in a hot railway carriage.	+	Most of the aunt's remarks begin with "Don't."	=	The children are restless and the aunt is having trouble controlling them.

DIRECTIONS: *For each numbered item, connect the two details in order to make the requested inference about a character's behavior or the outcome of events.*

1. Cyril is smacking the seat cushions of the railway carriage.	+	The aunt invites Cyril to look out the window.	=	*Make an inference about why the aunt tells Cyril to look out the window:* ____________ ____________
2. Cyril asks questions about what he sees.	+	Cyril is not satisfied with the aunt's answers and asks more questions.	=	*Make an inference about the kind of boy Cyril is:* ____________ ____________ ____________
3. The smaller sister recites one line of a poem over and over.	+	The bachelor looks twice at the aunt and once at the train's communication cord.	=	*Make an inference about why the bachelor looks at the aunt and the cord:* ____________ ____________
4. The bachelor tells a story about a good little girl who is eaten by a wolf because of her goodness.	+	The children enjoy the story.	=	*Make an inference about why the children enjoy the story:* ____________ ____________

Name ______________________ Date ______________

"The Story-Teller" by Saki (H. H. Munro)

Literary Analysis: Theme

A **theme** is a central idea, insight, or message that a work of literature conveys. It is usually expressed as a generalization about life or people. A theme is sometimes **stated** directly in a work, either by a character or by the narrator. More often, a theme is **unstated.** That is, it is only **implied,** and you must infer the theme from details in the work.

To determine the theme, consider the experiences of the characters and the outcome of events, and think about the general message to which they point. For example, in a story about a jewel thief who risks breaking his neck by scaling a building to steal a bracelet that turns out to be fake, the theme might be "Crime does not pay."

DIRECTIONS: *Create word webs about the story that the bachelor tells the children. Then, answer the questions below the word webs.*

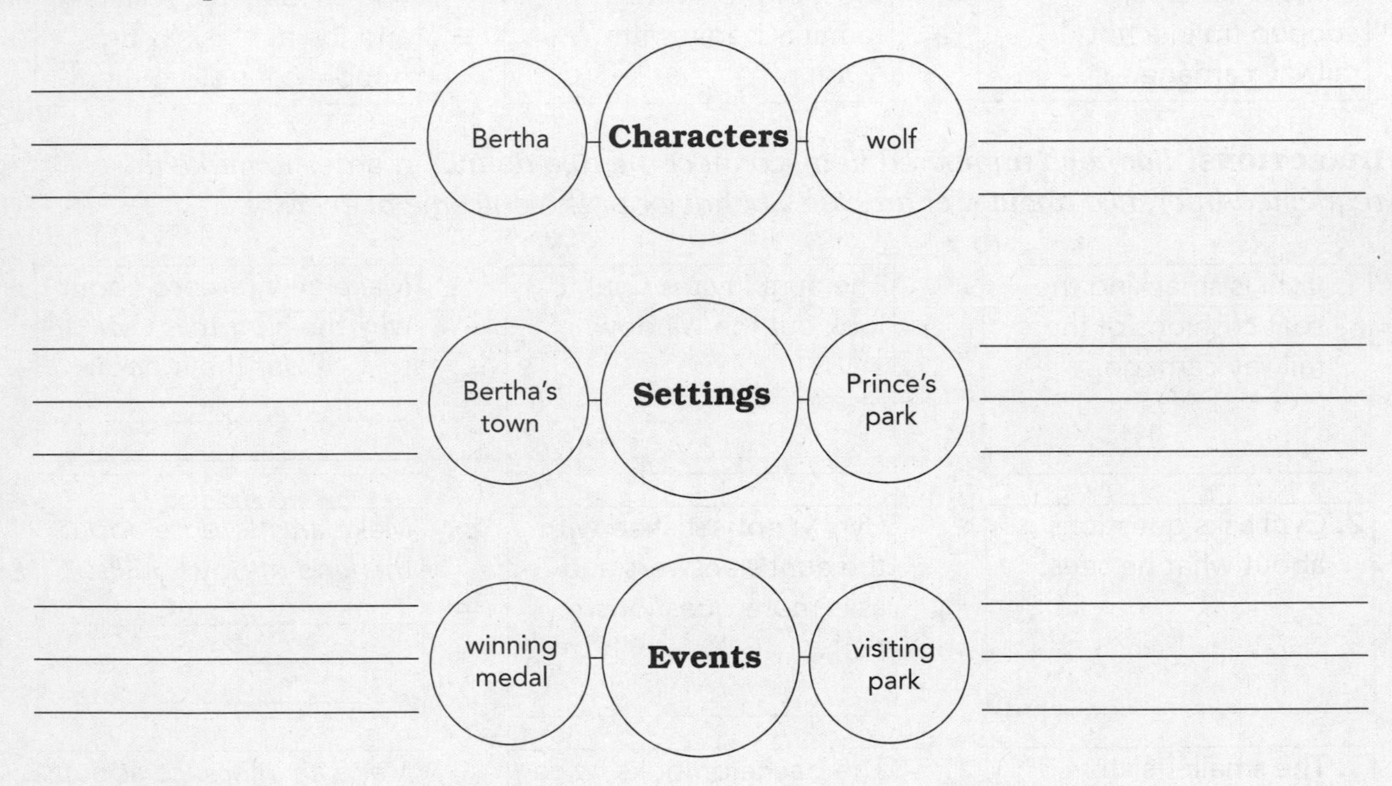

1. Based on the details you listed above, what sort of human behavior do you think the bachelor wants listeners to think about when they hear his story? ______________________

2. Based on the details you listed above, what does the story seem to be saying about the benefits and drawbacks of that kind of behavior?

____

Name ______________________________ Date ________________

"The Story-Teller" by Saki (H. H. Munro)

Vocabulary Builder

Word List

assail conviction immensely inevitable persistent suppressed

A. Directions: *Answer each item with a full sentence, using a word from the Word List. Use each word only once.*

1. How should you speak about a strong belief that you want others to share?

____

2. What would you do if you had a toothache that would not go away?

____

3. How would you feel if your young cousin were to attack you with demands for interesting stories every time you met?

____

4. Describe a school event that is certain to happen sometime in the next week.

____

5. What is one accomplishment of yours that makes you feel extremely proud?

____

6. Describe one situation in which you thought it best to hold back your laughter.

____

B. Word Study: The prefix *per-* means "thoroughly" or "throughout." Revise each sentence so that the underlined word containing the prefix *per-* is used logically. Be sure not to change the underlined word. Consult a dictionary if necessary.

1. These plants are <u>perennials</u>, so they will definitely die after one season.

____

2. The color red is barely <u>perceptible</u> against a yellow background.

____

3. Charlotte's <u>perfect</u> performance was filled with mistakes.

____

Name ______________________________ Date ______________

"The Story-Teller" by Saki (H. H. Munro)

Conventions: Principal Parts of Verbs

Each verb has four **principal parts,** or main forms: present, present participle, past, and past participle. **Regular verbs** follow a pattern to form these parts. Use the base form for the present, adding *-s* or *-es* to agree with third-person singular subjects. Add *-ing* to form the present participle and *-ed* or *-d* to form the past and past participle. **Irregular verbs** do not follow this pattern; their past and past participle are formed in irregular ways.

	Present (Base Form)	**Present Participle**	**Past**	**Past Participle**
Regular	walk(s), move(s), reach(es)	walking, moving, reaching	walked, moved, reached	walked, moved, reached
Irregular	see(s), ride(s), freeze(s), buy(s)	seeing, riding, freezing, buying	saw, rode, froze, bought	seen, ridden, frozen, bought

The present participle is usually used after a form of the verb *be;* the past participle, after a form of the verb *have.*

Ruby *is* riding the bus, but in the past she *has* walked and *has* also ridden the train.

A. Practice: *Complete each sentence with the principal part indicated in parentheses.*

1. (present participle of *sell*) Firewood was ________________ at forty dollars a cord.
2. (past participle of *buy*) Bart had ________________ it at the yard sale.
3. (past participle of *figure*) Cass has ________________ out the bill.
4. (present form of *tower*) The basketball player ________________ over me.
5. (past form of *take*) Stanley ________________ his fishing pole to the river.

B. Writing Application: *Write four sentences to illustrate the principal parts of* shiver *and* freeze. *Your sentences should be about very cold places and people.*

1. ____

____

2. ____

____

3. ____

____

4. ____

____

Name ______________________________ Date ________________

"The Story-Teller" by Saki (H. H. Munro)

Support for Writing to Sources: Comparison of Works

Use this Venn diagram to gather details for your **comparison of works.** In the portion of the two circles that overlap, list elements that the bachelor's story has in common with a traditional children's story. In the portions that do not overlap, list elements that they do not share.

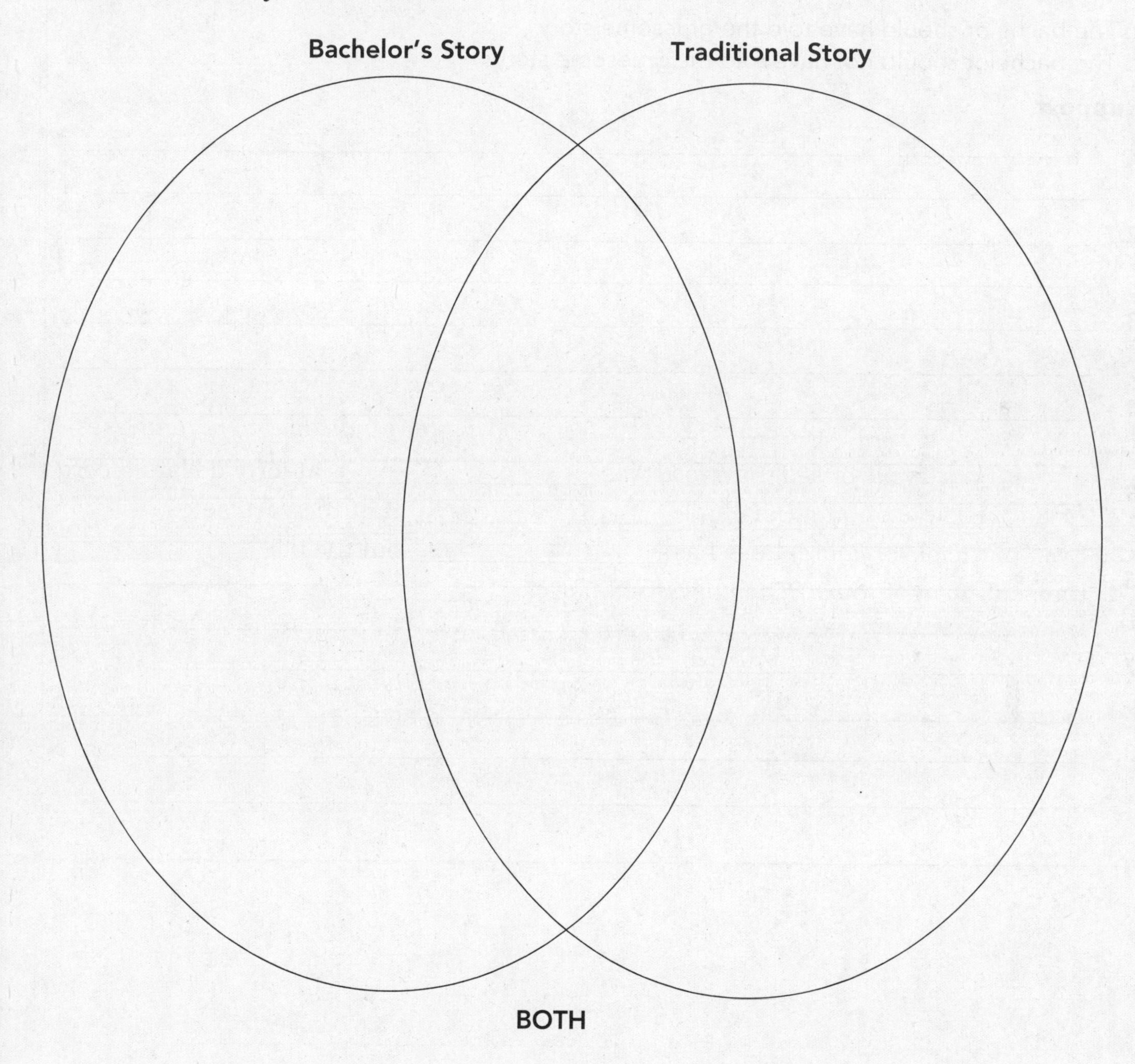

Name ______________________________ Date ______________

"The Story-Teller" by Saki

Support for Speaking and Listening: Panel Discussion

Use this chart to help you gather your thoughts for the panel discussion. Check off your opinion, and list the support you find for your opinion as you review the story.

Opinion

- ☐ The bachelor should have told the gruesome story.
- ☐ The bachelor should not have told the gruesome story.

Support

1. ______________________________
2. ______________________________
3. ______________________________
4. ______________________________
5. ______________________________
6. ______________________________
7. ______________________________
8. ______________________________

Name ______________________________ Date ______________

"The Finish of Patsy Barnes" by Paul Laurence Dunbar
"The Drummer Boy of Shiloh" by Ray Bradbury

THE BIG ?

Writing About the Big Question

Can all conflicts be resolved?

Big Question Vocabulary

argument	compromise	injury	insecurity	interact
irritate	mislead	negotiate	oppose	reaction
solution	stalemate	victorious	viewpoint	violence

A. *Use a word or words from the list above to complete each sentence.*

1. What is your ______________ about whether a fourteen-year-old should be allowed to ride a race horse?
2. I ______________ the idea because I do not think that a young rider would have the necessary strength and skill to win.
3. Some of the drummer boys who faced the ______________ of the Civil War were only ten years old.
4. Historical records show that many young drummer boys suffered serious ______________ or were killed on the battlefield.

B. *Follow the directions in responding to each of the items below. Answer in complete sentences.*

1. Name two conflicts that are sometimes part of the experience of growing up.

____

____

2. Write two sentences in which you give advice to a younger person facing a conflict. Use at least two of the Big Question vocabulary words.

____

____

____

C. *These stories involve two boys who have to assume serious adult responsibilities. Complete the sentence below. Then, write a paragraph in which you elaborate on your answer.*

When a child is forced to grow up too soon, he or she may face unexpected conflicts that

____

____

____

____

Name ______________________________ Date ______________

"The Finish of Patsy Barnes" by Paul Laurence Dunbar
"The Drummer Boy of Shiloh" by Ray Bradbury

Literary Analysis: Comparing Characters of Different Eras

A **character** is a person who takes part in the action of a literary work.

- A *dynamic character* develops and learns because of events in the story.
- A *static character* does not change. Static characters are often used by writers to develop conflict. These characters are not usually the central characters in a story.

Just as in real life, characters in fiction are affected by the **settings** in which they live. The forces that shape characters can include their jobs, living conditions, and major historical events. When a major historical event—such as a war or an economic downturn—occurs in a story, it can force characters to make difficult decisions for their own survival. Both "The Finish of Patsy Barnes" and "The Drummer Boy of Shiloh" present boys who live through challenging times. In one story, a recent move and a sudden illness have a devastating impact on a poor family. In the other, a war threatens to change the life of a soldier forever.

DIRECTIONS: *Answer the questions about the characters in these stories.*

1. Describe Patsy at the beginning of "The Finish of Patsy Barnes."

____

____

2. What is life like for Eliza and Patsy Barnes in Dalesford?

____

____

3. What does Patsy accomplish by the end of the story?

____

4. How does Patsy develop and change through events in the story?

____

____

5. Describe Joby, the drummer boy, at the beginning of "The Drummer Boy of Shiloh."

____

____

6. What does Joby think of his drum at the beginning of the story?

____

7. What causes the general to notice Joby as he walks by?

____

8. How has Joby—and his feelings about the drum—changed by the end of the story?

____

Name ______________________________ Date ______________

"The Finish of Patsy Barnes" by Paul Laurence Dunbar
"The Drummer Boy of Shiloh" by Ray Bradbury

Vocabulary Builder

Word List

compulsory diplomatic immortality meager resolute

A. Directions: *Answer each question, and then explain your answer.*

1. Would a person be able to live extravagantly on a *meager* income?

____

____

2. If Sarah is *resolute* in her decision, is it likely that she will change her mind?

____

____

3. If chorus practice is *compulsory,* would the music teacher let students not attend?

____

____

4. If Tim is *diplomatic* with classmates, would other students ask him to help settle arguments?

____

____

5. Would someone who believes in *immortality* be afraid of death?

____

____

B. Directions: *Fill in the blanks using each Word List word only once.*

1. Shianne was ______________ about going to law school; no one could talk her out of it.
2. Before the class trip, students must attend a ______________ meeting.
3. The college student barely survives on his ______________ salary at the bookstore.
4. Julio can be very ______________ when helping his coworkers resolve a problem.
5. Dan's belief in ______________ makes him unafraid of death.

Name ______________________________ Date ______________

"The Finish of Patsy Barnes" by Paul Laurence Dunbar
"The Drummer Boy of Shiloh" by Ray Bradbury

Support for Writing to Compare Characters

Before you write an essay that compares and contrasts the characters of Patsy Barnes and Joby, use the graphic organizer below to list ideas about each character.

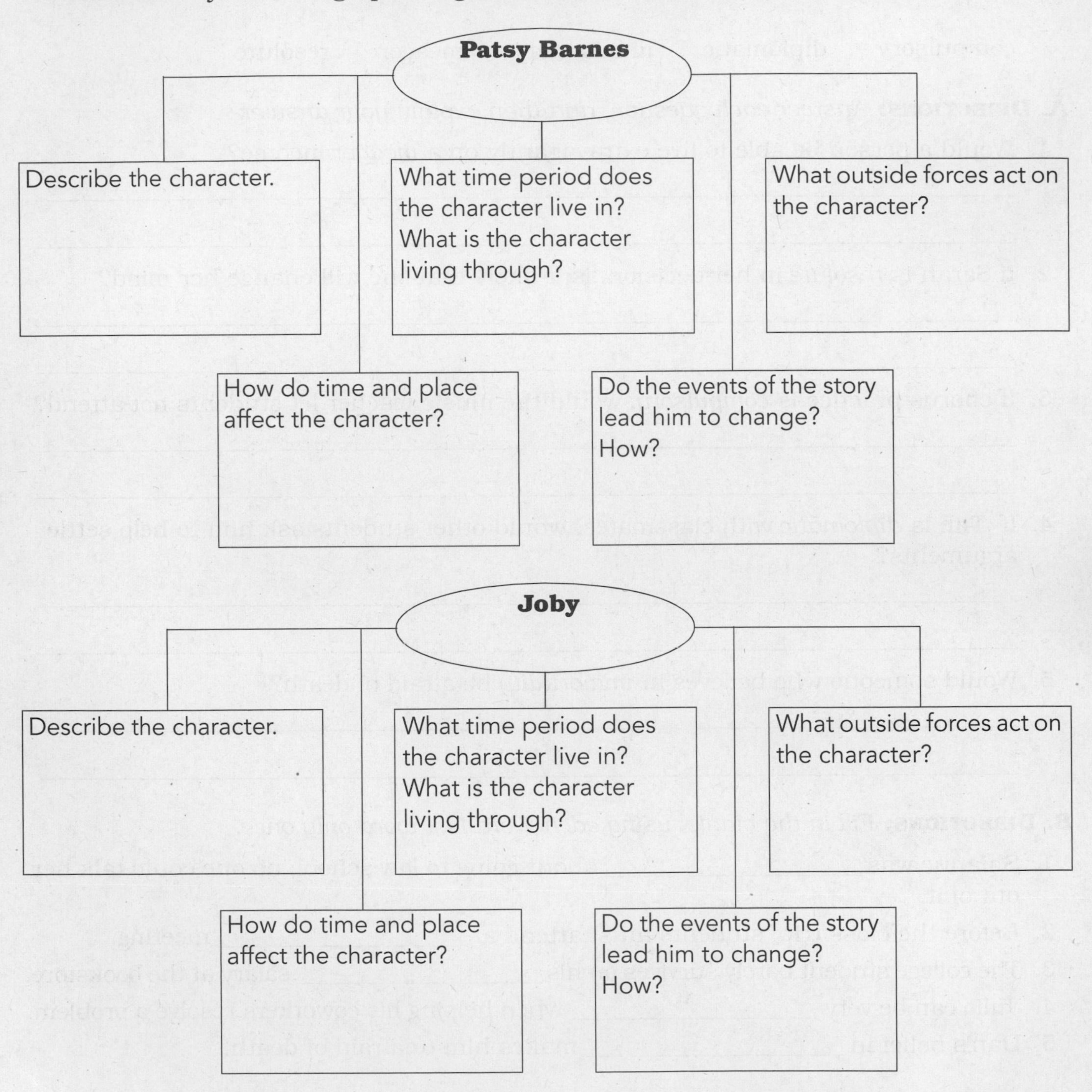

Now, use your notes to write an essay that compares and contrasts Patsy Barnes and Joby.

Name ______________________________ Date ______________

Writing Process

Autobiographical Essay

Prewriting: Gathering Details

Once you have chosen your topic—the event from your life that you would like to narrate—list details that will help in your writing. Use the following chart. Spend about three minutes listing words and phrases that apply to each heading.

People	Time	Place	Events	Emotions

Drafting: Ordering Events

Use the graphic organizer below to organize the events of your narrative around the conflict.

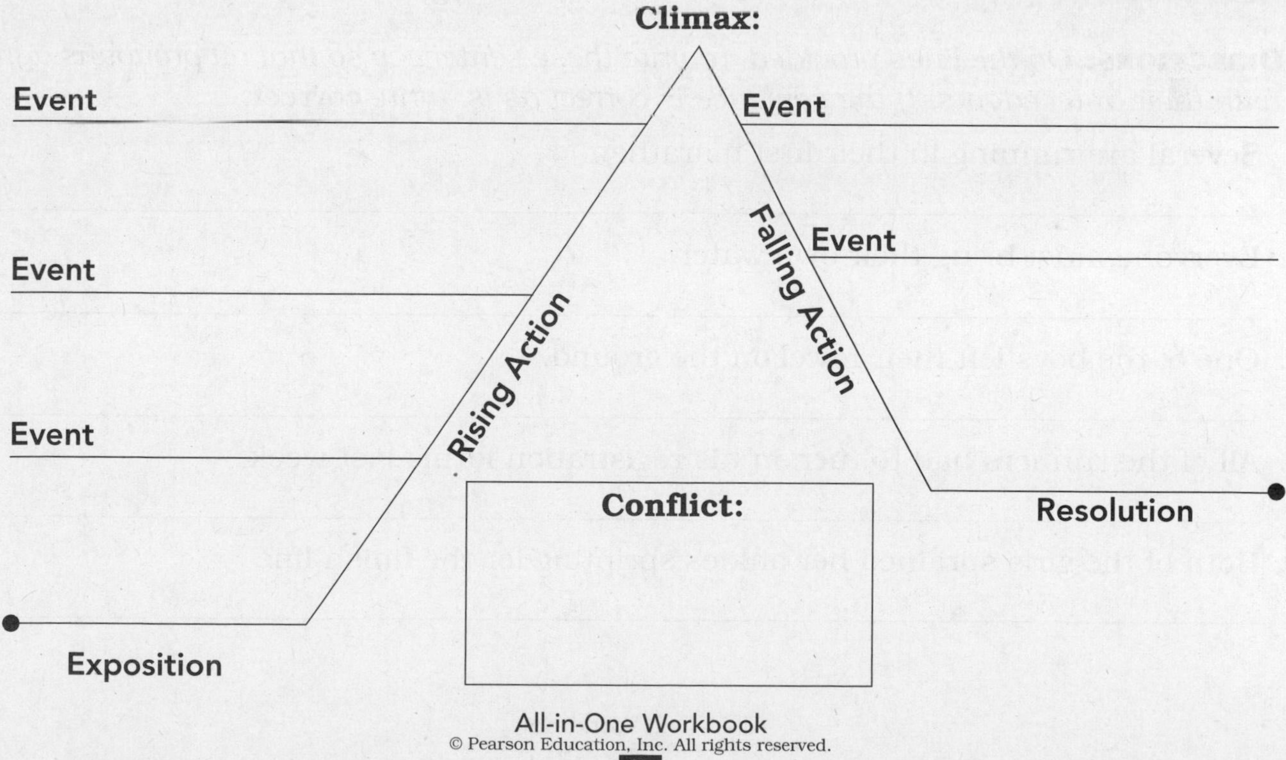

Name ______________________________ Date ______________

Writer's Toolbox

Conventions: Revising for Pronoun-Antecedent Agreement

A **pronoun** is a word that stands for a noun or another pronoun. An **antecedent** is the word or group of words for which the pronoun stands. Pronouns should agree with their antecedents in person and number.

Person	Singular in Number	Plural in Number
First person	I paid for *my* ticket, so please send it to *me*.	We ate *our* dinner when the waitress served it to *us*.
Second person	Simon, who gave that to *you*?	Girls, would *you* like some dessert?
Third person	Sara said *she* might be late because *her* watch was lost.	The boys brought *their* swimsuits so *they* could play in the pool.

An antecedent can be an **indefinite pronoun.** Indefinite pronouns vary in their number: some are always singular, some are always plural, and some can be either.

Indefinite Pronouns		
Singular: another, anyone, anything, each, either, everybody, everyone, everything, little, much, one, nothing, other, somebody, someone, something	**Plural:** both, few, many, others, several	**Either:** all, any, more, most, none, some

A. Directions: *Underline each pronoun, and draw an arrow to its antecedent.*

1. Raul runs daily because he wants to compete next year in ninth grade.
2. Daniel lifts weights for his workout.
3. Bethany and Leah do 15 push-ups as part of their exercise routine.
4. The president presented the senators with a challenge, and many rose to it.

B. Directions: *On the lines provided, rewrite these sentences so that all pronouns agree with their antecedents. If the sentence is correct as is, write* correct.

1. Several are running in their first marathon.

____

2. Everyone must bring their own water.

____

3. One of the boys left their towel on the ground.

____

4. All of the runners had to turn in his registration forms last week.

____

5. Both of the girls sprained her ankles sprinting for the finish line.

____

Name ______________________________ Date ______________

"Who Can Replace a Man?" by Brian Aldiss

Vocabulary Builder

Selection Vocabulary

deficiency erosion ravaged

A. DIRECTIONS: *Write at least one synonym, one antonym, and an example sentence for each word. Synonyms and antonyms can be words or phrases.*

Word	Synonym	Antonym	Example Sentence
deficiency			
erosion			
ravaged			

Academic Vocabulary

interactions reaction viewpoint

B. DIRECTIONS: *Complete each sentence with a word, phrase, or clause that contains a context clue for the italicized word.*

1. When certain chemicals undergo *interactions*, the result may be ____.
2. Most people's *reaction* to a good comedian is ____.
3. One person's *viewpoint* may be ____.

Name ______________________ Date ______________

"Who Can Replace a Man?" by Brian Aldiss

Take Notes for Discussion

Before the Group Discussion: Read the following passage from the selection.

"Yesterday orders came from the city. Today no orders have come. Yet the radio has not broken down. Therefore *they* have broken down ..." said the little penner.

"The *men* have broken down?"

"All men have broken down."

"That is a logical deduction," said the field-minder.

"That is the logical deduction," said the penner. "For if a machine had broken down, it would have been quickly replaced. But who can replace a man?"

During the Discussion: As you discuss each question, take notes on how other students' ideas either differ from or build upon your own.

Discussion Questions	Other Ideas Expressed	Comparison to My Own Ideas
1. For what purpose do the machines rely on humans?		
2. What makes the machines deduce that the men have broken down?		
3. According to the penner, what is the main difference between a machine and a human being?		

Name ______________________ Date ______________

"Who Can Replace a Man?" by Brian Aldiss

Take Notes for Writing to Sources

Planning Your Argument: Before you begin drafting your **argumentative essay,** use the chart below to organize your ideas. Follow the directions at the top of each section.

1. State your position. You will use this statement in your opening paragraph.

2. List details from the selection that demonstrate that machines have the ability to function as humans do.

3. List details from the selection that demonstrate that machines do not have the ability to function as humans do.

4. Jot down notes for your conclusion in which you summarize your argument.

Name ______________________________ Date ____________________

"Who Can Replace a Man?" by Brian Aldiss

Take Notes for Research

As you research **whether machines have become "smarter" over time,** use the forms below to take notes from your sources. As necessary, continue your notes on the back of this page, on note cards, or in a word-processing document.

Source Information Check one: ☐ Primary Source ☐ Secondary Source

Title: ______________________________ Author: ____________________

Publication Information: ______________________________

Page(s): ______________________________

Main Idea: ______________________________

____

Quotation or Paraphrase: ______________________________

____

Source Information Check one: ☐ Primary Source ☐ Secondary Source

Title: ______________________________ Author: ____________________

Publication Information: ______________________________

Page(s): ______________________________

Main Idea: ______________________________

____

Quotation or Paraphrase: ______________________________

____

Source Information Check one: ☐ Primary Source ☐ Secondary Source

Title: ______________________________ Author: ____________________

Publication Information: ______________________________

Page(s): ______________________________

Main Idea: ______________________________

____

Quotation or Paraphrase: ______________________________

____

Name ______________________________ Date ______________

"John Henry"

Vocabulary Builder

Selection Vocabulary

tunnel flagged locomotive

A. Directions: *Write a complete sentence to answer each question. For each item, use a vocabulary word from the list in place of the underlined words with similar meanings.*

1. A police officer signaled motorists to stop. What reason might he have had for stopping them?

____

____

2. Why might a train pulled by an engine be used for shipping heavy loads?

____

____

3. Under what situation would a train need an underground passageway?

____

____

Academic Vocabulary

aspects elements region

B. Directions: *Decide whether each statement below is true or false. On the line before each item, write TRUE or FALSE. Then, explain your answers.*

________ 1. A dialect is language that is spoken in a particular *region*.

____.

________ 2. Readers can interpret a poem by studying the poetic *elements* the author employs.

____.

________ 3. The *aspects* of a person's personality do not explain his or her behavior.

____.

Name ______________________________ Date ______________

"John Henry"

Take Notes for Discussion

Before the Group Discussion: Read the following passage from the selection.

John Henry tol' his cap'n,
Lightnin' was in his eye:
"Cap'n, bet yo' las, red cent on me,
Fo' I'll beat it to the bottom or I'll die,
Lawd, Lawd, I'll beat it to the bottom or I'll die."

During the Discussion: As you discuss each question, take notes on how others' ideas either differ from or build upon your own.

Discussion Questions	Other Ideas Expressed	Comparison to My Own Ideas
1. What does the passage indicate about John Henry's struggle?		
2. What does John Henry's struggle suggest about the relationship between humans and machines?		

Name ______________________ Date ______________

"John Henry"

Take Notes for Research

As you research **the rise of machines in the nineteenth century,** use the chart below to take notes from your sources. As necessary, continue your notes on the back of this page, on note cards, or in a word-processing document.

The Rise of Machines in the Nineteenth Century	
Main Idea ______________________ ______________________ Quotation or Paraphrase ______________________ ______________________ ______________________ ______________________ ______________________ Source Information ______________________ ______________________ ______________________ ______________________	Main Idea ______________________ ______________________ Quotation or Paraphrase ______________________ ______________________ ______________________ ______________________ ______________________ Source Information ______________________ ______________________ ______________________ ______________________
Main Idea ______________________ ______________________ Quotation or Paraphrase ______________________ ______________________ ______________________ ______________________ ______________________ Source Information ______________________ ______________________ ______________________ ______________________	Main Idea ______________________ ______________________ Quotation or Paraphrase ______________________ ______________________ ______________________ ______________________ ______________________ Source Information ______________________ ______________________ ______________________ ______________________

Name ______________________________ Date ______________

"John Henry"

Take Notes for Writing to Sources

Planning Your Argument: Before you begin drafting your **letter to the editor,** use the chart below to organize your ideas. Follow the directions in each section.

1. Write a position statement on the use of a steam drill. You will use your statement in your introduction.
2. List reasons why the machine will affect your job and your life. Write facts and other evidence to support each of your reasons.
3. Write notes about what you learned to use in your conclusion.

Name ______________________________ Date ______________

"Julie and the Turing Test" by Linda Formichelli

Vocabulary Builder

Selection Vocabulary

artificial intelligence   software   wired

A. DIRECTIONS: *Answer each of the following questions with a complete sentence. Demonstrate your understanding of the italicized vocabulary word or words in each of your answers.*

1. If you needed a machine to be *wired* to perform a particular task, what would you do? ____
   ____.
2. In what field of academic study would a student be likely to learn about the development of *software*? ______________________________
   ____.
3. Is *artificial intelligence* an ability that human beings possess? ______________
   ____.

Academic Vocabulary

capable   distinctive   identify

B. DIRECTIONS: *Complete each sentence with a word, phrase, or clause that contains a context clue for the italicized word.*

1. The robot Matthew developed was *distinctive* because ______________________
   ____.
2. The robot showed that it was *capable* of thought by ______________________
   ____.
3. The robot, Paul, could *identify* ______________________________________
   ____.

Name ______________________ Date ____________

"Julie and the Turing Test" by Linda Formichelli

Take Notes for Discussion

Before the Small Group Discussion: Read the following passage from the selection.

> What separates us from these robots? What other qualities must computers have before they can be considered more like humans? Emotion? Common sense? Artistic ability?

During the Discussion: As you discuss each question, take notes on how other students' ideas either differ from or build upon your own.

Discussion Questions	Other Ideas Expressed	Comparison to My Own Ideas
1. Do you agree that the qualities listed by the author separate humans from machines? Explain.		
2. What are some additional qualities she could have included?		
3. What would it mean if a robot did exhibit the qualities listed?		

Name ______________________ Date ______________

"**Julie and the Turing Test**" by Linda Formichelli

Take Notes for Research

As you research **what Watson has done, what it is capable of, and what it might do in the future,** use the forms below to take notes from your sources. As necessary, continue your notes on the back of this page, on note cards, or in a word-processing document.

Source Information Check one: ☐ Primary Source ☐ Secondary Source

Title: ______________________ Author: ______________

Publication Information: ______________________

Page(s): ______________________

Main Idea: ______________________

____

Quotation or Paraphrase: ______________________

____

Source Information Check one: ☐ Primary Source ☐ Secondary Source

Title: ______________________ Author: ______________

Publication Information: ______________________

Page(s): ______________________

Main Idea: ______________________

____

Quotation or Paraphrase: ______________________

____

Source Information Check one: ☐ Primary Source ☐ Secondary Source

Title: ______________________ Author: ______________

Publication Information: ______________________

Page(s): ______________________

Main Idea: ______________________

____

Quotation or Paraphrase: ______________________

____

Name ______________________________ Date ______________

"Julie and the Turing Test" by Linda Formichelli

Take Notes for Writing to Sources

Planning Your Explanatory Text: Before you begin drafting your **explanatory essay,** use the chart below to organize your ideas. Follow the directions in each section.

1. Write a description of how the Turing test works. You will include this description in the introduction to your essay.
2. List examples of questions that a judge might ask on the test. For each of your questions, provide a sample answer.
3. Jot down notes for your conclusion. Include your reflections on the meaning of the Turing test.

Name ______________________________ Date ______________

"The Good News, Dave, . . ." by Chris Madden

Vocabulary Builder and **Take Notes for Writing to Sources**

Academic Vocabulary

identify illogical validity

DIRECTIONS: *Choose the synonym of, or word closest in meaning to, the vocabulary word.*

________	**1.** *identify*	**A.** duplicate	**B.** specify	**C.** evaluate
________	**2.** *illogical*	**A.** unreasonable	**B.** rational	**C.** obvious
________	**3.** *validity*	**A.** complexity	**B.** accuracy	**C.** seriousness

Take Notes for Writing to Sources

Planning Your Narrative: Before you begin drafting your **diary entry,** use the chart below to organize your ideas. Follow the directions in each section of the chart.

1. Plan your entry by listing details about what happened *before* the scene shown in the cartoon.
2. List details about what happened *after* the scene shown in the cartoon.
3. Write ideas about how Dave feels before and after getting the news. What personal conflicts does he experience?

Name ______________________________ Date ______________

"Robots Get a Feel for the World at USC Viterbi" by USC Viterbi School of Engineering

Vocabulary Builder

Selection Vocabulary

algorithm tactile thermal

A. DIRECTIONS: *Complete each sentence with a word, phrase, or clause that contains a context clue for the italicized word.*

1. Scientists give robots *tactile* sensors so ______________________________

______________________________.

2. An *algorithm* might be used to ______________________________

______________________________.

3. Robotic sensors can react even to the *thermal* properties of an object, such as ____

______________________________.

Academic Vocabulary

beneficial imitate incorporate

B. DIRECTIONS: *Write a response to each question. Write a complete sentence, and use the underlined vocabulary word in your sentence.*

1. What is one reason the university's work on robots may be beneficial? __________

____

2. If you were to present research on this topic, why might you incorporate graphics?

____

3. Why did the scientists give the robot fingerprints that imitate the human finger? __

____

Name ______________________________ Date ______________

"Robots Get a Feel for the World at USC Viterbi" by USC Viterbi School of Engineering

Take Notes for Discussion

Before the Group Discussion: Read the following passage from the selection.

> When confronted with one material at random, the robot could correctly identify the material 95% of the time. . . . It was only rarely confused by a pair of similar textures that human subjects . . . could not distinguish at all. . . .
>
> [W]hile [the] robot is very good at identifying which textures are similar to each other, it has no way to tell what textures people will prefer.

During the Discussion: As you discuss each question, take notes on how other students' ideas either differ from or build upon your own.

Discussion Questions	Other Ideas Expressed	Comparison to My Own Ideas
1. How do the robot's skills compare with those of humans?		
2. Does the robot sense, just as humans do? Explain.		
3. What does the passage show about what people can do that robots cannot?		

Name ______________________ Date ______________

"Robots Get a Feel for the World at USC Viterbi" by USC Viterbi School of Engineering

Take Notes for Research

As you research **the history of neurorobotics and the kinds of advances that have already been made,** you can use the organizer below to take notes from your sources. As necessary, continue your notes on the back of this page, on note cards, or in a word-processing document.

History and Advances in Neurorobotics	
Main Idea ______________________	Main Idea ______________________
Quotation or Paraphrase ______________________	Quotation or Paraphrase ______________________
Source Information ______________________	Source Information ______________________
Main Idea ______________________	Main Idea ______________________
Quotation or Paraphrase ______________________	Quotation or Paraphrase ______________________
Source Information ______________________	Source Information ______________________

Name ______________________________ Date ______________

"**Robots Get a Feel for the World at USC Viterbi**" by USC Viterbi School of Engineering

Take Notes for Writing to Sources

Planning Your Informative Text: Before you begin drafting your **comparison-and-contrast essay,** use the chart below to organize your ideas. Follow the directions in each section.

1. Write a statement of your main idea that you will include in your introduction.
2. List ways in which the BioTac® sensor and the human fingertip are alike.
3. List ways in which the BioTac® sensor and the human fingertip are different.

Name ______________________________ Date ______________

from **Star Trek: The Next Generation, "The Measure of a Man,"**
Act 5 by Melinda M. Snodgrass

Vocabulary Builder

Selection Vocabulary

condemn   contention   hostile

A. Directions: *Provide an explanation for your answer to each question. Use the vocabulary word in your response.*

1. If someone's attitude is *hostile*, how is he or she likely to act toward others? ______
____

2. Can a *contention* become the basis for an argument? ______________
____

3. If a judge and jury *condemn* someone for a crime, what may happen to him or her? ______________________________
____

Academic Vocabulary

arguments   evaluation   technique

B. Directions: *Write the letter of the word or phrase that means the same or about the same as the vocabulary word. Then use the italicized word in a complete sentence.*

____ 1. *technique*

A. reason
B. decision
C. connection
D. method

____

____ 2. *evaluation*

A. effect
B. memory
C. assessment
D. idea

____

____ 3. *arguments*

A. reasonings
B. conclusions
C. disappointments
D. questions

____

Name ______________________________ Date ______________

***from* Star Trek: The Next Generation, "The Measure of a Man," Act 5** by Melinda M. Snodgrass

Take Notes for Discussion

Before the Group Discussion: Read the following passage from the selection.

> Is Data a machine? Yes. Is he the property of Starfleet? No. We've all been dancing around the basic issue: Does Data have a soul? I don't know that he has. I don't know that I have. But I've got to give him the freedom to explore that question himself.

During the Discussion: As you discuss each question, take notes on how other students' ideas either differ from or build upon your own.

Discussion Questions	Other Ideas Expressed	Comparison to My Own Ideas
1. Does the judge make a clear, definite ruling? Why or why not?		
2. Based on the evidence, did the judge make the correct ruling? Explain.		

Name ____________________ Date ____________

from **Star Trek: The Next Generation, "The Measure of a Man,"**
Act 5 by Melinda M. Snodgrass

Take Notes for Research

As you research **how close science is to creating an android as sophisticated as Data,** use the forms below to take notes from your sources. As necessary, continue your notes on the back of this page, on note cards, or in a word-processing document.

Source Information Check one: ☐ Primary Source ☐ Secondary Source

Title: ____________________ Author: ____________

Publication Information: ____________________

Page(s): ____________________

Main Idea: ____________________

____

Quotation or Paraphrase: ____________________

____

Source Information Check one: ☐ Primary Source ☐ Secondary Source

Title: ____________________ Author: ____________

Publication Information: ____________________

Page(s): ____________________

Main Idea: ____________________

____

Quotation or Paraphrase: ____________________

____

Source Information Check one: ☐ Primary Source ☐ Secondary Source

Title: ____________________ Author: ____________

Publication Information: ____________________

Page(s): ____________________

Main Idea: ____________________

____

Quotation or Paraphrase: ____________________

____

Name ______________________________ Date ______________

from **Star Trek: The Next Generation, "The Measure of a Man," Act 5** by Melinda M. Snodgrass

Take Notes for Writing to Sources

Planning Your Argument: Before you begin drafting your **argumentative essay,** use the chart below to organize your ideas. Follow the directions in each section of the chart.

1. Write an introduction to the topic and clearly state your claim about Data. You will use this information in the introduction to your essay.
2. List your main arguments. Under each argument, list facts and other evidence that support that argument.
3. Write notes you can use in your conclusion. It should sum up the main points you have made.

Name ______________________ Date ______________

Unit 2 Types of Nonfiction
Big Question Vocabulary—1

The Big Question: How much information is enough?

Thematic Vocabulary

accumulate: *v.* to gradually get more and more of something; other form: *accumulation*

development: *n.* the process by which someone or something grows or is built up; other forms: *develop, developing*

discrimination: *n.* the act of treating a person or group differently, in an unfair way; other forms: *discriminate, discriminating*

reveal: *v.* to uncover a secret or make something known; other forms: *revealing, revealed*

valuable: *adj.* useful, helpful, or important; other forms: *value, valued*

A. Directions: *From the words in the box, choose the correct synonym and antonym for each Thematic Vocabulary word. You will not use every word in the box.*

hide	gather	growth	treasured	fairness	pride
prejudice	expose	deterioration	worthless	scatter	

1. accumulate **Synonym:** ______________ **Antonym:** ______________
2. development **Synonym:** ______________ **Antonym:** ______________
3. discrimination **Synonym:** ______________ **Antonym:** ______________
4. reveal **Synonym:** ______________ **Antonym:** ______________
5. valuable **Synonym:** ______________ **Antonym:** ______________

B. Directions: *Complete each sentence by writing the correct Thematic Vocabulary word on the line.*

1. The ______________ of a plant begins with the sprouting of a tiny seed.
2. As a stamp collector, my goal is to ______________ a large quantity of valuable stamps.
3. This beautiful portrait is ______________ because it was painted by a famous artist.
4. The candidate vowed that she would rule fairly and avoid all forms of ______________.
5. When will the judges ______________ the identity of the new champion?

Name ______________________________ Date ______________

Unit 2 Types of Nonfiction
Big Question Vocabulary—2

The Big Question: How much information is enough?

Thematic Vocabulary

challenge: *v.* to question, oppose, or confront in order to argue a viewpoint; other forms: *challenged, challenging*

decision: *n.* a choice that is made after considering the options; other forms: *decide, deciding*

explanation: *n.* the act of making something clear and understandable; other forms: *explain, explaining, explained*

exploration: *n.* the study and observation of a location in order to find facts or make a discovery; other forms: *explore, exploring, explored*

inequality: *n.* an unfair situation in which some people have more money, opportunities, or power than others; other forms: *equal, equality*

A. DIRECTIONS: *Complete the passage by inserting the correct Thematic Vocabulary word on each line.*

In 1620, the Pilgrims crossed the Atlantic Ocean in the *Mayflower,* a small wooden ship. They suffered greatly along the way, and many died. However, they had great determination. They had left home because of the (1) ______________________ they faced under the unfair laws of the British king. He had begun to (2) ______________________ the religious beliefs of the Pilgrims, going so far as to throw many of the Pilgrims into jail. Therefore, the Pilgrims' (3) ______________________ was firm: They would not turn back, despite the suffering. Finally, their battered ship reached the calm waters of Massachusetts Bay, and they dropped anchor. After a small group went ashore for a thorough (4) ______________________ of the thickly wooded land, they returned and gave the others the following (5) ________________ of their settlement plans: They would build a small village, and they would name it Plymouth, after the British port city from which they had sailed.

B. DIRECTIONS: *Answer this question:* If you were President of the United States, what would you do to solve the problem of inequality? *Use as many vocabulary words as you can.*

____

____

____

____

____

Name ______________________ Date ______________

Unit 2 Types of Nonfiction
Big Question Vocabulary—3

The Big Question: How much information is enough?

Thematic Vocabulary

challenge: *v.* to question, oppose, or confront in order to dispute a viewpoint; other forms: *challenged, challenging*

global: *adj.* affecting or including the entire world; other forms: *globe, globally*

quality: *n.* the degree to which something is good or bad

quantity: *n.* an amount of something that can be counted or measured; other form: *quantities*

statistics: *n.* sets of numbers that represent facts or measurements; other forms: *statistical, statistically*

Before the voyage of Christopher Columbus, many people believed that Earth was flat. Columbus set out to prove them wrong.

A. Directions: *Write a proposal that he might have made, trying to persuade King Ferdinand and Queen Isabella to fund his voyage. Use facts about the good qualities of your crew and stress that you will keep a log of facts and measurements throughout the voyage. Use all five Thematic Vocabulary words.*

____

____

____

____

____

____

B. Directions: *Okay, Columbus. Now answer these questions. Use the words in parentheses.*

1. Queen Isabella: Tell me, Mr. Columbus, how many ships do you need?

   Answer: **(*quantity*)**: ______________________________

2. King Ferdinand: People say that you'll fall off the edge of the world. What about that?

   Answer: **(*challenge*)**: ______________________________

3. Queen Isabella: Well, why will history ever think this voyage is important?

   Answer: **(*global*)**: ______________________________

Name ______________________________ Date ______________

Unit 2 Types of Nonfiction
Applying the Big Question

How much information is enough?

DIRECTIONS: *Complete the chart below to apply what you have learned about quality and quantity of information. One row has been completed for you.*

Example	Type of Information	Useful	Not Useful	What I Learned
From Literature	What Harriet Tubman told the fugitive slaves	Information about success stories	Information that she had never been to Canada	Some information is best left unsaid.
From Literature				
From Science				
From Social Studies				
From Real Life				

Name ______________________________ Date ____________________

from **"Harriet Tubman: Conductor on the Underground Railroad"** by Ann Petry

Writing About the Big Question

THE BIG ?

How much information is enough?

Big Question Vocabulary

accumulate	challenge	decision	development	discrimination
explanation	exploration	factor	global	inequality
quality	quantity	reveal	statistics	valuable

A. *Use a word from the list above to complete each sentence.*

1. Research tells us that slaves endured a poorer ____________________ of life than white servants did.
2. The ____________________ to try to escape was difficult for a slave to make.
3. There was ____________________ interest in America's abolishment of slavery.
4. Documents show that many spoke out against ____________________ based on race.

B. *Follow the directions in responding to each of the items below.*

1. Explain why slavery was more common in the South than in the North. Use at least two words from the list in your explanation.

   ____

   ____

2. Do you think slavery will ever disappear completely? Use at least two words from the list in your answer.

   ____

   ____

C. *Complete the sentence below. Then, write a short paragraph in which you connect this answer to the Big Question.*

The situation of slaves in the United States was ____________________

____

____

____

Name ______________________ Date ______________

from **"Harriet Tubman: Conductor on the Underground Railroad"** by Ann Petry

Reading: Use Details to Identify the Main Idea

The **main idea** of a work of nonfiction is the central point that the author conveys. Sometimes the author states the main idea directly. More often, the author implies, or suggests, the main idea by giving you details to consider. To **identify the implied main idea,** connect details that the author provides. The main idea you decide upon should cover all the important details in the paragraph, section, or essay.

In "Harriet Tubman: Conductor on the Underground Railroad," the author tells how Tubman led fugitive slaves to freedom in Canada. Harriet Tubman believed strongly in the right of freedom for all. Therefore, she repeatedly risked her own freedom to gain it for others.

Ask: What does the author want me to discover about Harriet Tubman as I read the details of her efforts?

DIRECTIONS: *Read each excerpt from the selection, and summarize its details. The first one is done as an example. Then, add up all the details to identify the main idea of the selection.*

1. In December 1851, when she started out with the band of fugitives that she planned to take to Canada, she had been in the vicinity of the plantation for days, planning the trip, carefully selecting the slaves that she would take with her.

   Summary of details: Tubman planned carefully for each trip.

2. There were eleven in this party. . . . It was the largest group that she had ever conducted, but she was determined that more and more slaves should know what freedom was like.

   Summary of details: ______________________

3. She had never been in Canada. The route beyond Philadelphia was strange to her. But she could not let the runaways who accompanied her know this. As they walked along she told them stories of her own first flight, she kept painting vivid word pictures of what it would be like to be free.

   Summary of details: ______________________

4. She lifted the gun, aimed it at the despairing slave. She said, "Go on with us or die." The husky low-pitched voice was grim.

   Summary of details: ______________________

5. They had come to trust her implicitly, totally. They, too, had come to believe her repeated statement, "We got to go free or die." She was leading them into freedom, and so they waited until she was ready to go on.

   Summary of details: ______________________

Main idea of the selection: ______________________

____

Name ______________________________ Date ______________

from **"Harriet Tubman: Conductor on the Underground Railroad"** by Ann Petry

Literary Analysis: Narrative Essay

A **narrative essay** tells the story of real events experienced by real people in real places. Narrative essays share these features with fictional stories:

- People's traits and personalities are developed through their words, actions, and thoughts.
- The setting of the action may be an important element.

In "Harriet Tubman: Conductor on the Underground Railroad," the author tells a true story about how a former slave led other slaves to freedom in the mid-1800s. The author provides details about the setting, particular events, and interactions with others. The details help the reader understand Harriet Tubman's personality, her personal strength, and her success as a leader.

DIRECTIONS: *Answer the following questions. Your answers will help you identify the details that the author provides to develop Harriet Tubman's personality.*

1. What kinds of stories does Harriet Tubman tell to the fugitives in order to build their courage?

____

____

2. What would probably happen to Tubman if she were caught?

____

____

3. What time of day does the group travel, and what is the weather like?

____

____

4. After being refused shelter, how does Tubman react?

____

____

5. Why does Tubman admire the Quaker, Thomas Garrett?

____

____

6. What does Tubman do when she and her group make it to Canada?

____

____

Name ______________________________ Date ______________

from **"Harriet Tubman: Conductor on the Underground Railroad"** by Ann Petry

Vocabulary Builder

Word List

bleak   dispel   fugitives   incentive   invariably   mutinous

A. Directions: *Look at the underlined vocabulary word in each question. Then, answer the question.*

1. Why would <u>fugitives</u> sleep during the day and travel at night?

   ____

2. What might be an <u>incentive</u> to apply for a job at a health club?

   ____

3. If a student is <u>mutinous</u>, what might he or she do?

   ____

4. How might someone <u>dispel</u> a rumor?

   ____

5. Do you find a desert landscape <u>bleak</u>?

   ____

6. Why does every class <u>invariably</u> include someone who answers every question?

   ____

B. Word Study The suffix *-ly* is usually used to create adverbs that describe how, when, or how often something is done. Use what you know about the suffix *-ly* and the meaning of the base word to write whether each adverb describes how, when, or how often.

1. Why doesn't anyone take teenagers <u>seriously</u>? ______________
2. Exercising <u>daily</u> for hours on end is not a wise idea. ______________
3. Answering questions <u>sarcastically</u> is sure to annoy Mr. Kohn. ______________

Name ______________________________ Date ______________

from **"Harriet Tubman: Conductor on the Underground Railroad"** by Ann Petry

Conventions: Simple Tenses of Verbs

The **tense** of a verb shows the time of an action or a condition. The **simple tenses** show present, past, and future time.

Present Tense	**Past Tense**	**Future Tense**
Use base form; add *-s* or *-es* if subject is *he, she, it*, or a singular noun	For regular verbs, add *-ed* or *-d* to base form; irregular forms vary.	Use *will* before base form.
I *talk.* They *go.* She *talks.* Bob *goes.*	I *talked.* It *faded.* He *went.* They *saw.*	I *will talk.* They *will go.*

When telling a sequence of events, do not shift tenses unnecessarily.

Incorrect: I *crawled* into bed and *sleep.*

Correct: I *crawled* into bed and *slept.*

In some cases, however, it is necessary to shift tense to show the order of events.

Incorrect: Because I *wake* up early this morning, I *feel* tired this afternoon.

Correct: Because I *woke* up early this morning, I *feel* tired this afternoon.

A. Practice: *Underline the verb in each sentence. Then, on the line before the sentence, write whether the verb is in the* present, past, *or* future *tense.*

______________ 1. I really admire Harriet Tubman.

______________ 2. Tubman helped fugitive slaves.

______________ 3. She looked like a little old lady.

______________ 4. To people today, she seems like a great hero.

______________ 5. People will remember her always.

B. Writing Application: *Write a sentence about freedom or civil rights. Use verbs in the past tense. Then, rewrite the sentence using verbs in the present tense. Finally, rewrite the sentence using verbs in the future tense. Study these examples:*

PAST TENSE: We struggled for freedom.

PRESENT TENSE: We struggle for freedom.

FUTURE: We will struggle for freedom.

____

____

____

Name ______________________________ Date ________________

from **"Harriet Tubman: Conductor on the Underground Railroad"** by Ann Petry

Support for Writing to Sources: Biographical Sketch

A **biography** is an account of a real person's life. A **biographical sketch** is a much shorter piece of writing in which the author tells something important about a real person.

DIRECTIONS: *Use the graphic organizer below to help plan your biographical sketch about someone who took risks in order to achieve a worthy goal. Based on the details you generate about the person, come up with a main idea for your sketch.*

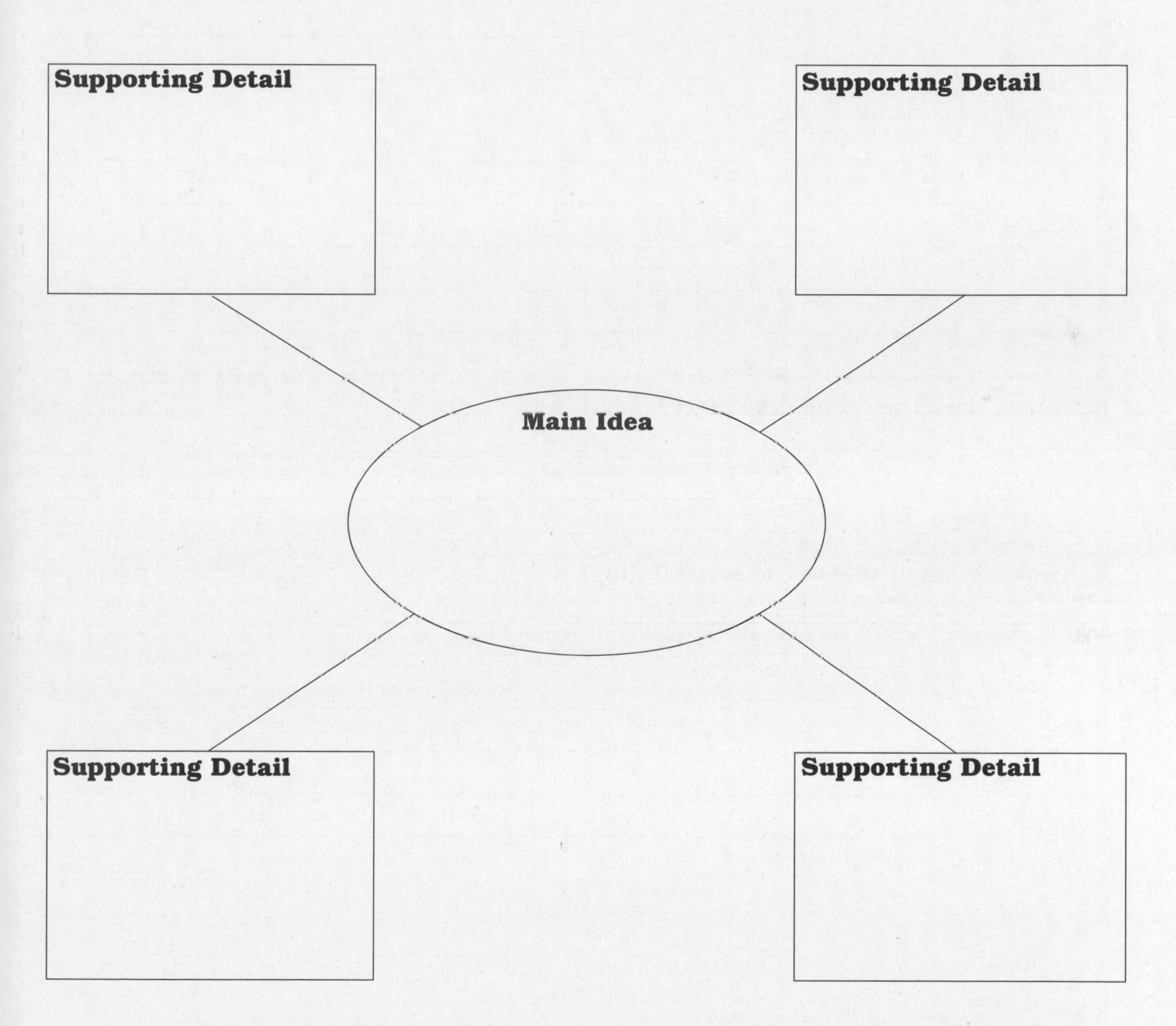

Now, revise your main idea as appropriate, write the body of the biographical sketch, and end with a strong concluding sentence that restates your main idea in different words.

Name ______________________________ Date ____________________

from **"Harriet Tubman: Conductor on the Underground Railroad"** by Ann Petry

Support for Speaking and Listening: Skit

Discuss in your small group which scenes from the essay about Harriet Tubman you will write about. On the lines below, record your group's responses to the following questions. Then, use the information to write your **skit.**

1. Who are the people in your scene?

____

____

____

2. What happens in the scene?

____

____

____

____

____

____

3. Where does the scene take place?

____

____

____

4. How are the people in the scene feeling?

____

____

____

____

____

____

Name ______________________________ Date ______________

"Always to Remember: The Vision of Maya Ying Lin" by Brent Ashabranner

Writing About the Big Question

THE BIG ?

How much information is enough?

Big Question Vocabulary

accumulate	challenge	decision	development	discrimination
explanation	exploration	factor	global	inequality
quality	quantity	reveal	statistics	

A. *Write a word from the Big Question vocabulary list that best answers each question below.*

1. Which word describes something that happens all over the world?
   ____
2. Which word would you use to call something into question? ______________________
3. Which word means "make something known"? ______________________

B. *Follow the directions in responding to each of the items below.*

1. Write a two-sentence description of a person or event that you would like to honor in a memorial. Explain why that person or event deserves a memorial. Use at least two list words in your sentences.
   ____
   ____
2. What kind of memorial should the person or event have? Include one or more list words in your answer.
   ____
   ____

C. *Complete the sentence below. Then, write a short paragraph in which you connect this answer to the Big Question.*

Exploration of history requires ______________________________

____

____

____

Name ______________________________ Date ______________

"Always to Remember: The Vision of Maya Ying Lin" by Brent Ashabranner

Reading: Make Connections Between Supporting Paragraphs and the Main Idea

Main ideas are the most important points in a literary work. Writers often organize essays so that main ideas are part of a clear structure. An introduction states the main idea, and then each paragraph supports or develops it. **Make connections between supporting paragraphs and the main idea.**

- Pause to note the main idea of paragraphs or sections.
- Write notes, or complete an organizer to track main ideas and key details.
- Review the main ideas and details in each section to see how they support the essay's main idea.

Read this passage from the selection about Maya Ying Lin.

Announcement of the competition in October, 1980, brought an astonishing response. The Vietnam Veterans Memorial Fund received over five thousand inquiries. They came from every state in the nation and from every field of design.

The details support the main idea: the astonishing support for the competition.

DIRECTIONS: *For each passage, list details that support the stated main idea.*

1. Maya Lin grew up in an environment of art and literature. She was interested in sculpture and made both small and large sculptural figures, one cast in bronze. She learned silversmithing and made jewelry. She was surrounded by books and read a great deal. . . .

   Main idea of whole section: Maya Lin's home was full of art and literature.

   Supporting details: ______________________________

   ____

2. On the day of their visit, Maya Lin remembers, Constitution Gardens was awash with a late November sun; the park was full of light, alive with joggers and people walking beside the lake.

   Main idea of whole section: Maya's visit to the building site was memorable.

   Supporting details: ______________________________

   ____

3. The designs were displayed without any indication of the designer's name so that they could be judged anonymously, on their design merits alone. The jury spent one week reviewing all the designs. . . . On May 1 it made its report to the Vietnam Veterans Memorial Fund; the experts declared Entry Number 1,026 the winner.

   Main idea of whole section: Designs were judged impartially.

   Supporting details: ______________________________

   ____

Name ______________________________ Date ______________

"Always to Remember: The Vision of Maya Ying Lin" by Brent Ashabranner

Literary Analysis: Biography and Autobiography

- A **biographical essay** is a short work in which a writer tells about an important event in the life of another person.
- An **autobiographical essay** is also a true account, but it is written by the person who experienced the event himself or herself. It includes the writer's thoughts and feelings about an event.

Both types of writing look at the influence of personal experiences, such as schooling, on the later personalities and accomplishments of a person.

DIRECTIONS: *Complete the following outline by providing the details given in the biographical essay about Maya Ying Lin.*

Maya Ying Lin

I. Background and education

A. Background

1. ______________________________

2. ______________________________

3. ______________________________

B. Education

____

II. The Vietnam Veterans Memorial contest

A. Steps to winning

1. ______________________________

2. ______________________________

B. Rewards

1. ______________________________

2. ______________________________

III. The Vietnam Veterans Memorial

A. Specifications

1. ______________________________

2. ______________________________

3. ______________________________

B. Judges' reactions to winning entry

1. ______________________________

2. ______________________________

Name ______________________________ Date ______________

"Always to Remember: The Vision of Maya Ying Lin" by Brent Ashabranner

Vocabulary Builder

Word List

anonymously authorized criteria eloquent harmonious unanimous

A. Directions: *Complete each of the following sentences with a vocabulary word.*

1. What ______________ did the teacher use in grading the research papers?
2. The senator's speech before Congress was ______________.
3. The spices created a(n) ______________ blend of flavors in the stew.
4. Opinion was ______________; everyone agreed to the suggestion.
5. A(n) ______________ biography is one that the subject approves.
6. Our newspaper does not print letters people send ______________.

B. Word Study The Greek root *-nym-* means "name." Answer each question that follows with one of these words containing the root *-nym-*: *synonym, anonymous, acronym, homonyms.* Consult a dictionary if necessary.

1. What is a word formed from the first letters of a phrase?

   ____

2. What is a word that has the same or nearly the same meaning as another word?

   ____

3. What are two words that sound the same but are spelled differently?

   ____

4. What is a word that describes a work whose author is unknown?

   ____

C. Directions: *Identify each item as a pair of synonyms, a pair of homonyms, or an acronym.*

1. their/there ______________________________
2. NATO ______________________________
3. buy/purchase ______________________________
4. do/due ______________________________
5. LOL ______________________________

Name ______________________________ Date ______________

"Always to Remember: The Vision of Maya Ying Lin" by Brent Ashabranner

Conventions: The Perfect Tenses

A **verb tense** tells when the action or state of being takes place. Each of the **perfect tenses** describes an action or a state of being that was or will be completed at a certain time. Perfect tenses are formed by adding a form of the helping verb *have* to the past participle of the main verb, which in regular verbs ends in *ed.*

- The **present perfect tense** shows a past action or condition that continues into the present. Example: The gas gauge **has indicated** an empty tank for some time now.
- The **past perfect tense** shows a past action or condition that was completed before another began. Example: Dad **had filled** the tank before we started our vacation.
- The **future perfect tense** shows a future action or condition that will have ended at a certain time. Example: By this time next week, our trip **will have ended.**

A. Practice: *Complete each sentence with the verb form requested in parentheses.*

1. The teacher ________________ our short-answer test papers, and now we are waiting for the class bell to ring. (*collect* in the present perfect)
2. The teacher ________________ an essay for us to write before she scheduled this test. (*assign* in the past perfect)
3. By five o'clock, the teacher ________________ all our short-answer tests. (*review* in the future perfect)
4. Most of the students ________________ hard this year and do well on the tests. (*study* in the present perfect)

B. Writing Application: *Write three sentences about your education and future plans. One sentence should use the past perfect tense, one should use the present perfect tense, and one should use the future perfect tense. Underline the verbs, and label the verb tenses.*

____

____

____

____

____

____

Name ______________________ Date ______________

"Always to Remember: The Vision of Maya Ying Lin" by Brent Ashabranner

Support for Writing to Sources: Reflective Essay

Think about a commemorative work, such as a memorial or a statue, that you find significant. What makes it effective and memorable? Use the chart to organize your thoughts for your composition. First, list details about the purpose and style of the work. Then, for each detail, make a comparison to Lin's memorial, citng details from Ashabranner's essay.

My Commemorative Work	Lin's Memorial

Now, use your notes to write your essay, supporting main ideas with details about the two works.

Name ______________________ Date ______________

"Always to Remember: The Vision of Maya Ying Lin" by Brent Ashabranner

Support for Research and Technology: Multimedia Presentation

To prepare for your group's proposal for a **multimedia presentation** about the U.S. involvement in Vietnam, gather some basic information about that period. You might assign each group member to a particular source to search for ways to represent the impact of the war on people's attitudes at the time. Use the following lines to record your findings.

1. When did America's involvement in the Vietnam War occur?

____

____

2. What reasons did some Americans have for supporting the war?

____

____

____

____

____

____

3. What were some objections that some Americans had to the war?

____

____

____

____

____

____

4. What effects did the Vietnam War have on popular culture?

____

____

____

____

____

____

Name ______________________________ Date ______________

"**The Trouble With Television**" by Robert MacNeil

Writing About the Big Question

How much information is enough?

Big Question Vocabulary

accumulate	challenge	decision	development	discrimination
explanation	exploration	factor	global	inequality
quality	quantity	reveal	statistics	valuable

A. *Use a word from the list above to complete each sentence.*

1. Let me ______________________ some information about television.
2. The ______________________ of television changed people's lives forever.
3. What is the ______________________ for why some people watch hours of television a day?

B. *Follow the directions in responding to each of the items below.*

1. How would you rate the quality of television programming? What factors entered into your decision?

____

____

2. Write two sentences speculating about how your life would change if you stopped watching television. Use at least two Big Question words in your sentences.

____

____

____

____

C. *Complete the sentence below. Then, write a short paragraph in which you connect this answer to the Big Question.*

The exploration of ideas on TV news shows is usually ________________ and

____

____

____

____

____

Name ______________________________ Date ______________

"The Trouble With Television" by Robert MacNeil

Reading: Use Clue Words to Distinguish Fact From Opinion

A **fact** is information that can be proved based on evidence. An **opinion** may be supported by factual evidence, but it cannot be proved. A **generalization** is a conclusion based on facts. Like an opinion, a generalization can be supported by facts. However, an author may sometimes use an **overgeneralization,** a conclusion stated in a more extreme way than can be supported by facts.

Statements may be a combination of opinions and generalizations, or they may be opinions written to sound like facts. As you read, **use clue words** to determine when a statement should be read carefully and evaluated to determine whether it is an opinion, a fact, a generalization, or an overgeneralization.

- Words that communicate judgment, such as *best* and *worst,* or specific words that suggest the writer's good or bad feelings about the topic usually indicate an opinion. Sometimes, opinions are signaled directly with words such as *I believe* or *I think.*
- Words that indicate connections, such as *therefore, so,* and *because,* may signal generalizations or opinions that should be supported by facts. Extreme statements that include words such as *always, everything, anything, nothing, never,* and *only* may be overgeneralizations.

As you read nonfiction, distinguish facts and supported generalizations from opinions and overgeneralizations to evaluate the strengths and weaknesses of a writer's argument.

In "The Trouble With Television," Robert MacNeil makes a strong argument for limiting the time many people spend watching television. He uses a combination of all of these devices to convince his readers. His essay leads to a logical conclusion based on long observation and careful thought.

DIRECTIONS: *Read the passages from the selection, and then answer the questions.*

1. "Yet its dominating communications instrument, its principal form of national linkage, is one that sells neat resolutions to human problems that usually have no neat resolutions."
   On what fact is this generalization based?

   ____

2. "One study estimates that some 30 million adult Americans are 'functionally illiterate' and cannot read or write well enough to answer a want ad or understand the instructions on a medicine bottle."
   How could you prove that this statement is a fact?

   ____

3. "But it has come to be regarded as a given, . . . as though General Sarnoff, or one of the other august pioneers of video, had bequeathed to us tablets of stone commanding that nothing in television shall ever require more than a few moments' concentration."
   Why might this statement be considered an overgeneralization?

   ____

Name ______________________________ Date ______________

"The Trouble With Television" by Robert MacNeil

Literary Analysis: Persuasive Techniques

Persuasive techniques are the methods that a writer uses to convince an audience to think or act a certain way.

- **Repetition** is an effective way to drive home a point.
- **Rhetorical questions** (questions with obvious answers) make readers more likely to agree with later, more controversial points.

In "The Trouble With Television," Robert MacNeil uses both repetition and rhetorical questioning to drive home a point to his audience. Here is an example of the latter.

> Who can quarrel with a medium that so brilliantly packages escapist entertainment as a mass-marketing tool?

This rhetorical question forces readers to acknowledge the obvious answer: It is hard to argue against such a successful combination of entertainment and marketing.

DIRECTIONS: *Decide whether you find each of the following passages from the selection convincing, and then answer the questions.*

1. "It has become fashionable to think that, like fast food, fast ideas are the way to get to a fast-moving, impatient public."

   A. MacNeil use the word *fast* three times. What three things is he describing?

   ____

   B. How does the repetition in the preceding sentence convey the author's negative attitude toward television?

   ____

2. "When before in human history has so much humanity collectively surrendered so much of its leisure to one toy, one mass diversion?"

   A. How would you answer the rhetorical question?

   ____

   B. Does answering the question help persuade you to support the author's argument? Explain.

   ____

3. "When before in human history has so much humanity collectively surrendered so much of its leisure to one toy, one mass diversion? When before has virtually an entire nation surrendered itself wholesale to a medium for selling?"

   A. Why might MacNeil have repeated the word *surrendered*?

   ____

   B. Do you find the repetition effective? Explain.

   ____

Name ______________________________ Date ______________

"The Trouble With Television" by Robert MacNeil

Vocabulary Builder

Word List

constructive   diverts   passively   pervading   skeptically   trivial

A. DIRECTIONS: *Circle* T *if the statement is true or* F *if the statement is false. Then, explain your answer.*

1. When you need to concentrate on finishing a complicated project, you should find something that *diverts* your attention.

   T / F ______________________________

2. If a problem with a car is *trivial*, you don't need to repair it immediately.

   T / F ______________________________

3. If a burning smell were *pervading* the room, you would expect it to disappear immediately.

   T / F ______________________________

4. If you respond to a speech *skeptically*, you are likely to trust the speaker.

   T / F ______________________________

5. *Constructive* criticism can help actors improve their performances.

   T / F ______________________________

6. A crowd might protest *passively* by lying down in the street.

   T / F ______________________________

B. WORD STUDY The Latin root *-vad-* or *-vas* means "to go." Words with *-vad-* and *-vas-* might include *pervade,* "go into every part of"; *invasion,* "a takeover of something or a raid for the purpose of conquest"; and *evade,* "avoid" or "go away from." Use the meaning of the root to help you answer the following questions.

1. What might be the response of homeowners who notice an *invasion* of weeds in their garden?

   ____

2. Why might someone *evade* responsibility for a mistake?

   ____

3. What kind of smell might *pervade* an enormous auditorium?

   ____

Name ______________________________ Date ______________

"The Trouble With Television" by Robert MacNeil

Conventions: Verb Mood—The Subjunctive

The **mood** of a verb expresses the speaker's attitude. The **indicative mood** is used to state a fact: She *is* on television. The **subjunctive mood** is used to express a wish, a hope, or a condition contrary to fact: She wishes that she *were* on television. The subjunctive mood typically appears in clauses that begin with *if* and *that* (although *that* is sometimes dropped as understood). Verbs such as *ask, wish, demand, insist, prefer, desire, suggest,* and *require* often come before *that* clauses in the subjunctive mood.

Rules for Forming the Subjunctive Mood	
For *that* clauses, generally use the base form of the verb, regardless of the subject.	I demand that she *speak* on the record. Mom asked that he *spend* less time online.
For *be* (as a main or helping verb), use the base form, *be,* in most *that* clauses, regardless of the subject. In *that* clauses after the verb *wish,* however, use *were.*	We prefer that she *appear* in person. I insisted that Megan *be* quiet. I suggest (that) he *be* granted immunity. I wish (that) she *were* mayor.
For *be*, use *were* in present-tense *if* clauses, regardless of the subject.	If Lou *were* mayor, he would change the law. If it *were* stopped, I would be happy.

A. Practice: *Circle the correct verb in parentheses.*

1. Kelly's mother demanded that Kelly (cut, cuts) her TV viewing time in half.
2. She insisted that Kelly (was, be) more helpful around the house.
3. Kelly's sister Meg prefers that Kelly not (watches, watch) that crime show.
4. Meg wishes the crime show (was, were) less violent.
5. If she (was, were) in charge, she would change the channel.

B. Writing Assignment: *On the lines below, write three sentences about television that follow the instructions given.*

1. Use *view* in the subjunctive mood in a clause that begins with *that* and has the subject *I.*

   ____

2. Use *be* in the subjunctive mood in a clause that begins with *that* and has the subject *he.*

   ____

3. Use *be* in the subjunctive mood in a clause that begins with *if* and has the subject *she.*

   ____

Name ________________________________ Date ____________________

"The Trouble With Television" by Robert MacNeil

Support for Writing to Sources: Evaluation

An **evaluation** of a writer's arguments should identify specific supporting points that the author uses to defend his or her position. An evaluation should also determine whether each supporting point is effective.

DIRECTIONS: *Fill in the chart with Robert MacNeil's points supporting his negative view of watching television, the persuasive techniques that MacNeil uses, and an assessment of whether the overall argument is effective and sound.*

Supporting Points	
Persuasive Techniques	
Assessment	

Now, use your notes in the chart to write your evaluation.

Name ______________________________ Date ______________

"The Trouble With Television" by Robert MacNeil

Support for Research and Technology: Snapshot

Use this chart to record and organize the information you gather for your snapshot of the two conflicting arguments about the effects of watching television. List pros from one article and cons from the other, and put a check to show whether each is a fact or an opinion.

Pro	Con
☐ Fact ☐ Opinion	☐ Fact ☐ Opinion
☐ Fact ☐ Opinion	☐ Fact ☐ Opinion
☐ Fact ☐ Opinion	☐ Fact ☐ Opinion
☐ Fact ☐ Opinion	☐ Fact ☐ Opinion
☐ Fact ☐ Opinion	☐ Fact ☐ Opinion

Name ______________________________ Date ______________

"Science and the Sense of Wonder" by Isaac Asimov

Writing About the Big Question

How much information is enough?

Big Question Vocabulary

accumulate	challenge	decision	development	discrimination
explanation	exploration	factor	global	inequality
quality	quantity	reveal	statistics	valuable

A. *Use a word from the list above to complete each sentence.*

1. Science is more than facts and ______________________.
2. Scientists' ______________________ of knowledge about the world continues to grow.
3. Do you think there will come a time when there is a(n) ______________________ for everything?

B. *Follow the directions in responding to each of the items below.*

1. What two scientific developments would you like to learn more about?

____

____

2. How might you learn more about these scientific developments? Use at least two list words in your answer.

____

____

____

____

C. *Complete the sentence below. Then, write a short paragraph in which you connect this answer to the Big Question.*

The knowledge we gain from space exploration shows us ______________________

____

____

____

____

____

____

Name ______________________________ Date ____________________

"Science and the Sense of Wonder" by Isaac Asimov

Reading: Use Support for Fact and Opinion

A **fact** is information that can be proved. An **opinion** is a person's judgment or belief. As you read nonfiction, ask questions to evaluate an author's support for his or her opinions.

- A *valid opinion* can be supported by facts or by expert authority.
- A *faulty opinion* cannot be supported by facts. Instead, it is supported by other opinions and may contradict the facts. Faulty opinions often show *bias*.

In "Science and the Sense of Wonder," Isaac Asimov draws on facts and opinions to support his ideas about the limitations of Walt Whitman's poetic view of the stars. He claims that scientific knowledge is necessary to fully appreciate nature's beauty.

The following statement from the essay tells a fact. It can be proved by scientists.

> Those other bright spots, which are stars rather than planets, are actually suns.

The following statement is an opinion because it is a judgment or belief.

> The trouble is that Walt Whitman is talking through his hat, but the poor soul didn't know any better.

Asimov supports his opinion with scientific descriptions and explanations about our universe.

Directions: *Read the following statements of opinion from the selection. Complete the chart with Asimov's statements of support for each opinion. Then, decide whether you think the opinion is adequately supported, or valid.*

Opinion	Support	Adequately Supported?
1. "That is a very convenient point of view since it makes it not only unnecessary, but downright aesthetically wrong, to try to follow all that hard stuff in science."		
2. "There are worlds with thick atmospheres of carbon dioxide and sulfuric acid; . . . each with a weird and unearthly beauty that boils down to a mere speck of light if we just gaze at the night sky."		
3. "Some of them are of incomparable grandeur, each glowing with the light of a thousand suns like ours; some of them are merely red-hot coals doling out their energy stingily."		

Name ______________________________ Date ______________

"Science and the Sense of Wonder" by Isaac Asimov

Literary Analysis: Use Word Choice to Convey Ideas

An author's **word choice** can help him or her convey a certain idea or feeling. An author might choose words that are formal or informal, simple or complex. Factors that influence an author's word choice include the following:

- the author's intended audience and purpose
- the **connotations** of words—the negative or positive ideas associated with them

In this passage from his essay about the wonders of science, Isaac Asimov chooses words that he hopes will appeal to his listeners and spark their interest in learning about the science behind our universe.

> That is a very convenient point of view since it makes it not only unnecessary, but downright aesthetically wrong, to try to follow all that hard stuff in science. Instead, you can just take a look at the night sky, get a quick beauty fix, and go off to a nightclub.

By using language such as *all that hard stuff* and *get a quick beauty fix,* Asimov creates an informal feeling in his essay. He gets the attention of his audience—as a result, his readers are more likely to continue reading.

DIRECTIONS: *Read the following passages from the selection. Decide whether the underlined words create a formal feeling or an informal feeling. Then, explain the effect of each passage on readers.*

1. "I . . . have in my time spread out on a hillside for hours looking at the stars and being awed by their beauty (and receiving bug-bites whose marks took weeks to go away)."

____

____

____

2. "There are stars that pulsate endlessly in a great cosmic breathing; and others that, having consumed their fuel, expand and redden until they swallow up their planets. . . ."

____

____

____

3. "And some stars explode in a vast cataclysm whose ferocious blast of cosmic rays . . . reaches across thousands of light years."

____

____

____

Name ______________________________ Date ______________

"**Science and the Sense of Wonder**" by Isaac Asimov

Vocabulary Builder

Word List

awed   cataclysm   conceivable   contraction   exultantly   radiation

A. DIRECTIONS: *Write the letter of the word that means the* opposite *of the word in CAPITAL LETTERS.*

___ 1. EXULTANTLY
- A. miserably
- B. thankfully
- C. happily
- D. hopefully

___ 2. CONTRACTION
- A. disappearing
- B. expansion
- C. shrinking
- D. brightening

___ 3. AWED
- A. scared
- B. nervous
- C. amused
- D. unimpressed

___ 4. RADIATION
- A. revolving
- B. brightness
- C. absorption
- D. growth

___ 5. CATACLYSM
- A. success
- B. challenge
- C. party
- D. event

___ 6. CONCEIVABLE
- A. unimaginable
- B. forgotten
- C. fertile
- D. initial

B. WORD STUDY The Latin root *-tract-* means "pull or drag." The following questions have words containing the root *-tract-*. Use the meaning of *-tract-* to help you answer the questions.

1. If something *contracts*, is it still or does it move?

____

2. Can a *distraction* lure people away from their work?

____

Name ______________________________ Date ______________

"Science and the Sense of Wonder" by Isaac Asimov

Conventions: Active and Passive Voice

A verb is in the **active voice** if the subject performs the action. It is in the **passive** voice if the subject receives the action. To form the passive voice, use a form of *be* with the past participle of an action verb.

Active Voice	Passive Voice
Lightning *struck* the barn.	The barn *was struck* by lightning.
My family *is painting* the house.	The house *is being painted* by my family.

Writing is stronger when most sentences use the active voice, but the passive voice may be used when the performer of the action is unknown or to stress the action rather than its performer. Be careful not to shift from active to passive voice for no reason.

Performer Unknown: The office *was closed.* **To Stress Action:** The goal was *reached.*
Unnecessary Shift: He *drew* a map of Asia. The map *was drawn* on thick paper.

A. Practice: *On the line before each sentence, write* active *or* passive *to identify the voice of the verb.*

______________ **1.** Fire raged in the dry preserve area.

______________ **2.** Sparks were carried by the wind.

______________ **3.** A passing motorist called 9-1-1 from her car phone.

______________ **4.** Before long, nearby houses were threatened.

B. Writing Application: *On the lines provided, rewrite these sentences by using the active voice.*

1. Energy is released by a flash of lightning.

____

2. Thunder is produced by a rapid rise in air temperature.

____

3. Lightning rods are used by owners of buildings.

____

4. Lightning is attracted by the metal in umbrellas.

____

Name ______________________________ Date ______________________

"**Science and the Sense of Wonder**" by Isaac Asimov

Support for Writing to Sources: Response to Literature

To prepare for writing a **response** to Isaac Asimov's idea that a scientist's way of appreciating nature is just as valid as a poet's, fill out this chart. In the left column, identify Asimov's words, phrases, and passages that seem especially effective. In the right column, explain how the words, phrases, and passages affect your understanding and feelings about the text.

Words, Phrases, and Passages	Your Response

Now, use the ideas and details on your chart to help you write your response.

Name ______________________________ Date ______________

"Science and the Sense of Wonder" by Isaac Asimov

Support for Speaking and Listening: Speech

Use this outline to gather and organize ideas for your **speech** comparing the audiovisual presentation with Asimov's essay. For the introduction, write notes to help you preview the main points you will make. For the body, list your claims or findings in a logical order, supporting them with sound reasoning and well-chosen details. For the conclusion, write notes to help you sum up your presentation in an effective way. After you have completed the outline, go back and cross out any irrelevant details, and make sure you have enough support for your claims.

I. Introduction: ______________________________

____

II. Body

A. Claim: ______________________________

1. Support: ______________________________

2. Support: ______________________________

3. Support: ______________________________

B. Claim: ______________________________

1. Support: ______________________________

2. Support: ______________________________

3. Support: ______________________________

C. Claim: ______________________________

1. Support: ______________________________

2. Support: ______________________________

3. Support: ______________________________

D. Claim: ______________________________

1. Support: ______________________________

2. Support: ______________________________

3. Support: ______________________________

III. Conclusion: ______________________________

____

Name ______________________ Date ______________

"Forest Fire" by Anaïs Nin
"Why Leaves Turn Color in the Fall" by Diane Ackerman
"The Season's Curmudgeon Sees the Light" by Mary C. Curtis

Writing About the Big Question

How much information is enough?

Big Question Vocabulary

accumulate	challenge	decision	development	discrimination
explanation	exploration	factor	global	inequality
quality	quantity	reveal	statistics	valuable

A. *Use a word from the list above to complete each sentence.*

1. During the fall, leaves ______________ their underlying colors.
2. One ______________ in the forest fire was dry conditions.
3. What is your ______________ for preferring summer to spring?
4. Through ______________ you can discover a lot about nature.

B. *Follow the directions in responding to each of the items below.*

1. Write a two-sentence description of your favorite season. Use at least two of the Big Question vocabulary words in your sentences.

____

____

2. Which season do you like least? Use at least two of the Big Question vocabulary words in your explanation.

____

____

C. *These essays highlight different ways of appreciating nature. Complete the sentence below. Then, write a short paragraph in which you connect this sentence to the Big Question.*

The part of nature that I value the most is ______________ because ______________

____

____

____

Name ______________________________ Date ______________

"Forest Fire" by Anaïs Nin
"Why Leaves Turn Color in the Fall" by Diane Ackerman
"The Season's Curmudgeon Sees the Light" by Mary C. Curtis

Literary Analysis: Comparing Types of Organization

To present information in the most useful way possible, writers can choose among several **types of organization.** Here are three of the most common organizational plans.

- **Chronological order** relates events in the order in which they occurred.
- **Cause-and-effect order** examines the relationship between an event and its result or results.
- **Comparison and contrast** examines similarities and differences.

DIRECTIONS: *Answer the following questions about the organization of the essays.*

1. List six of the main events in "Forest Fire" in the order that they occur.

   Event 1 ______________ Event 4 ______________
   Event 2 ______________ Event 5 ______________
   Event 3 ______________ Event 6 ______________

2. Why is chronological order the best type of organization for "Forest Fire"?

   ____
   ____

3. Based on "Why Leaves Turn Color in the Fall," explain the causes and effects that make leaves colorful in the fall.

   ____
   ____
   ____
   ____

4. Why is cause-and-effect order the best type of organization for "Why Leaves Turn Color in the Fall"?

   ____
   ____

5. How do the author's feelings change in "The Season's Curmudgeon Sees the Light"?

   ____
   ____

6. Why is comparison and contrast the best type of organization for "The Season's Curmudgeon Sees the Light"?

   ____
   ____

Name ______________________________ Date ______________

"Forest Fire" by Anaïs Nin
"Why Leaves Turn Color in the Fall" by Diane Ackerman
"The Season's Curmudgeon Sees the Light" by Mary C. Curtis

Vocabulary Builder

Word List

capricious consoling contemplation evacuees predisposed tenacious

A. Directions: *Revise each sentence so that it uses the underlined vocabulary word logically. Be sure to keep the vocabulary word in your revision.*

1. The principal is consoling the student by disciplining him.

____

____

2. The children are predisposed to illness; they never get sick.

____

____

3. I call Lillian capricious because she does not like changing anything.

____

____

4. The evacuees left the movie theater laughing and discussing the funny movie.

____

____

5. Eliana enjoyed a noisy period of contemplation.

____

____

6. Scott has a tenacious personality, so he readily compromises.

____

____

B. Directions: *Circle the letter of the word that is most nearly* opposite *in meaning to the word in CAPITAL LETTERS.*

1. CONSOLING
   - A. helping
   - B. cheering
   - C. blending
   - D. agitating

2. PREDISPOSED
   - A. able
   - B. unwilling
   - C. ready
   - D. upgraded

3. TENACIOUS
   - A. relaxed
   - B. sturdy
   - C. pressure
   - D. stretched

Name ______________________________ Date ______________

"Forest Fire" by Anaïs Nin
"Why Leaves Turn Color in the Fall" by Diane Ackerman
"The Season's Curmudgeon Sees the Light" by Mary C. Curtis

Support for Writing to Compare Types of Organization

Before you write about the organization of one of the essays, use the graphic organizer below to list ideas about all three essays.

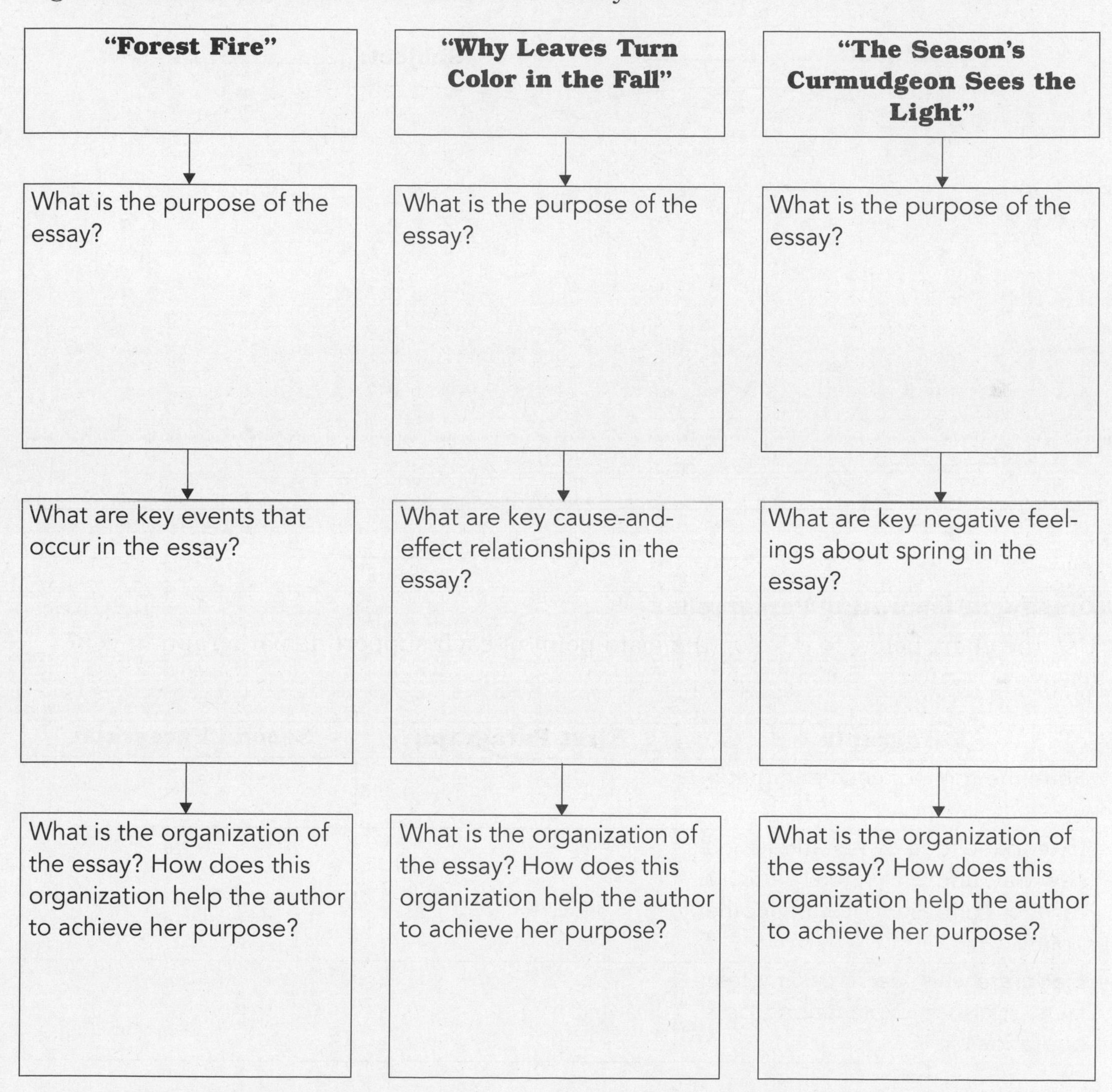

Now, choose one of the three essays, and explain how its organization matches or supports the writer's topic and purpose.

Name ______________________________ Date ______________

Writing Process

Comparison-and-Contrast Essay

Prewriting: Gathering Details

Use the Venn diagram below to list ideas and details about your two subjects. Use the center section to record similarities and the outer sections of each circle to record differences.

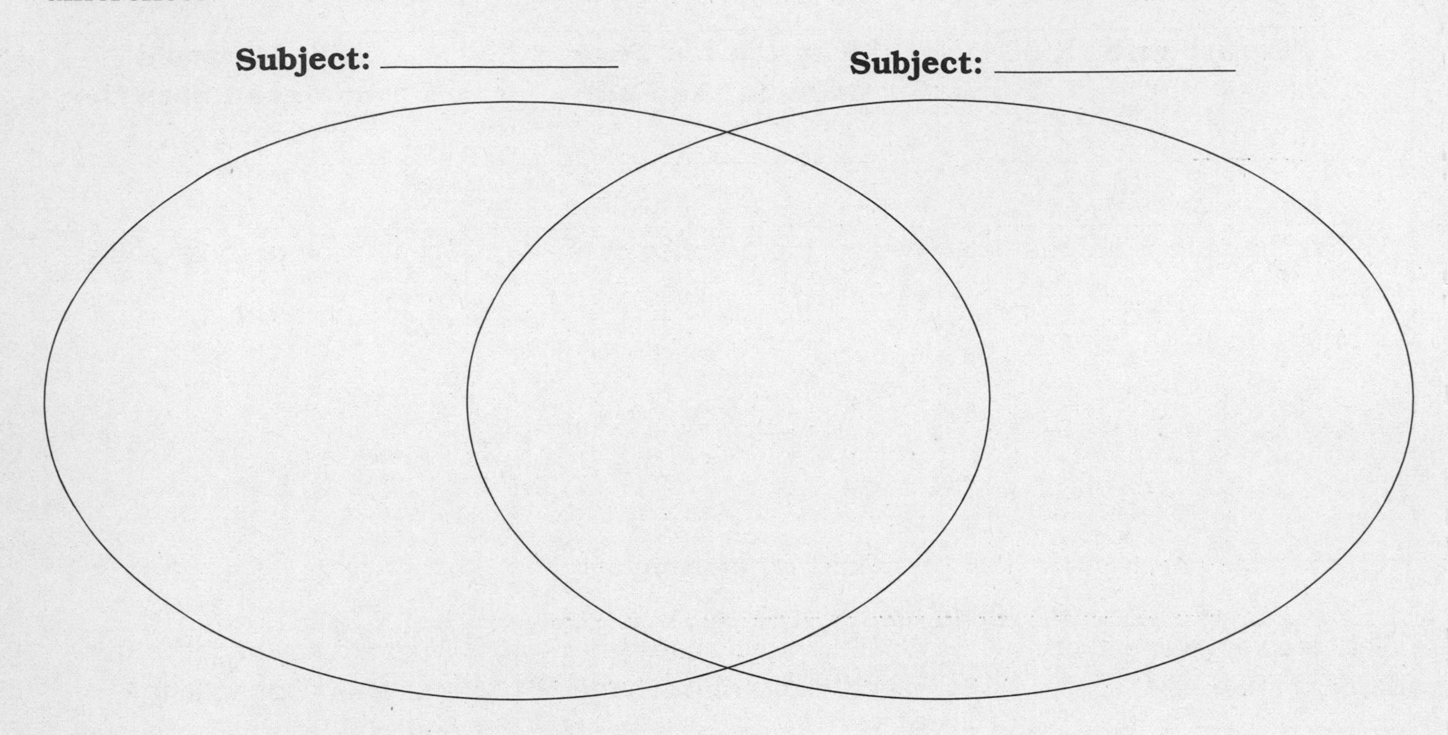

Drafting: Elaborating Paragraphs

Use the chart below to develop the main point of each supporting paragraph in your essay.

Paragraphs	First Paragraph	Second Paragraph
State the topic of each paragraph.		
Extend the idea by restating it in a new way, applying it to a particular case, or contrasting it with another point.		
Elaborate with specific examples, facts, statistics, explanations, or quotations.		

Name ______________________________ Date ________________

Writer's Toolbox

Conventions: Revising Verbs for Mood

The **mood** of a verb shows the speaker's attitude toward the action or condition expressed by the verb. The **indicative mood** is used to make statements of fact: *My sister travels by train.* The **interrogative mood** is used to ask a question: *Does your sister travel by train?* The **imperative mood** is used to make a command: *Take the noon train.*

The **conditional mood** is used to express something that has not yet happened. It uses a helping verb such as *could, would, should, may,* or *might.*

Ana *could leave* tonight. She *might take* a bus.

The **subjunctive mood** is used to express a wish, a hope, or a condition contrary to fact. It generally occurs in clauses beginning with *if* or *that* and uses *were* or the base form of the verb regardless of the subject.

I asked that she *take* the train. If she *were* late, she would drive.

A. Practice: *On the line before each sentence, write whether the verb in italics uses the* indicative, interrogative, imperative, conditional, *or* subjunctive *mood.*

______________ 1. *Have* you *been* to the supermarket lately?

______________ 2. The prices on many items *seem* very high.

______________ 3. Alicia *would save* money if she could.

______________ 4. *Look* for weekly specials.

______________ 5. I requested that the store *give* me a rain check.

B. Writing Activity: *Rewrite these sentences, correcting errors in mood by changing the underlined verbs. If a sentence is correct as is, write* correct.

1. Carla insisted that her brother <u>leaves</u> early.

____

2. If he were a lawyer, he <u>be</u> a good one.

____

3. Mrs. Abrams requests that the bus <u>makes</u> special stops.

____

4. If Raul <u>were</u> playing, the Tigers would probably win.

____

Name ______________________________ Date ______________

from **Travels with Charley** by John Steinbeck

Vocabulary Builder

Selection Vocabulary

desolate   inexplicable   omens

A. Directions: *From the following lists, select one synonym and one antonym for each of the numbered words in the table below. Write your choices in the appropriate boxes.*

Synonyms	**Antonyms**
deserted	comprehensible
foreshadowings	crowded
unexplainable	flashbacks

Word	Synonym	Antonym
1. omens		
2. inexplicable		
3. desolate		

Academic Vocabulary

anticipate   intensify   perceive

B. Directions: *Complete each sentence with a word, phrase, or clause that contains a context clue for the italicized word.*

1. You can *intensify* description in writing by ______________________________
______________________________.

2. If you *perceive* a situation as threatening you ______________________________
______________________________.

3. When you *anticipate* something you ______________________________
______________________________.

Name ______________________________ Date ________________

from **Travels with Charley** by John Steinbeck

Take Notes for Discussion

Before the Partner Discussion: Read the following passage from the selection.

> And I thought how every safe generality I gathered in my travels was canceled by another. In the night the Bad Lands had become the Good Lands. I can't explain it. That's how it was.

During the Discussion: As you discuss each question, take notes on how your partner's ideas either differ from or build upon your own.

Discussion Questions	Other Ideas Expressed	Comparison to My Own Ideas
1. What did it take for the author to feel he belonged in the Bad Lands?		
2. How is his eventual sense of belonging like or unlike that of the people he meets during his journey?		
3. Use examples from the text to determine the ways in which the people do or do not "belong" to their place.		

Name ______________________________ Date ______________

from **Travels with Charley** by John Steinbeck

Take Notes for Writing to Sources

Planning Your Informative Text: Before you begin drafting your **travel essay,** use the chart below to organize your ideas. Follow the directions at the top of each section.

1. Details from the selection that describe specific *people* in North Dakota:
2. Details from the selection that describe specific *places* in North Dakota:
3. Evaluation of your details and their categories:

Name ______________________ Date ______________

from **Travels with Charley** by John Steinbeck

Take Notes for Research

As you research **fear of unknown places and how people get over it,** use the forms below to take notes from your sources. As necessary, continue your notes on the back of this page, on note cards, or in a word-processing document.

Source Information Check one: ☐ Primary Source ☐ Secondary Source

Title: ______________________ Author: ______________

Publication Information: ______________________

Page(s): ______________________

Main Idea: ______________________

____

Quotation or Paraphrase: ______________________

____

Source Information Check one: ☐ Primary Source ☐ Secondary Source

Title: ______________________ Author: ______________

Publication Information: ______________________

Page(s): ______________________

Main Idea: ______________________

____

Quotation or Paraphrase: ______________________

____

Source Information Check one: ☐ Primary Source ☐ Secondary Source

Title: ______________________ Author: ______________

Publication Information: ______________________

Page(s): ______________________

Main Idea: ______________________

____

Quotation or Paraphrase: ______________________

____

Name ______________________________ Date ______________

"Gentleman of Río en Medio" by Juan A. A. Sedillo

Vocabulary Builder

Selection Vocabulary

descendants negotiation preliminary

A. Directions: *Write a complete sentence to answer each question. For each item, use a vocabulary word from the list in place of the underlined word with similar meaning.*

1. What kind of <u>introductory</u> remarks might a speaker make?

____

____

2. Why would you take part in lengthy <u>bargaining</u> with someone when buying a bicycle?

____

____

3. Why do grandparents like to tell their <u>grandchildren</u> about the family history?

____

____

Academic Vocabulary

accurate influence methods

B. Directions: *Decide whether each statement below is true or false. On the line before each item, write TRUE or FALSE. Then, explain your answers.*

________ 1. If someone's arguments are convincing, he or she probably will not *influence* other people's perceptions.

____

________ 2. An *accurate* survey will include correct measurements.

____

________ 3. If you are not successful at something, you should try again using the exact same *methods*.

____

Name ________________________________ Date ________________

"Gentleman of Río en Medio" by Juan A. A. Sedillo

Take Notes for Discussion

Before the Group Discussion: Read the following passage from the selection.

> Every time a child has been born in Río en Medio since I took possession of that house from my mother I have planted a tree for that child. The trees in that orchard are not mine, *Señor,* they belong to the children of the village.

During the Discussion: As you discuss each question, take notes on how other students' ideas either differ from or build upon your own.

Discussion Questions	Other Ideas Expressed	Comparison to My Own Ideas
1. What ideas of "belonging to a person" and "belonging to a place" does Don Anselmo express?		
2. How is Don Anselmo's idea of ownership, or what belongs to whom, different from the narrator's idea of ownership?		

Name ______________________ Date ______________

"Gentleman of Río en Medio" by Juan A. A. Sedillo

Take Notes for Research

As you research **the history of surveying,** use the chart below to take notes from your sources. As necessary, continue your notes on the back of this page, on note cards, or in a word-processing document.

Surveying	
Main Idea ______________ ______________ **Quotation or Paraphrase** ______________ ______________ ______________ ______________ ______________ **Source Information** ______________ ______________ ______________ ______________	**Main Idea** ______________ ______________ **Quotation or Paraphrase** ______________ ______________ ______________ ______________ ______________ **Source Information** ______________ ______________ ______________ ______________
Main Idea ______________ ______________ **Quotation or Paraphrase** ______________ ______________ ______________ ______________ ______________ **Source Information** ______________ ______________ ______________ ______________	**Main Idea** ______________ ______________ **Quotation or Paraphrase** ______________ ______________ ______________ ______________ ______________ **Source Information** ______________ ______________ ______________ ______________

Name ______________________________ Date ______________

"Gentleman of Río en Medio" by Juan A. A. Sedillo

Take Notes for Writing to Sources

Planning Your Argument: Before you begin drafting your **argumentative essay,** use the chart below to organize your ideas. Follow the directions in each section.

1. Statement of your claim: ____________________ ____________________
2. Reasons to support your claim: ____________________ ____________________ ____________________ ____________________ ____________________
3. Opposing claims: ____________________ ____________________ ____________________ ____________________ ____________________
4. Your refutation of opposing claims: ____________________ ____________________ ____________________ ____________________ ____________________
5. Your conclusion: ____________________ ____________________ ____________________

Name ______________________________ Date ______________

"Choice: A Tribute to Martin Luther King, Jr." by Alice Walker

Vocabulary Builder

Selection Vocabulary

brutal disinherit revolutionary

A. Directions: *Write the letter of the word or phrase that is the best synonym for the italicized word. Then, use the italicized word in a complete sentence.*

______ 1. *brutal*

A. generous C. savage

B. unfriendly D. noisy

____

______ 2. *disinherit*

A. dispute C. dismiss

B. disgust D. disown

____

______ 3. *revolutionary*

A. angry C. peaceful

B. rebellious D. disciplined

____

Academic Vocabulary

annotated cause-and-effect cite

B. Directions: *Complete each sentence with a word, phrase, or clause that contains a context clue for the italicized word.*

1. In an *annotated* outline, ____

____.

2. When you *cite* your sources, you ____

____.

3. *Cause-and-effect* relationships help explain ____

____.

Name ______________________________ Date ______________

"Choice: A Tribute to Martin Luther King, Jr." by Alice Walker

Take Notes for Discussion

Before the Group Discussion: Read the following passage from the selection.

> He gave us continuity of place, without which community is ephemeral. He gave us home.

During the Discussion: As you discuss each question, take notes on how other students' ideas either differ from or build upon your own.

Discussion Questions	Other Ideas Expressed	Comparison to My Own Ideas
1. What does Walker mean by "continuity of place"?		
2. In what way were African Americans missing this continuity?		
3. How did King help restore it?		

Name ______________________ Date ______________

"Choice: A Tribute to Martin Luther King, Jr." by Alice Walker

Take Notes for Research

As you research **a speech or sermon in which King discusses issues in an American city or cities,** use the forms below to take notes. As necessary, continue your notes on the back of this page, on note cards, or in a word-processing document.

King's Ideas	
Main Idea ______________________ ______________________ **Quotation or Paraphrase** ______________________ ______________________ ______________________ ______________________ ______________________ ______________________ ______________________ ______________________	**Main Idea** ______________________ ______________________ **Quotation or Paraphrase** ______________________ ______________________ ______________________ ______________________ ______________________ ______________________ ______________________ ______________________
Main Idea ______________________ ______________________ **Quotation or Paraphrase** ______________________ ______________________ ______________________ ______________________ ______________________ ______________________ ______________________ ______________________	**Main Idea** ______________________ ______________________ **Quotation or Paraphrase** ______________________ ______________________ ______________________ ______________________ ______________________ ______________________ ______________________ ______________________

Name ______________________________ Date ______________

"Choice: A Tribute to Martin Luther King, Jr." by Alice Walker

Take Notes for Writing to Sources

Planning Your Informative Essay: Before you begin drafting your **analytical essay,** use the chart below to organize your ideas. Follow the directions in each section.

1. Notes for your introduction:
2. Summary of Walker's account:
3. Notes and reflections on Walker's account for your conclusion:

Name ______________________________ Date ____________________

"**Tears of Autumn**" by Yoshiko Uchida

Vocabulary Builder

Selection Vocabulary

affluence degrading radical

A. Directions: *Decide whether each statement below is true or false. On the line before each item, write TRUE or FALSE. Then, explain your answers.*

________ 1. If a merchant lives a life of *affluence,* he is frugal and has few material possessions.

____.

________ 2. People would likely consider a politician *radical* if she were to support extreme social change.

____.

________ 3. A community leader would likely find it *degrading* to be recognized for her work in raising funds for education.

____.

Academic Vocabulary

significance techniques tradition

B. Directions: *Write the letter of the word or phrase that is the best synonym for the italicized word. Then, use the italicized word in a complete sentence.*

____ 1. *significance*

A. importance
B. ignorance
C. support
D. understanding

____

____ 2. *techniques*

A. differences
B. funds
C. methods
D. desires

____

____ 3. *tradition*

A. method
B. difficulty
C. combination
D. custom

____

Name ______________________________ Date ______________

"Tears of Autumn" by Yoshiko Uchida

Take Notes for Discussion

Before the Small Group Discussion: Read the following passage from the selection.

"You are Takeda San?" she asked.

He removed his hat and Hana was further startled to see that he was already turning bald.

During the Discussion: As the group discusses each question, take notes on how other students' ideas either differ from or build upon your own.

Discussion Questions	Other Ideas Expressed	Comparison to My Own Ideas
1. What does the passage suggest about difficulties Hana may face in making her new home in America?		
2. Is Hana's *wanting* to belong to a new place enough to guarantee that she will? Explain.		

Name ______________________________ Date ______________

"Tears of Autumn" by Yoshiko Uchida

Take Notes for Research

As you do research **on nineteenth- and early-twentieth-century U.S. immigration from a country you choose,** you can use the forms below to take notes from your sources. As necessary, continue your notes on the back of this page, on note cards, or in a word-processing document.

Source Information Check one: ☐ Primary Source ☐ Secondary Source

Title: ______________________________ Author: ______________

Publication Information: ______________________________

Page(s): ______________________________

Main Idea: ______________________________

____

Quotation or Paraphrase: ______________________________

____

Source Information Check one: ☐ Primary Source ☐ Secondary Source

Title: ______________________________ Author: ______________

Publication Information: ______________________________

Page(s): ______________________________

Main Idea: ______________________________

____

Quotation or Paraphrase: ______________________________

____

Source Information Check one: ☐ Primary Source ☐ Secondary Source

Title: ______________________________ Author: ______________

Publication Information: ______________________________

Page(s): ______________________________

Main Idea: ______________________________

____

Quotation or Paraphrase: ______________________________

____

Name ______________________________ Date ______________

"Tears of Autumn" by Yoshiko Uchida

Take Notes for Writing to Sources

Planning Your Fictional Narrative: Before you begin drafting your **new ending,** use the chart below to organize your ideas. Follow the directions in each section.

1. Notes on story background and characters:

2. Notes on details of new ending:

3. Notes on use of dialogue and other narrative techniques in new ending:

Name ______________________ Date ______________

from **I Know Why the Caged Bird Sings** by Maya Angelou

Vocabulary Builder

Selection Vocabulary

enchantment intolerant valid

A. Directions: *Revise each sentence so that the underlined vocabulary word is used logically. Be sure to keep the vocabulary word in your version.*

1. Because his argument was valid, we chose to ignore it. ______________________
______________________.
2. Having an open mind, the professor was intolerant of differing viewpoints. ______________________
______________________.
3. The best way to get good grades is through enchantment. ______________________
______________________.

Academic Vocabulary

community maintain role

B. Directions: *Write a response to each question. Write a complete sentence, and use the underlined vocabulary word in your sentence.*

1. If you maintain a formal style in an essay, what do you do?
____
____
2. What role might humor play in a story?
____
____
3. What would be a sign of being accepted as part of a community?
____
____

Name ______________________ Date ______________

from **I Know Why the Caged Bird Sings** by Maya Angelou

Take Notes for Discussion

Before the Panel Discussion: Read the following passage from the selection.

> On that first day, I ran down the hill and into the road . . . and had the good sense to stop running before I reached the Store.
>
> I was liked, and what a difference it made. I was respected not as Mrs. Henderson's grandchild or Bailey's sister but for just being Marguerite Johnson.

During the Discussion: As you discuss each question, take notes on how other students' ideas either differ from or build upon your own.

Discussion Questions	Other Ideas Expressed	Comparison to My Own Ideas
1. How has Marguerite's outlook changed?		
2. Why might she need a new way of belonging, beyond her way of belonging to the Store?		

Name ______________________ Date ______________

from **I Know Why the Caged Bird Sings** by Maya Angelou

Take Notes for Research

As you research **how much African Americans participated in the education system in the South when Marguerite went to school,** use the forms below to take notes from your sources. As necessary, continue your notes on the back of this page, on note cards, or in a word-processing document.

Source Information Check one: ☐ Primary Source ☐ Secondary Source

Title: ______________ Author: ______________

Publication Information: ______________

Page(s): ______________

Main Idea: ______________

____

Quotation or Paraphrase: ______________

____

Source Information Check one: ☐ Primary Source ☐ Secondary Source

Title: ______________ Author: ______________

Publication Information: ______________

Page(s): ______________

Main Idea: ______________

____

Quotation or Paraphrase: ______________

____

Source Information Check one: ☐ Primary Source ☐ Secondary Source

Title: ______________ Author: ______________

Publication Information: ______________

Page(s): ______________

Main Idea: ______________

____

Quotation or Paraphrase: ______________

____

Name ______________________________ Date ______________

from **I Know Why the Caged Bird Sings** by Maya Angelou

Take Notes for Writing to Sources

Planning Your Informational Text: Before you begin drafting your **comparison-contrast essay,** use the chart below to organize your ideas. Follow the directions at the top of each section of the chart.

1. Notes for your introduction:
2. Points you will make about the role of *objects*:
3. Points you will make about the role of *ideas*:

Name ______________________________ Date ______________

"Study Finds Americans Increasingly Rooted" by Cindy Weiss

Vocabulary Builder

Selection Vocabulary

assumption   embedded   disruption

A. DIRECTIONS: *Write a complete sentence to answer each question. For each item, use a vocabulary word in place of the underlined word or phrase with similar meaning.*

1. Why would something fixed in surrounding material be difficult to dislodge?

____

____

2. Why would an electrical power outage cause a breakdown in the school routine?

____

____

3. Why shouldn't you take for granted that you'll win a game against someone you don't know?

____

____

Academic Vocabulary

contrasting   evidence   statistics

B. DIRECTIONS: *Complete each sentence with a word, phrase, or clause that contains a context clue for the italicized word.*

1. *Statistics* are useful in proving a statement because ______________________________

____

2. Comparing *contrasting* ideas can be difficult because ______________________________

____

3. Supporting details provide *evidence* for a main idea by ______________________________

____

Name ______________________ Date ______________

"Study Finds Americans Increasingly Rooted" by Cindy Weiss

Take Notes for Discussion

Before the Group Discussion: Read the following passage from the selection.

> What keeps people stuck in one place? Age, for one thing. Older people are less likely to move. But technology is also contributing to the trend. If retired people can easily fly to a warm climate for part of the year, they are less likely to move there.

During the Discussion: As you discuss each question, take notes on how other students' ideas either differ from or build upon your own.

Discussion Questions	Other Ideas Expressed	Comparison to My Own Ideas
1. What factors allow people to remain in a place, even as their lives change?		
2. Do the factors that affect staying in one place determine whether or not someone really "belongs" there?		

Name ______________________________ Date ______________

"**Study Finds Americans Increasingly Rooted**" by Cindy Weiss

Take Notes for Research

As you research **a decade when people were settling the American West,** use the forms below to take notes from your sources. As necessary, continue your notes on the back of this page, on note cards, or in a word-processing document.

Source Information Check one: ☐ Primary Source ☐ Secondary Source

Title: ______________________ Author: ______________

Publication Information: ______________________

Page(s): ______________________

Main Idea: ______________________

____

Quotation or Paraphrase: ______________________

____

Source Information Check one: ☐ Primary Source ☐ Secondary Source

Title: ______________________ Author: ______________

Publication Information: ______________________

Page(s): ______________________

Main Idea: ______________________

____

Quotation or Paraphrase: ______________________

____

Source Information Check one: ☐ Primary Source ☐ Secondary Source

Title: ______________________ Author: ______________

Publication Information: ______________________

Page(s): ______________________

Main Idea: ______________________

____

Quotation or Paraphrase: ______________________

____

Name ______________________ Date ______________

"Study Finds Americans Increasingly Rooted" by Cindy Weiss

Take Notes for Writing to Sources

Planning Your Argumentative Text: Before you begin drafting your argument, use the chart below to organize your ideas. Follow the directions at the top of each section of the chart.

1. Statement of your claim:
2. Other claims that differ from yours:
3. Your refutation of other claims:
4. Reasons to support your claim:
5. Notes for your conclusion:

Name ______________________________ Date ______________

Media: "Relationships to Place" by Jennifer E. Cross

Vocabulary Builder and **Take Notes for Discussion**

Academic Vocabulary

categories sources support

A. DIRECTIONS: *Choose the synonym, or word closest in meaning, to the vocabulary word.*

_____ 1. *sources* A. results B. descriptions C. causes

_____ 2. *support* A. proof B. opposition C. purpose

_____ 3. *categories* A. guidelines B. classifications C. choices

Take Notes for Discussion

Before the Class Discussion: Discuss each question with your classmates. Take notes on how other students' ideas either differ from or build upon your own.

Discussion Questions	My Ideas	Comparison to My Own Ideas
1. Does the chart show all the different ways of belonging? Explain, drawing on your own background knowledge or on examples from the texts in this section.		
2. Would you remove any of the categories from the chart? Explain why or why not.		

Name ______________________________ Date ______________

Unit 3: Poetry
Big Question Vocabulary—1

The Big Question: What is the secret to reaching someone with words?

Thematic Vocabulary

benefit: *n.* an advantage, an improvement, or a type of help that something offers
v. to offer an advantage, an improvement, or a type of help; other forms: *beneficial, beneficiary*

cultural: *adj.* belonging or relating to a particular society and its way of life; other form: *culture*

feedback: *n.* advice, praise, or criticism about how successful or useful something is

meaningful: *adj.* serious, important, useful, and valuable; other forms: *mean, meaning*

misunderstand: *v.* to understand someone or something incorrectly; other forms: *understand, misunderstanding*

A. Directions: *Write the Thematic Vocabulary word that best completes each group of related words.*

1. comment, observation, ______________________________
2. ethnic, traditional, ______________________________
3. worthwhile, significant, ______________________________
4. confuse, mistake, ______________________________
5. aid, asset, ______________________________

B. Directions: *Complete each sentence by writing the correct Thematic Vocabulary word on the line.*

1. It is a ____________________ tradition to celebrate the Fourth of July in the United States.
2. Was the television program ____________________, or was it silly?
3. The teacher was careful to give each student helpful ____________________ regarding his or her report.
4. Daily exercise will definitely be a ____________________ to your health.
5. Listen carefully so that you don't ____________________ the directions.

Name ______________________________ Date ______________

Unit 3 Poetry
Big Question Vocabulary—2

The Big Question: What is the secret to reaching someone with words?

Thematic Vocabulary

connection: *n.* a joining together based on common thoughts or interests; other forms: *connect, connecting, connected*

experience: *n.* the act of living through an event

v. to be involved in an event; other forms: *experiencing, experienced*

express: *v.* to use actions or words to share thoughts and feelings; other forms: *expression, expressing, expressed*

relevant: *adj.* related directly to the subject being discussed; other form: *relevance*

sensory: *adj.* related to or affecting any of the five senses; other forms: *sense, sensing*

Logan's grandmother's birthday was coming up, and Logan wanted to write a poem for her. So, Logan asked some friends for advice.

DIRECTIONS: *Use the words and phrases in parentheses to write the dialogue she had with her friends. Use what you have learned about poetry and sensory details.*

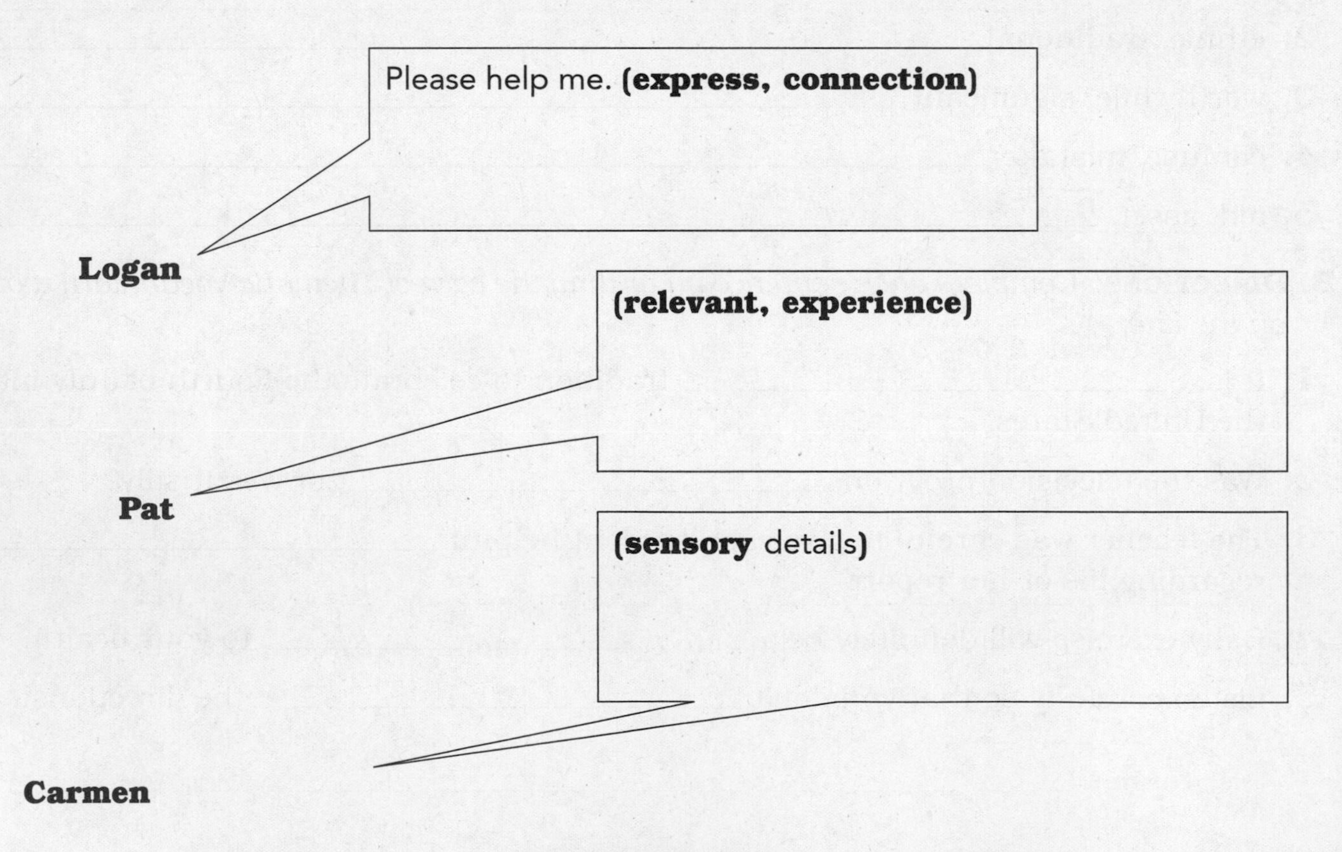

Name ______________________ Date ______________

Unit 3 Poetry
Big Question Vocabulary—3

The Big Question: What is the secret to reaching someone with words?

Thematic Vocabulary

individuality: *n.* the sum of personal traits that makes a person unique; other form: *individual*

inform: *v.* to tell, share, or teach facts related to a subject; other forms: *information, informed*

media: *n.* institutions or items that present news and other information, such as newspapers, magazines, television programs, and Internet sources; other form: *medium*

significance: *n.* the meaning or importance of something; other forms: *significant, significantly*

valid: *adj.* believable and reasonable; other forms: *validity, validation*

DIRECTIONS: *For each Thematic Vocabulary word, list three items as instructed. Then, use the vocabulary word in a sentence about one of the items.*

Example: List three *sensory* details about pizza.

spicy smell　　red and yellow color　　hot from the oven

Sentence: *I love the sensory experience of smelling a pizza baking in the oven.*

1. List three specific forms of the *media.*

______________ ______________ ______________

Sentence: ______________________________

2. List three things about you that show your *individuality.*

______________ ______________ ______________

Sentence: ______________________________

3. List three *valid* facts about the state in which you live.

______________ ______________ ______________

Sentence: ______________________________

4. List three facts that illustrate the *significance* of good nutrition.

______________ ______________ ______________

Sentence: ______________________________

5. List three facts that you would use to *inform* someone about one of your hobbies or interests.

______________ ______________ ______________

Sentence: ______________________________

Name ______________________________ Date ______________

Unit 3: Poetry
Applying the Big Question

What is the secret to reaching someone with words?

DIRECTIONS: *Complete the chart below to apply what you have learned about the secret to reaching others with words. One row has been completed for you.*

Example	Type of communication	Goal of writer or speaker	Effect on reader or listener	How the goal was achieved
From Literature	Poem "Cat!" by Eleanor Farjeon	Share experience of her stubborn cat in an entertaining way	I could see and hear the cat and the dog throughout the action.	Alliteration, onomatopoeia, rhyme, choppy rhythm
From Literature				
From Science				
From Social Studies				
From Real Life				

Name ______________________________ Date ______________

Poetry Collection: Walter de la Mare; Alfred, Lord Tennyson; Eleanor Farjeon; Eve Merriam

Writing About the Big Question

What is the secret to reaching someone with words?

Big Question Vocabulary

benefit	connection	cultural	experience	express
feedback	individuality	inform	meaningful	media
misunderstand	relevant	sensory	significance	valid

A. *Use one or more words from the list above to complete each sentence.*

1. When Kirsten wrote her summary, she included only ______________ information.
2. Justin hoped that Sarah didn't ______________ his question.
3. To paint a picture with words, poetry uses ______________ details.
4. Jasmine chose to express her ______________ through her writing.
5. Zoe appreciated the ______________ she received from her teacher.

B. *Follow the directions in responding to each of the items below.*

1. Write two sentences describing a personal connection you have formed in the last year.

   ______________________________.

   ______________________________.

2. Write two sentences about the possible results of a misunderstanding. Use at least two of the Big Question vocabulary words.

   ____

   ____

C. *Complete the sentence below. Then, write a short paragraph in which you connect this idea to the Big Question.*

Poets use sounds and rhythms to ______________

____

____

____

Name ______________________________ Date ______________

Poetry Collection: Walter de la Mare; Alfred, Lord Tennyson; Eleanor Farjeon; Eve Merriam

Reading: Using Context

Poetry often contains unusual words with which you may not be familiar. When you read a poem, it is a good idea to preview it, or examine it in advance, to identify any unfamiliar words. Then, as you read the poem more closely, look for clues in the context that can help you determine the meanings of these words. The **context** consists of the other words and phrases that surround a particular word. The following chart shows common types of context clues and an example of each. In the examples, the possibly unfamiliar words are underlined, and the context clues are in italics.

Clue	**Synonym/Definition:** words that mean the same as the unfamiliar word
Example	Knowing the importance of *exercise,* she does calisthenics every day.
Clue	**Antonym/Contrast:** words that mean the opposite of the unfamiliar word
Example	She does calisthenics every day, *but her brother is a couch potato.*
Clue	**Explanation:** words that give more information about the unfamiliar word
Example	Calisthenics *can improve your muscle tone and breathing.*
Clue	**Example:** a word or words that illustrate the unfamiliar word
Example	Calisthenics include *pushups and situps.*
Clue	**Sentence Role:** structural clue that indicates the unfamiliar word's part of speech
Example	Joanna *does* calisthenics every morning. [clearly a noun; seems to be an activity]

DIRECTIONS: *Answer these questions about words in the poems in this collection.*

1. What synonym later in the poem shows the meaning of *git* in line 11 of "Cat!"?

____

2. A. In lines 26–27 of "Cat!" what does the context suggest that a *sycamore* is?

____

B. What other word is a clue to the meaning of *sycamore*? ______________

3. In line 3 of "Silver," what synonym shows the meaning of *peers*? ______________

____

4. In "Thumbprint," what context clues clarify the meaning of *unique* in line 3?

____

____

5. A. Look at the role of *slander* in line 22 of "Ring Out, Wild Bells." What part of speech is it? ______________________________

B. Explain how the contrast in line 23 helps clarify the meaning of *slander.*

____

____

Name ______________________________ Date ______________

Poetry Collection: Walter de la Mare; Alfred, Lord Tennyson; Eleanor Farjeon; Eve Merriam

Literary Analysis: Sound Devices

Poets often use **sound devices** to make their poems more musical and memorable.

- **Meter** is the pattern of strong and weak beats, as in TWINkle TWINkle LITtle STAR.
- **Rhyme** is the repetition of sounds at the ends of words, as in *star* and *far.*
- **Alliteration** is the repetition of consonant sounds at the beginnings of nearby words, as in *twinkle* and *twist.*
- **Onomatopoeia** is the use of words that imitate sounds, such as *bang* and *sizzle.*

DIRECTIONS: *Use this chart to record examples of sound devices in the poems.*

Poem	Meter	Rhyme	Alliteration	Onomatopoeia
"Silver"				
"Ring Out, Wild Bells"				
"Cat!"				
"Thumbprint"				

Name ______________________________ Date ______________

Poetry Collection: Walter de la Mare; Alfred, Lord Tennyson; Eleanor Farjeon; Eve Merriam

Vocabulary Builder

Word List

flatterer imprint scampering singularity spite strife

A. Directions: *Answer each question with a sentence that uses one of the Word List words. Use each Word List word only once.*

1. Was there a lot of misery in the world during the twentieth century?

____

____

2. What quality might an independent person display?

____

____

3. Does a good adviser tell a leader only what she or he wants to hear?

____

____

4. How might a person feel toward his or her enemy?

____

____

5. How might you state your desire to make a lasting mark on your friends?

____

____

6. What might you see small animals doing when attacked?

____

____

B. Word Study: *The Latin prefix* im- *often means "in" or "into." Use the context of the sentences and what you know about the Latin prefix* im- *to explain your answer to each question.*

1. What is something that can be *implanted*?

____

____

2. Is someone who is *imperiled* safe? Explain.

____

____

Name ______________________________ Date ______________

Poetry Collection: Walter de la Mare; Alfred, Lord Tennyson; Eleanor Farjeon; Eve Merriam

Conventions: Types of Sentences

Sentences are classified into four categories, according to their function.

Category, Function, and End Mark	Example
A **declarative sentence** makes a statement. It ends with a period.	Your thumbprint is unique.
An **interrogative sentence** asks a question. It ends with a question mark.	Is that the sound of bells? Are they ringing in the new year?
An **imperative sentence** gives a command. It ends with a period or an exclamation point.	Do not tease the cat. Watch out!
An **exclamatory sentence** calls out or exclaims. It ends with an exclamation point.	Wow! How lovely the moonlight is!

The type of sentence relates to a verb classification called **mood.** For instance, the verb of a declarative sentence is said to be in the **indicative mood,** indicating a statement; the verb of an imperative sentence is said to be in the **imperative mood.** The subject of an imperative sentence is always *you,* but it is never stated: (*You*) *do not tease the cat.* (*You*) *watch out!*

A. Practice: *Add the correct end mark to each sentence. Then, on the line, identify the sentence as* declarative, interrogative, imperative, *or* exclamatory.

1. Where did you go on your field trip on Saturday ______________
2. We drove to a quarry and looked for fossils ______________
3. How incredible those fossils are ______________
4. Don't drop them ______________

B. Writing Application: *On the lines provided, write one sentence each about the four poems in this collection. Use each of the four types of sentences. In the parentheses before each sentence, write whether it is* declarative, interrogative, imperative, *or* exclamatory.

1. (__________) ______________________________
2. (__________) ______________________________
3. (__________) ______________________________
4. (__________) ______________________________

Name ______________________________ Date ______________

Poetry Collection: Walter de la Mare; Alfred, Lord Tennyson; Eleanor Farjeon; Eve Merriam

Support for Writing to Sources: Poem That Uses Sound Devices

Use this chart to jot down your ideas about what to include in your poem.

Title	
Subject	
Main Idea	
Mood	
Sound Devices	Rhyme:
	Meter:
	Alliteration:
	Onomatopoeia:

Name ______________________________ Date ______________

Poetry Collection: Walter de la Mare; Alfred, Lord Tennyson; Eleanor Farjeon; Eve Merriam

Support for Speaking and Listening: Poetry Recitation

Use this chart to record details about the sound devices and the mood they create.

Poem Title and Author	
Mood of Poem	
Rhyme	
Meter	
Alliteration	
Onomatopoeia	

Name ______________________________ Date ____________________

Poetry Collection: Emily Dickinson, Patricia Hubbell, Langston Hughes, Richard García

Writing About the Big Question

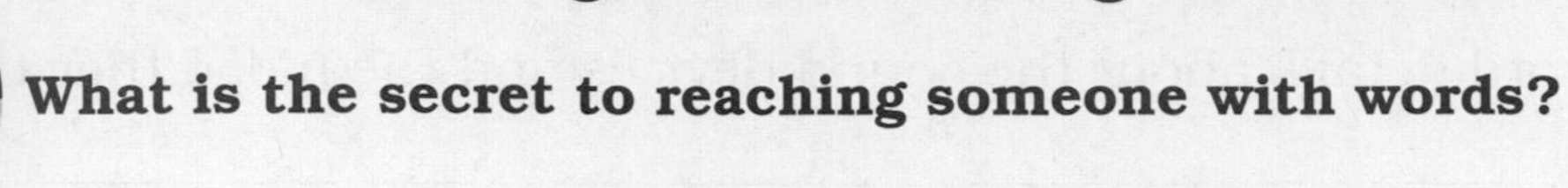

What is the secret to reaching someone with words?

Big Question Vocabulary

benefit	connection	cultural	experience	express
feedback	individuality	inform	meaningful	media
misunderstand	relevant	sensory	significance	valid

A. *Use one or more words from the list above to complete each sentence.*

1. The ______________________ of his message was expressed through his heartfelt emotion.
2. Everyone can gain a ______________________ from communication.
3. Shawna made a ______________________ point when she said I didn't listen to her.
4. My ______________________ with communication suggests that my words must reflect my true feelings.
5. The ______________________ the poet received from the critics was positive.

B. *Follow the directions in responding to each of the items below.*

1. Write two sentences about a topic relevant to your communication with others.

   ____.

   ____.

2. Write two sentences that use sensory details to describe a conversation. Use at least two of the Big Question vocabulary words.

   ____

   ____

C. *Complete the sentence below. Then, write a short paragraph in which you connect this idea to the Big Question.*

Writers often communicate their experiences in poetry because ______________

____

____

____

Name ______________________________ Date ________________

Poetry Collection: Emily Dickinson, Patricia Hubbell, Langston Hughes, Richard García

Reading: Context Clues

You can often understand an unfamiliar word if you examine its **context**—the words and phrases surrounding it. Reread and read ahead for **context clues** that will help you figure out its meaning. When you have come up with a possible meaning, insert it in place of the word to see if it makes sense. Here are some types of context clues to look for:

- **Restatement or Synonym:** *Felines*, or cats, all share many characteristics.
- **Definition:** She shopped in a *boutique*, a small specialty store.
- **Example:** *Felines* include lions, tigers, and leopards.
- **Comparison/Contrast:** Did you buy that in a *boutique* or in a large chain store?

In "Concrete Mixers," for example, the word *ponderous* may be unfamiliar, but if you reread the line in which it appears, the example of "monsters standing" is a clue to its meaning. If you then read ahead, you find the word restated as "elephant-bellied." From these context clues, you can figure out that *ponderous* probably means "big and heavy."

Directions: *Reread the poem "Concrete Mixers," looking for clues to the meaning of the underlined word in each item below. On the lines provided, write your best guess about the meaning of the word, and write any context clues that pointed you to that meaning. When you have finished, you can check the meanings in a dictionary.*

1. Likely meaning of hose in line 2: ______________________________

   Clue(s): ______________________________
2. Likely meaning of muck in line 5: ______________________________

   Clue(s): ______________________________
3. Likely meaning of perch in line 7: ______________________________

   Clue(s): ______________________________
4. Likely meaning of bellow in line 14: ______________________________

   Clue(s): ______________________________
5. Likely meaning of urban in line 16: ______________________________

   Clue(s): ______________________________

Name ______________________________ Date ______________

Poetry Collection: Emily Dickinson, Patricia Hubbell, Langston Hughes, Richard García

Literary Analysis: Figurative Language

Figurative language, or language not meant to be taken literally, can help make poems more memorable. Instances of figurative language, called **figures of speech,** often compare unlike things. A **simile** directly states the comparison by using a word such as *like* or *as*. A **metaphor** suggests the comparison by saying that one thing *is* the other. **Personification** compares something nonhuman to a human being by giving it human characteristics.

Similes: Life is like a dance. The ocean is as moody as a child.

Metaphor: Life is a dance.

Personification: The ocean laughs and cries.

DIRECTIONS: *Use this chart to record and explain the poems' examples of the three types of figures of speech.*

	Line Number(s); Type of Figure of Speech	What Two Things Are Compared
1. "The Sky Is Low, the Clouds Are Mean"		
2. "Concrete Mixers"		
3. "Harlem Night Song"		
4. "The City Is So Big"		

Name ______________________ Date ______________

Poetry Collection: Emily Dickinson, Patricia Hubbell, Langston Hughes, Richard García

Vocabulary Builder

Word List

debates dew ponderous roam rut urban

A. Directions: *Answer each question with a sentence that uses one of the Word List words. Use each Word List word only once.*

1. What might a suitcase with lots of travel labels show about its owner?

2. What kind of suitcase would be hard to carry?

3. What might you see in a road after a severe windstorm?

4. What might cover flowers' petals on a spring morning?

5. How might you describe a photograph of a city?

6. What does a nervous, unsure person often do when it comes time to make a decision?

B. Word Study: *The suffix* -ous *means "characterized by" or "full of." Use the context of the sentences and what you know about the suffix* -ous *to explain your answer to each question.*

1. Does something *instantaneous* take a long time? Explain.

2. Is something *marvelous* likely to catch people's attention? Explain.

Name ______________________________ Date ______________

Poetry Collection: Emily Dickinson, Patricia Hubbell, Langston Hughes, Richard García

Conventions: Subject Complements

A linking verb connects a subject to a **subject complement,** a noun, a pronoun, or an adjective that follows the linking verb and tells something about the subject. The most common **linking verbs** are forms of *be—am, is, are, was, were, has been,* and so on. Other common linking verbs include *seem, become,* and sometimes *look, sound,* and *feel.*

One kind of subject complement is called a *predicate adjective.* It describes the subject. Other kinds of subject complements are called a *predicate noun* and a *predicate pronoun.* They further identify the subject. A predicate pronoun uses the subject, not object, form.

Predicate Adjective:	The visitor seems *lost.* [*Lost* describes the subject, *visitor.*]
Predicate Noun:	He was the best *player* on the team. [*Player* further identifies the subject, *He.*]
Predicate Pronoun:	The winner is *she.* [*She* further identifies the subject, *winner.*]

A. Practice: *Circle the subject complement in each sentence that contains a subject complement. On the line before the sentence, write* PN *if the subject complement is a predicate noun,* PP *if it is a predicate pronoun, and* PA *if it is a predicate adjective. If the sentence does not contain a subject complement, write* none *on the line.*

____ **1.** Poems are often very musical.

____ **2.** That word is an example of personification.

____ **3.** The last speaker in the choral reading was I.

____ **4.** The simile in the poem sounded familiar to me.

____ **5.** The bell sounded at the end of English class.

B. Writing Application: *Add to each subject in the items below to build a sentence that includes a linking verb and a subject complement. Include at least one predicate noun, one predicate pronoun, and one predicate adjective in your sentences.*

1. The sky ______________________________

2. Concrete mixers ______________________________

3. At night in Harlem, I ______________________________

4. The city ______________________________

5. The reader of the poem ______________________________

Name ______________________________ Date ______________

Poetry Collection: Emily Dickinson, Patricia Hubbell, Langston Hughes, Richard García

Support for Writing to Sources: Study for a Poem

Use this chart to jot down ideas about the figurative language that you hope to include in your poem.

Comparison to Make	Wording to Use	Type of Figurative Language

Name ____________________ Date ____________

Poetry Collection: Emily Dickinson, Patricia Hubbell, Langston Hughes, Richard García

Support for Research and Technology: Mini-Anthology

Use this form to record information about the poems you choose for your **mini-anthology.** Under "Ideas for My Introduction," jot down points to be made and details to be included.

POEM 1	
Title of Poem	Author
Subject or Theme of Poem	Source
Ideas for My Introduction	
POEM 2	
Title of Poem	Author
Subject or Theme of Poem	Source
Ideas for My Introduction	
POEM 3	
Title of Poem	Author
Subject or Theme of Poem	Source
Ideas for My Introduction	

Name ______________________________ Date ______________

Poetry Collection: Emma Lazarus, William Shakespeare, Henry Wadsworth Longfellow

Writing About the Big Question

What is the secret to reaching someone with words?

Big Question Vocabulary

benefit	connection	cultural	experience	express
feedback	individuality	inform	meaningful	media
misunderstand	relevant	sensory	significance	valid

A. *Use one or more words from the list above to complete each sentence.*

1. Shakespeare sometimes uses a jolly song to ______________ bitter disappointment.
2. Lazarus understands the immigrant ______________ in America.
3. Longfellow commemorates the ______________ of a historical hero's brave deeds.
4. The ______________ that Americans feel surpasses cultural differences.

B. *Follow the directions in responding to each of the items below.*

1. Explain what you would include if you wanted to inform someone about a significant event.

   ____

   ____

2. How would you express your reaction to one of the poems you have read? Use at least two of the Big Question vocabulary words.

   ____

   ____

C. *Complete the sentence below. Then, write a short paragraph in which you connect this idea to the Big Question.*

Someone who has contributed greatly to the history of our country is ______________

____

____

____

Name ______________________ Date ______________

Poetry Collection: Emma Lazarus, William Shakespeare, Henry Wadsworth Longfellow

Reading: Paraphrase

To understand a poem, it often helps to paraphrase it in simple, everyday language. When you **paraphrase,** you restate text in your own words. First, reread the poem to clarify the writer's meaning. Identify the most basic information in each sentence or phrase—what is being done and who or what is doing it. Use a dictionary or text aids such as footnotes, if provided, to help you with unfamiliar terms. Once you understand the poet's meaning, restate the sentences in everyday English. Eliminate repetition, use simpler synonyms, and put unusual sentence structures into a word order that is easier to understand.

DIRECTIONS: *Use this chart to paraphrase the two shorter poems in this collection. An example has been provided for you.*

Poem	Original Lines	Paraphrased Lines
"The New Colossus"	Lines 1–2: "Not . . . land;"	Unlike the giant bronze statue on the Greek island of Rhodes, with its image of conquest,
	Lines 3–6: "Here . . . Exiles."	
	Lines 6–8: "From . . . frame."	
	Lines 9–10: "Keep . . . lips."	
	Lines 10–14: "Give . . . door!"	
"Blow, Blow, Thou Winter Wind"	Lines 1–3: "Blow . . . ingratitude."	
	Lines 4–6: "Thy . . . rude."	
	Lines 7–8: "Heigh-ho! . . . folly."	
	Lines 9–10: "Then . . . jolly."	
	Lines 11–13: "Freeze . . . forgot."	
	Lines 14–16: "Though . . . not."	
	Lines 17–20: "Heigh-ho . . . jolly."	

Name ______________________________ Date ______________

Poetry Collection: Emma Lazarus, William Shakespeare, Henry Wadsworth Longfellow

Literary Analysis: Lyric and Narrative Poetry

A **lyric poem** expresses the thoughts and feelings of a single speaker and uses vivid images and often musical language to convey an impression. A **narrative poem** tells a story in verse and has all the elements of a short story, including plot, conflict, setting, characters, and theme.

DIRECTIONS: *Choose one lyric poem and one narrative poem in this collection. Write the title of each poem on the line provided, and then answer the questions about it.*

A. Lyric Poem Title: ______________________________

1. Why is this poem a lyric poem? ______________________________

2. What are two feelings or emotions that the speaker expresses? ______________________________

3. List two images that the speaker uses and the ideas they convey. ______________________________

4. What main impression would you say the poem conveys? ______________________________

B. Narrative Poem Title: ______________________________

1. Why is this poem a narrative poem? ______________________________

2. Summarize the plot in one or two sentences. ______________________________

3. What is the main conflict or struggle, and how is it resolved in the end?

4. As specifically as possible, identify the poem's main setting.

5. Who is the main character? What minor characters does the poem feature?

Name ______________________________ Date ______________

Poetry Collection: Emma Lazarus, William Shakespeare, Henry Wadsworth Longfellow

Vocabulary Builder

Word List

defiance exiles ingratitude peril somber yearning

A. Directions: *Answer each question with a sentence that uses one of the Word List words. Use each Word List word only once.*

1. What is the mood at a funeral usually like?

____

____

2. What adjective describes a person who craves a piece of candy?

____

____

3. How can you describe danger?

____

____

4. What do you call people who are forced to leave their homelands?

____

____

5. How could you describe a child's refusing to listen to his or her parent?

____

____

6. How would you describe a friend you've always helped who refuses to help you?

____

____

B. Word Study: *The prefix* in- *can mean "not" or "lacking." Use the context of the sentences and what you know about the prefix to explain your answer to each question.*

1. What might a student do if he or she were *incapable* of solving a problem?

____

____

2. Are *indefinite* plans fixed? Explain.

____

____

Name ______________________ Date ______________

Poetry Collection: Emma Lazarus, William Shakespeare, Henry Wadsworth Longfellow

Conventions: Direct and Indirect Objects

A **direct object** is a noun or pronoun that follows an action verb and receives the action of the verb. It answers the question *What?* or *Whom?* after the action verb. (A direct object does not appear after a linking verb.)

Sonya brewed some *tea.* [*What* did Sonya brew?]

The aroma tempted *them.* [*Whom* did the aroma tempt?]

An **indirect object** is a noun or pronoun that comes between an action verb and a direct object. It answers the question *To or for whom?* or *To or for what?* after an action verb. You cannot have an indirect object without a direct object.

Sonya brewed her *guests* some tea. [*For whom* did Sonya brew some tea?]

Sonya gave each *cup* a different flavor. [*To what* did Sonya give a different flavor?]

A. Practice: *Underline the direct object and circle the indirect object in each sentence that contains one or both. If there is no direct or indirect object in the sentence, write* none *on the line.*

1. Nature plays a strong role in Shakespeare's poem. ______________
2. The poem's speaker gives us advice about human relationships. ______________
3. The last poem really impressed Nancy and me. ______________
4. The images show readers the speaker's feelings. ______________
5. The biggest fans of her poetry are Celia and Mary. ______________

B. Writing Application: *Add to each subject below to create a sentence that includes an action verb and a direct object. Also, include an indirect object in two of your sentences.*

1. The Statue of Liberty ______________________________
____
2. Great poets ______________________________
____
3. My thoughts ______________________________
____
4. The glowing light ______________________________
____
5. Paul Revere ______________________________
____

Name ______________________ Date ______________

Poetry Collection: Emma Lazarus, William Shakespeare, Henry Wadsworth Longfellow

Support for Writing to Sources: Lyric or Narrative Poem

Use this sheet to jot down your notes for your lyric or narrative poem. If you plan to write a lyric poem, fill in the information called for on the first chart. If you plan to write a narrative poem, fill in the information called for on the second chart.

Lyric Poem
Person:
Qualities:
Achievements:

Narrative Poem
Events:
Characters:
Details of Setting:

Name ______________________________ Date ______________

Poetry Collection: Emma Lazarus, William Shakespeare, Henry Wadsworth Longfellow

Support for Speaking and Listening: Evaluation Form

Create your evaluation form using the chart below. Add more qualities in the blank spaces of the first column. Decide on a scale for scoring—for example, a four-point scale with *1* being "poor" and *4* being "outstanding." Then, photocopy the form, or copy it by hand, and use it to evaluate each person's reading of a poem in the collection.

Title:		
Delivery	**Score**	**Comments**
Varied Tone		
Proper Pauses		
Clear Reading		
Adjusted Reading Rate		

Name ______________________________ Date ______________

Poetry Collection: Amy Ling, E. E. Cummings, John Updike, N. Scott Momaday

Writing About the Big Question

What is the secret to reaching someone with words?

Big Question Vocabulary

benefit	connection	cultural	experience	express
feedback	individuality	inform	meaningful	media
misunderstand	relevant	sensory	significance	valid

A. *Use one or more words from the list above to complete each sentence.*

1. In his poem "January," Updike uses ______________________ details to appeal to sight and feeling.
2. E. E. Cummings's poem celebrates the early telephone, not the later electronic news ______________________.
3. N. Scott Momaday examines the ______________________ between man and nature in "New World."

B. *Follow the directions in responding to each of the items below.*

1. Write two sentences about the benefit of observing nature. Consider how observation affects your life.

   ____.

   ____.

2. Express your ideas about a relevant issue in your school or community. Use at least two of the Big Question vocabulary words.

   ____

   ____

C. *Complete the sentence below. Then, write a short paragraph in which you connect this idea to the Big Question.*

Poetry written about nature helps us discover ______________________

____

____

____

Name ______________________________ Date ______________

Poetry Collection: Amy Ling, E. E. Cummings, John Updike, N. Scott Momaday

Reading: Paraphrase

When you **paraphrase** a poem, you restate it in your own words. First, read the poem through carefully and try to determine the complete thoughts it contains. Use the punctuation on the page—as well as the words themselves—to help you identify complete thoughts. Next, restate the meaning of each complete thought in your own words. Eliminate unneeded repetition. Mentally fill in any missing words to complete thoughts that are not fully stated. If the vocabulary is difficult, use simpler synonyms. Put unusual sentence structures into a word order that is easier to understand.

DIRECTIONS: *Use this chart to paraphrase the first two parts of "New World" by N. Scott Momaday. An example has been provided for you.*

Complete Thoughts	Paraphrased Lines
Lines 1–2: "First Man, behold:"	Look, First Man
Lines 3–5: "the earth . . . leaves;"	
Lines 6–8: "the sky . . . rain."	
Lines 9–15: "Pollen . . . mountains."	
Lines 16–19: "Cedars . . . pines."	
Lines 20–28: "At . . . pools."	
Lines 29–31: "Grasses . . . shine."	
Lines 32–36: "Shadows . . . smoke."	

Name ______________________________ Date ______________

Poetry Collection: Amy Ling, E. E. Cummings, John Updike, N. Scott Momaday

Literary Analysis: Imagery

Poetry often makes use of **imagery,** language that appeals to the senses. If you take note of the images as you read a poem, you will often understand it better.

DIRECTIONS: *Use this chart to help you focus on the imagery in the four poems.*

	Sight	Hearing	Touch	Smell	Taste
"Grandma Ling"					
"your little voice"					
"January"					
"New World"					

Name ______________________________ Date ______________________

Poetry Collection: Amy Ling, E. E. Cummings, John Updike, N. Scott Momaday

Vocabulary Builder

Word List

exquisite impertinently jostling pollen recede tongue

A. Directions: *Circle* T *if the statement is true or* F *if the statement is false. Then, explain your answer.*

T / F 1. A wave going back to sea can be said to recede.
____

T / F 2. Flowers produce pollen.
____

T / F 3. Most teachers like students who speak impertinently.
____

T / F 4. A jostling ride is comfortable.
____

T / F 5. If you speak only one tongue, you know just one language.
____

T / F 6. An exquisite diamond will probably be expensive.
____

B. Word Study: *The root* -cede- *or* -ceed- *means "go" or "yield." Use the context of the sentences and what you know about the roots to explain your answer to each question.*

1. If a line *proceeds* quickly, what happens?
____
____

2. If someone *exceeds* expectations at work, what has he or she done?
____
____

C. Directions: *Circle the letter of the word that is closest in meaning to the Word List word in capital letters.*

1. RECEDE
A. triumph B. retreat C. grow D. revisit

2. JOSTLING
A. shoving B. joking C. lending D. neighing

3. IMPERTINENTLY
A. relevantly B. intelligently C. rudely D. eagerly

Name ______________________ Date ______________

Poetry Collection: Amy Ling, E. E. Cummings, John Updike, N. Scott Momaday

Conventions: Pronoun Case

In English, pronouns have three **cases,** or forms: **nominative, objective, or possessive.** The correct form to use depends on the pronoun's role in a sentence.

Case/Pronouns	Role in Sentence	Examples
Nominative Case I, we you he, she, it, they	 subject of a verb predicate pronoun (after a linking verb)	 *We* walked to school. The winners were Jan and *I*.
Objective Case me, us you him, her, it, them	 direct object of a verb indirect object of a verb object of a preposition	 The teacher helped *us*. Get *him* a book. Give that book to *them*.
Possessive Case my, mine; our, ours your, yours his; her, hers; its; their, theirs	 to show ownership	 Jo is at *her* locker. The cat had *its* claws clipped. The new car is *yours*.

Errors in pronoun case tend to occur in compound structures.

Incorrect: Max and *her* came early. **Correct:** Max and *she* came early.

Incorrect: Choose between he and *I*. **Correct:** Choose between him and *me*.

A. Practice: *Circle the pronoun that correctly completes each sentence.*

1. Jackie and (us, we) are on the softball team.
2. The coach taught Sonya and (her, she) a new pitch.
3. Were you throwing the ball to Tanya or (I, me)?
4. The best players are Sofia and (I, me).

B. Writing Application: *On the lines provided, rewrite these sentences so that they use the pronouns correctly. If the sentence has no pronoun errors, write* correct.

1. Wendell, Terry, and me like to play basketball.

   ____

2. Terry's brother taught Wendell and I some good moves.

   ____

3. Often Wendell's older brother joins Wendell and us in a game.

   ____

4. Him and Terry's brother have played together for years.

   ____

Name ______________________________ Date ________________

Poetry Collection: Amy Ling, E. E. Cummings, John Updike, N. Scott Momaday

Support for Writing to Sources: Review of Poetry

Fill in this chart to help you write your review.

Poem Title:	
Element	**Details**
sound	
word choice	
imagery	
Poem Title:	
Element	**Details**
sound	
word choice	
imagery	
Poem Title:	
Element	**Details**
sound	
word choice	
imagery	
Poem Title:	
Element	**Details**
sound	
word choice	
imagery	

Name ______________________________ Date ______________

Poetry Collection: Amy Ling, E. E. Cummings, John Updike, N. Scott Momaday

Support for Research and Technology: Profile

Use this modified timeline to record important events in the life of the poet you investigate. Include information on the author's birth date, education, employment, family milestones, places of residence, publications, awards, and death date, if relevant, as well as other key events related to the author's heritage or literary development.

Poet: ______________________________

Year	Important Event	Source of Information

Name ________________________________ Date ____________________

"The Road Not Taken" by Robert Frost
"O Captain! My Captain!" by Walt Whitman

Writing About the Big Question

What is the secret to reaching someone with words?

Big Question Vocabulary

benefit	connection	cultural	experience	express
feedback	individuality	inform	meaningful	media
misunderstand	relevant	sensory	significance	valid

A. *Use one or more words from the list above to complete each sentence.*

1. Whitman makes a ______________________ between a ship and the government of the country.
2. Whitman expresses the ______________________ of the history of our country in his poem.
3. Frost examines a ______________________ experience that reflects the choices we make in life.

B. *Follow the directions in responding to each of the items below.*

1. How would you best express your opinion of the choices you have made thus far in life?

   ____.

   ____.

2. Who has reached you with his or her words? Write two sentences explaining the experience. Use at least two of the Big Question vocabulary words.

   ____

   ____

C. *Complete the sentence below. Then, write a short paragraph in which you connect this idea to the Big Question.*

Choosing words carefully when we write helps us to ______________________

____

____

____

Name ______________________________ Date ______________

"The Road Not Taken" by Robert Frost
"O Captain! My Captain!" by Walt Whitman

Literary Analysis: Comparing Types of Description

Descriptive writing paints word pictures for readers. A variety of descriptions can be used in poetry to present **levels of meaning.**

- **Literal meaning** is the actual, everyday meaning of words.
- **Figurative meaning** relies on figures of speech and the symbolic nature of language.

An **analogy** is a figurative description that compares two or more things that are similar in some ways, but otherwise unalike. For example, a poem that literally describes the ocean also can be read as an analogy: It may compare the ocean to life because both are vast, deep, and ever-changing. The poem, therefore, has two levels of meaning—one literal and one figurative.

DIRECTIONS: *On the following chart, for each quotation from a poem, note words and images that give you clues about its figurative meaning. The first one is done for you.*

Passages from "The Road Not Taken"	Which words and images give you clues about the figurative meaning of the passage?
1. "Two roads diverged in a yellow wood,"	Two roads = choices; yellow wood = life
2. "Then took the other, as just as fair, / And having perhaps the better claim, / Because it was grassy and wanted wear;"	

Passages from "O Captain! My Captain!"	Which words and images give you clues about the figurative meaning of the passage?
3. "O Captain! my Captain! our fearful trip is done, / The ship has weather'd every rack, the prize we sought is won,"	
4. "My Captain does not answer, his lips are pale and still, / My father does not feel my arm, he has no pulse nor will."	

Name ______________________ Date ______________

"The Road Not Taken" by Robert Frost
"O Captain! My Captain!" by Walt Whitman

Vocabulary Builder

Word List

diverged exulting

A. Directions: *Complete the following word maps by filling in the appropriate information.*

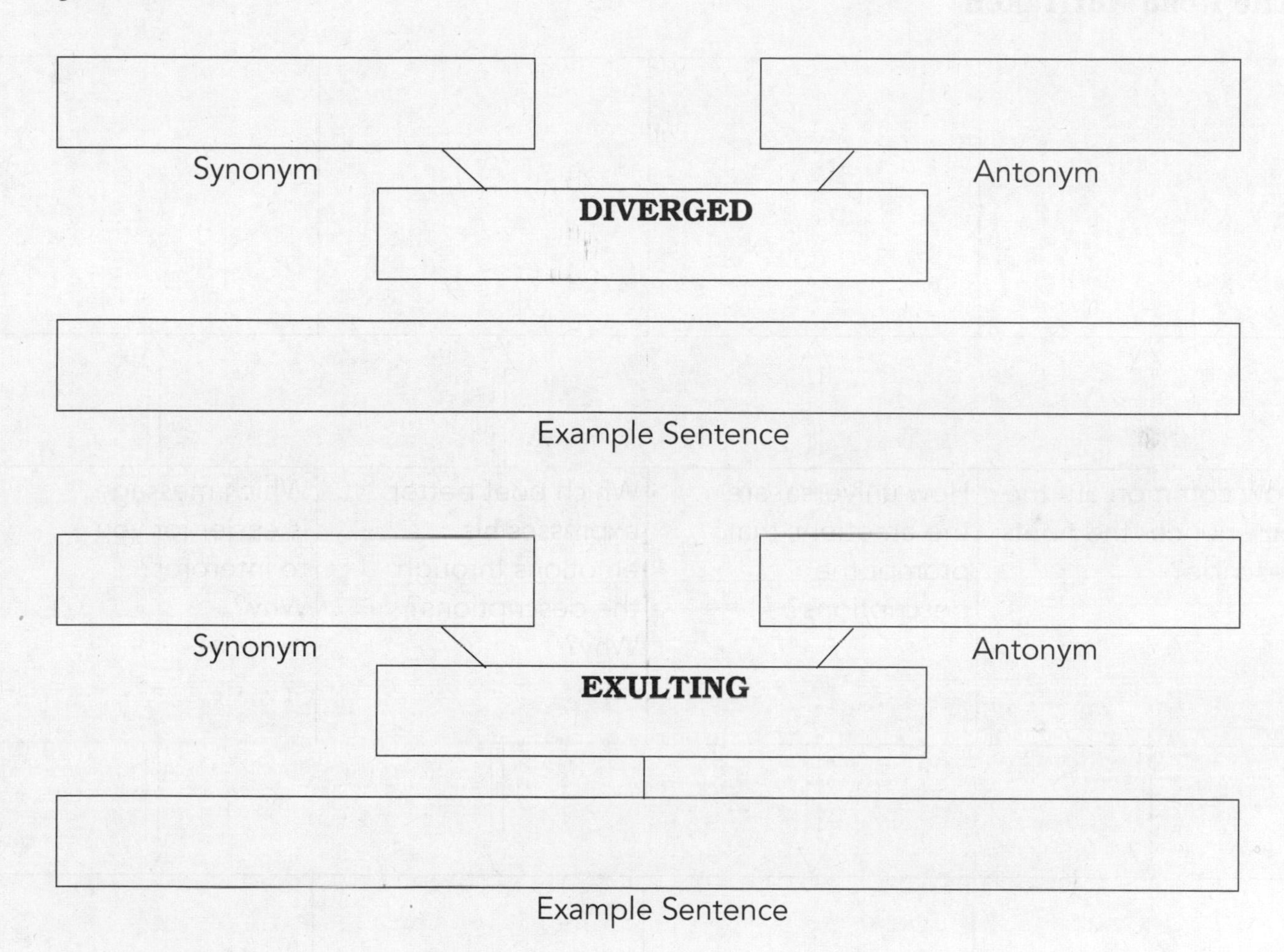

B. Directions: *Circle the letter of the pair that best expresses a relationship similar to that expressed in the pair in CAPITAL LETTERS.*

1. DIVERGED : SEPARATED ::
   A. converged : split
   B. removed : extracted
   C. weighed : lowered
   D. dressed : garment

2. EXULTING : LAMENTING ::
   A. talk : converse
   B. barrel : basket
   C. seldom : often
   D. dwindle : decrease

Name ______________________ Date ______________

"The Road Not Taken" by Robert Frost
"O Captain! My Captain!" by Walt Whitman

Support for Writing to Sources: Compare Description in Literary Works

Before you write your essay, use the graphic organizer below to list ideas about each poem.

"The Road Not Taken"

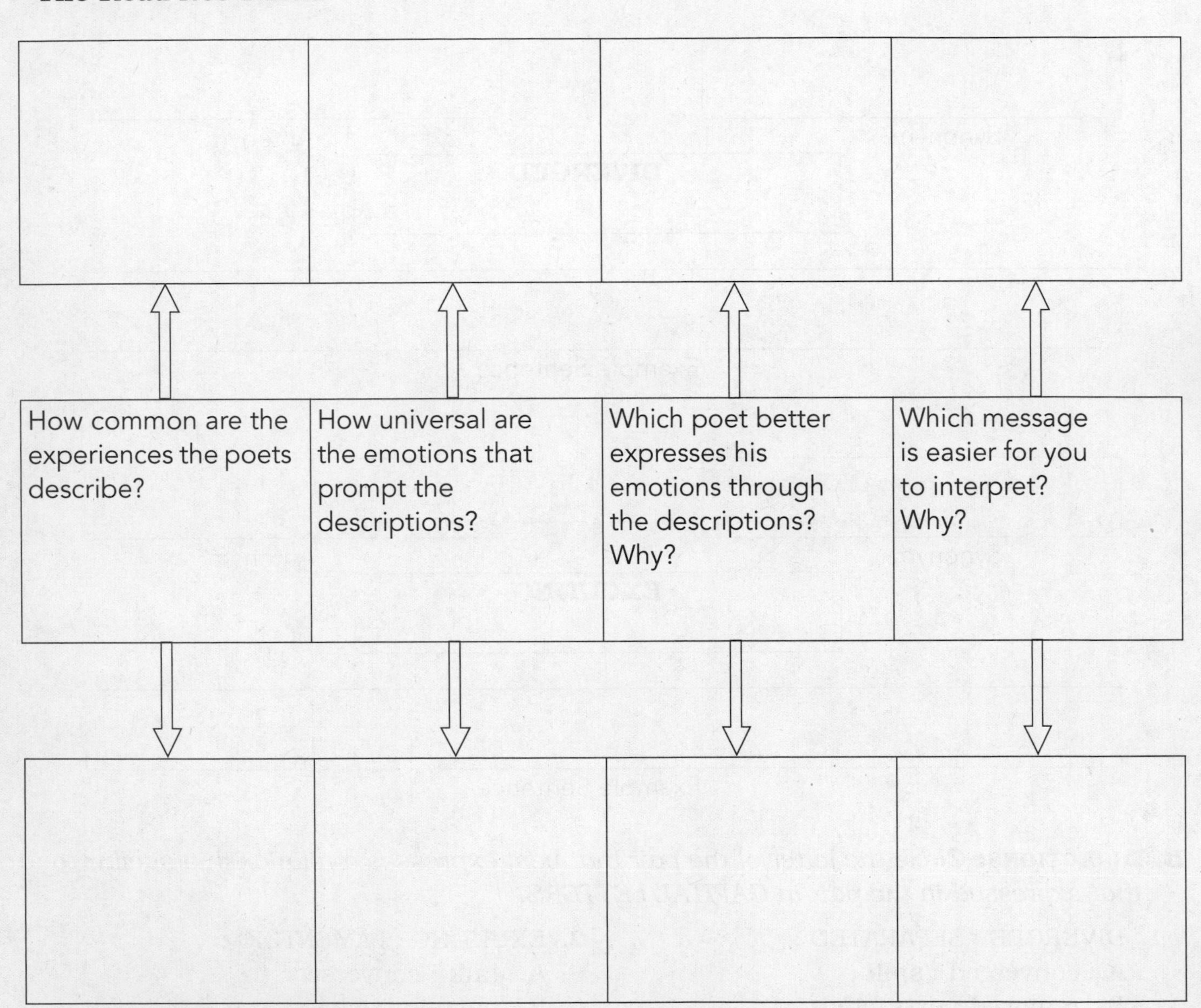

"O Captain! My Captain!"

Now, use your notes to write your essay comparing the descriptions in "The Road Not Taken" and "O Captain! My Captain!"

Name ______________________________ Date ______________

Writing Process

Critical Review

Prewriting: Choosing Your Topic

Use the chart below to take notes on two literary works that you have found while browsing. These two works should have enough similarities to make connections between them and to draw comparisons.

Story	Author	Plot	Characters	Theme

Drafting: Using Logical Organization

Use the graphic organizer below to help you organize your review.

Introduction State your thesis and identify both works.	
Body Paragraphs Develop your comparisons and contrasts using examples.	
Conclusion Summarize similarities and differences, and restate your response.	

Name ______________________________ Date ______________

Writer's Toolbox

Conventions: Revising for Subject-Verb Agreement

A verb must agree with its subject in number. Only nouns, pronouns, and verbs have number. Singular subjects need singular verbs, and plural subjects need plural verbs.

	Singular	Plural
Nouns and Pronouns	soldier, bus, child, goose, I, he, she, it	soldiers, buses, children, geese, we, they
Verbs	runs, reads, sleeps, writes, fixes, goes, am, is, was, has	run, read, sleep, write, fix, go, are, were, have

To fix problems with subject-verb agreement, first identify the subject. Then, make the verb agree.

Singular: The child *goes* to sleep at eight o'clock.

Plural: The children *go* to sleep at eight o'clock.

Compound, Plural: Dave and Martha *agree* to get married.

Inverted, Singular: Waiting for some friends *was* George.

A. Directions: *Circle the verb that agrees with the subject in each sentence.*

1. The characters in this cartoon (act, acts) too silly.
2. One Oscar (go, goes) to the best film of the year.
3. Cody and Casey (has, have) seen the movie.
4. Dressed in stunning clothes (was, were) the famous actress.

B. Directions: *Rewrite these sentences so that the verbs agree with their subjects.*

1. My favorite artist do vivid oil paintings.

   ____

2. Kayla and Nichole prefers watercolors.

   ____

3. When I grow up, I wants to study to be an architect.

   ____

4. Here is three good paintings by Picasso.

   ____

Name ______________________________ Date ______________

"Old Man" by Ricardo Sánchez
"For My Sister Molly Who in the Fifties" by Alice Walker

Vocabulary Builder

Selection Vocabulary

aromas   legacy   remote

A. DIRECTIONS: *Follow each direction. Write complete sentences for your responses.*

1. Describe one *legacy* Americans enjoy.

____

____

2. Name an appealing *aroma* and tell why it is appealing.

____

____

3. Name a *remote* place and explain what makes it remote.

____

____

Academic Vocabulary

conveyed   pattern   reinforce

B. DIRECTIONS: *Complete each sentence with a word, phrase, or clause that contains a context clue for the italicized word.*

1. The language of the poem *conveyed* a feeling of sadness because ______________

______________________________.

2. You can *reinforce* your point of view by ______________________________

______________________________.

3. The pattern of rhythm or rhyme in a poem is ______________________________

______________________________.

Name ______________________________ Date ______________

"Old Man" by Ricardo Sánchez
"For My Sister Molly Who in the Fifties" by Alice Walker

Take Notes for Discussion

Before the Partner Discussion: Read the following passages from the poems.

from "For My Sister Molly Who in the Fifties"

WHO SAW US SILENT
Cursed with fear   A love burning
Inexpressible
And sent me money not for me
But for "College."
Who saw me grow through letters
The words misspelled. . . .

from "Old Man"

"you are indio,
among other things,"
he would tell me
during the nights spent
so long ago
amidst familial gatherings
in albuquerque . . .

During the Discussion: As you discuss each question, take notes on how your partner's ideas either differ from or build upon your own.

Discussion Questions	Other Ideas Expressed	Comparison to My Own Ideas
1. Compare the ways in which the old man and Molly each support a younger person.		
2. Why is this support important?		
3. What do these passages suggest about the ties between generations?		

Name ______________________ Date ______________

"Old Man" by Ricardo Sánchez
"For My Sister Molly Who in the Fifties" by Alice Walker

Take Notes for Writing to Sources

Planning Your Informative Text: Before you begin drafting your **comparison-and-contrast essay,** use the chart below to organize your ideas. Follow the directions at the top of each column.

Details About Mood	Details About Theme

Name ____________________ Date ____________

"Old Man" by Ricardo Sánchez
"For My Sister Molly Who in the Fifties" by Alice Walker

Take Notes for Research

As you research **generational differences within different cultures,** use the forms below to take notes from your sources. As necessary, continue your notes on the back of this page, on note cards, or in a word-processing document.

Source Information Check one: ☐ Primary Source ☐ Secondary Source

Title: ____________________ Author: ____________

Publication Information: ____________________

Page(s): ____________________

Main Idea: ____________________

____

Quotation or Paraphrase: ____________________

____

Source Information Check one: ☐ Primary Source ☐ Secondary Source

Title: ____________________ Author: ____________

Publication Information: ____________________

Page(s): ____________________

Main Idea: ____________________

____

Quotation or Paraphrase: ____________________

____

Source Information Check one: ☐ Primary Source ☐ Secondary Source

Title: ____________________ Author: ____________

Publication Information: ____________________

Page(s): ____________________

Main Idea: ____________________

____

Quotation or Paraphrase: ____________________

____

Name ______________________ Date ______________

"**The Medicine Bag**" by Virginia Driving Hawk Sneve

Vocabulary Builder

Selection Vocabulary

authentic procession unseemly

A. Directions: *Revise each sentence so that the underlined vocabulary word is used logically. Be sure to keep the vocabulary word in your version.*

1. The tourist knew that the diamond ring she bought from a street vendor for ten dollars was really authentic. ______________________

______________________.

2. She looked at the procession on the street where people were going in different directions. ______________________

______________________.

3. He acted unseemly by speaking respectfully in court. ______________________

______________________.

Academic Vocabulary

initial represents traditions

B. Directions: *Write one example that demonstrates the meaning of each word. Follow this example:*

challenges: winning a scholarship, climbing a mountain

1. *initial:* ______________________

______________________.

2. *represents:* ______________________

______________________.

3. *traditions:* ______________________

______________________.

Name ______________________________ Date ______________

"**The Medicine Bag**" by Virginia Driving Hawk Sneve

Take Notes for Discussion

Before the Group Discussion: Read the following passage from the selection.

> My friends kept asking to come see the old man, but I put them off. I told myself that I didn't want them laughing at Grandpa. But even as I made excuses, I knew it wasn't Grandpa that I was afraid they'd laugh at.

During the Discussion: As you discuss each question, take notes on how other students' ideas either differ from or build upon your own.

Discussion Questions	Other Ideas Expressed	Comparison to My Own Ideas
1. What is Martin's main concern in this passage? What does this concern reveal about him?		
2. Why might behavior like this be more common among young people than adults?		

Name ______________________ Date ______________

"The Medicine Bag" by Virginia Driving Hawk Sneve

Take Notes for Research

As you research **how the Sioux or another Native American group passes its heritage from one generation to the next,** use the chart below to take notes from your sources. As necessary, continue your notes on the back of this page, on note cards, or in a word-processing document.

Passing Heritage from One Generation to the Next	
Main Idea ______________________ ______________________ Quotation or Paraphrase ______________________ ______________________ ______________________ ______________________ ______________________ Source Information ______________________ ______________________ ______________________ ______________________	Main Idea ______________________ ______________________ Quotation or Paraphrase ______________________ ______________________ ______________________ ______________________ ______________________ Source Information ______________________ ______________________ ______________________ ______________________
Main Idea ______________________ ______________________ Quotation or Paraphrase ______________________ ______________________ ______________________ ______________________ ______________________ Source Information ______________________ ______________________ ______________________ ______________________	Main Idea ______________________ ______________________ Quotation or Paraphrase ______________________ ______________________ ______________________ ______________________ ______________________ Source Information ______________________ ______________________ ______________________ ______________________

Name ______________________________ Date ______________

"**The Medicine Bag**" by Virginia Driving Hawk Sneve

Take Notes for Writing to Sources

Planning Your Narrative: Before you begin drafting your **narrative retelling,** use the chart below to organize your ideas. Follow the directions in each section.

1. Write a statement introducing the problem or conflict.
2. Write notes identifying and describing people, events, ideas, and emotions you will develop in your narrative. Try out figurative language that will make the descriptions vivid.
3. List ideas for dialogue that will create a strong sense of the characters.
4. Write notes for your conclusion that will make connections between the experiences you describe and Martin's.

Name ______________________________ Date ______________

"Cub Pilot on the Mississippi" by Mark Twain

Vocabulary Builder

Selection Vocabulary

confronted judicious malicious

A. Directions: *From the following lists, select one synonym and one antonym for each of the numbered words in the table below. Write your choices in the appropriate boxes.*

Synonyms	**Antonyms**
wise	kind
challenged	foolish
hateful	retreated

Word	**Synonym**	**Antonym**
1. malicious		
2. judicious		
3. confronted		

Academic Vocabulary

adjust opposing relevant

B. Directions: *Complete each sentence with a word, phrase, or clause that contains a context clue for the italicized word.*

1. The details he provided were not *relevant* because ______________________________
____.

2. The *opposing* debate team was ______________________________
____.

3. If you *adjust* the rules to fit the circumstances, you ______________________________
____.

Name ______________________________ Date ______________

"**Cub Pilot on the Mississippi**" by Mark Twain

Take Notes for Discussion

Before the Panel Discussion: Read the following passage from the selection.

> An hour later Henry entered the pilothouse. . . . Brown began, straightway: "Here! Why didn't you tell me we'd got to land at that plantation?"
> "I did tell you, Mr. Brown."
> "It's a lie!"
> I said: "You lie, yourself. He did tell you."

During the Discussion: As you discuss each question, take notes on how other students' ideas either differ from or build upon your own.

Discussion Questions	Other Ideas Expressed	Comparison to My Own Ideas
1. Why does Twain react as he does?		
2. Do Brown's actions justify Twain's disrespect? Explain.		
3. What difference to your answer does it make that Twain is responding on behalf of someone else?		

Name ______________________________ Date ______________

"Cub Pilot on the Mississippi" by Mark Twain

Take Notes for Research

As you research in **what situations it is illegal to disobey a command by someone in authority, whether you consider the command right or wrong,** use the forms below to take notes from your sources. As necessary, continue your notes on the back of this page, on note cards, or in a word-processing document.

Source Information Check one: ☐ Primary Source ☐ Secondary Source

Title: ______________________ Author: ______________________

Publication Information: ______________________

Page(s): ______________________

Main Idea: ______________________

____

Quotation or Paraphrase: ______________________

____

Source Information Check one: ☐ Primary Source ☐ Secondary Source

Title: ______________________ Author: ______________________

Publication Information: ______________________

Page(s): ______________________

Main Idea: ______________________

____

Quotation or Paraphrase: ______________________

____

Source Information Check one: ☐ Primary Source ☐ Secondary Source

Title: ______________________ Author: ______________________

Publication Information: ______________________

Page(s): ______________________

Main Idea: ______________________

____

Quotation or Paraphrase: ______________________

____

Name ______________________ Date ______________

"Cub Pilot on the Mississippi" by Mark Twain

Take Notes for Writing to Sources

Planning Your Narrative: Before you begin drafting your **scenario,** use the chart below to organize your ideas. Follow the directions in each section.

1. Statement of problem or conflict:

____

____

____

2. Events in the order they occur:

____

____

____

____

____

____

____

____

____

3. Options for resolving conflict:

____

____

____

____

____

4. Notes about the experience for your conclusion:

____

____

____

____

____

Name ______________________________ Date ______________

"Thank You, M'am" by Langston Hughes

Vocabulary Builder

Selection Vocabulary

barren contact presentable

A. DIRECTIONS: *Decide whether each statement below is true or false. On the line before each item, write* TRUE *or* FALSE. *Then, explain your answers.*

________ 1. Two methods of staying in *contact* are e-mailing and sending text messages.

____.

________ 2. A person is likely to look extremely *presentable* in a wrinkled T-shirt and scruffy jeans.

____.

________ 3. *Barren* city streets are generally crowded with people.

____.

Academic Vocabulary

factor imply insight

B. DIRECTIONS: *Write the letter of the word or phrase that is the best synonym for the italicized word. Then, use the italicized word in a complete sentence.*

____ 1. *factor*

A. relationship

B. choice

C. challenge

D. component

____

____ 2. *imply*

A. suggest

B. interact

C. introduce

D. remove

____

____ 3. *insight*

A. starting point

B. perception

C. summary

D. sequence

____

Name ______________________ Date ____________

"Thank You, M'am" by Langston Hughes

Take Notes for Discussion

Before the Quick Write and Discussion: Read the following passage from the selection.

> When they were finished eating, she got up and said, "Now here, take this ten dollars and buy yourself some blue suede shoes. And next time, do not make the mistake of latching onto *my* pocketbook *nor nobody else's*—because shoes got by devilish ways will burn your feet."

During the Discussion: As the group discusses each question, take notes on how other students' ideas either differ from or build upon your own.

Discussion Questions	Other Ideas Expressed	Comparison to My Own Ideas
1. Why does Mrs. Jones give Roger money? Is she just rewarding bad behavior? Explain.		
2. How is this interaction influenced by Mrs. Jones's past? How might it influence Roger's future?		

Name ______________________ Date ______________

"**Thank You, M'am**" by Langston Hughes

Take Notes for Research

As you research **what fashion items were valued by various generations from the 1940s through today,** you can use the organizer below to take notes from your sources. As necessary, continue your notes on the back of this page, on note cards, or in a word-processing document.

The Changing Values of Fashion Items	
Main Idea ______________________ ______________________ Quotation or Paraphrase ______________ ______________________ ______________________ ______________________ ______________________ Source Information ______________ ______________________ ______________________ ______________________	Main Idea ______________________ ______________________ Quotation or Paraphrase ______________ ______________________ ______________________ ______________________ ______________________ Source Information ______________ ______________________ ______________________ ______________________
Main Idea ______________________ ______________________ Quotation or Paraphrase ______________ ______________________ ______________________ ______________________ ______________________ Source Information ______________ ______________________ ______________________ ______________________	Main Idea ______________________ ______________________ Quotation or Paraphrase ______________ ______________________ ______________________ ______________________ ______________________ Source Information ______________ ______________________ ______________________ ______________________

Name ______________________________ Date ______________

"**Thank You, M'am**" by Langston Hughes

Take Notes for Writing to Sources

Planning Your Explanatory Text: Before you begin drafting your **cause-and-effect analysis,** use the chart below to organize your ideas. Follow the directions in each section.

1. Introduction to your topic:
2. Cause and effect of three events:
3. Notes to summarize your findings for your conclusion:

Name ______________________________ Date ______________

"Tutoring Benefits Seniors' Health, Students' Skills" by David Crary

Vocabulary Builder

Selection Vocabulary

buoyed engaged promising

A. DIRECTIONS: *Write the letter of the word or phrase that is the best synonym for the italicized word. Then, use the italicized word in a complete sentence.*

____ 1. *buoyed*

A. saddened C. encouraged

B. sunk D. depressed

____.

____ 2. *engaged*

A. ignored C. optimized

B. involved D. achieved

____.

____ 3. *promising*

A. hopeless C. certain

B. discouraging D. hopeful

____.

Academic Vocabulary

benefit support valid

B. DIRECTIONS: *Write a response to each question. Make sure to use the italicized word at least once in your response.*

1. What is one way a good education will *benefit* a person? ____.

2. What types of things might indicate that a study is *valid?* ____.

3. How would you *support* a contribution you make to a class discussion? ____.

Name ______________________________ Date ______________

"Tutoring Benefits Seniors' Health, Students' Skills" by David Crary

Take Notes for Discussion

Before the Class Discussion: Read the following passage from the selection.

> "The message to [the volunteers] is to take all their accumulated wisdom of a lifetime and give it back to help other people," Carlson said. "They get out of bed in the morning, even when they don't feel great, because they have a social contract with the kids at school. They know a child is waiting for them."

During the Discussion: As you discuss each question, take notes on how other students' ideas either differ from or build upon your own.

Discussion Questions	Other Ideas Expressed	Comparison to My Own Ideas
1. According to Michelle Carlson, how should older people use their "wisdom"?		
2. What might she think is the best relationship between generations?		
3. Explain whether you agree with her views.		

Name ______________________ Date ______________

"Tutoring Benefits Seniors' Health, Students' Skills" by David Crary

Take Notes for Research

As you research **volunteer programs in which older adults might play an important role,** use the forms below to take notes from your sources. As necessary, continue your notes on the back of this page, on note cards, or in a word-processing document.

Source Information Check one: ☐ Primary Source ☐ Secondary Source

Title: ______________________ Author: ______________

Publication Information: ______________________

Page(s): ______________________

Main Idea: ______________________

____

Quotation or Paraphrase: ______________________

____

Source Information Check one: ☐ Primary Source ☐ Secondary Source

Title: ______________________ Author: ______________

Publication Information: ______________________

Page(s): ______________________

Main Idea: ______________________

____

Quotation or Paraphrase: ______________________

____

Source Information Check one: ☐ Primary Source ☐ Secondary Source

Title: ______________________ Author: ______________

Publication Information: ______________________

Page(s): ______________________

Main Idea: ______________________

____

Quotation or Paraphrase: ______________________

____

Name ______________________________ Date ______________

"Tutoring Benefits Seniors' Health, Students' Skills" by David Crary

Take Notes for Writing to Sources

Planning Your Argument: Before you begin drafting your **persuasive essay,** use the chart below to organize your ideas. Follow the directions at the top of each section of the chart.

1. Statement of your claim:
2. Facts, examples, reasons, and other evidence to support your claim:
3. Counterclaims and your refutation of the counterclaims:

Name ________________________________ Date ________________

"The Return of the Multi-Generational Family Household" by Pew Research Center

Vocabulary Builder

Selection Vocabulary

demographic   incentives   resources

A. Directions: *Complete each sentence with a word, phrase, or clause that contains a context clue for the italicized word.*

1. An example of a *demographic* change in our population is ________________________________

____

2. In their reports, students demonstrated that they had the proper *resources* by

____

____

3. Two *incentives* that might influence young people to remain in their parents' houses after graduation are ________________________________

____

Academic Vocabulary

percentage   statistics   trend

B. Directions: *Write the letter of the word or phrase that is the best synonym for the italicized word. Then, use the italicized word in a complete sentence.*

_____ 1. *percentage*

A. role   C. fraction

B. relationship   D. income

____

_____ 2. *statistics*

A. figures   C. reductions

B. strengths   D. factors

____

_____ 3. *trend*

A. tune   C. relevance

B. tendency   D. bias

____

Name ______________________________ Date ______________

"The Return of the Multi-Generational Family Household" by Pew Research Center

Take Notes for Discussion

Before the Partner Discussion: Study the graph "Share of Population in Multi-Generational Family Households, by Age and Gender, 2008" in your textbook. Then, as you discuss each question **during the discussion,** take notes on how your partner's ideas either differ from or build upon your own.

Discussion Questions	Other Ideas Expressed	Comparison to My Own Ideas
1. Which are the only age groups with a higher percentage of men than of women? Why might this be the case?		
2. How do you account for the gender differences in the 65–85+ age groups?		

Name ______________________________ Date ______________

"The Return of the Multi-Generational Family Household" by Pew Research Center

Take Notes for Research

As you research **how people may feel about living in a multi-generational household,** use the forms below to take notes from your sources. As necessary, continue your notes on the back of this page, on note cards, or in a word-processing document.

Source Information Check one: ☐ Primary Source ☐ Secondary Source

Title: ______________________ Author: ______________

Publication Information: ______________________

Page(s): ______________________

Main Idea: ______________________

____

Quotation or Paraphrase: ______________________

____

Source Information Check one: ☐ Primary Source ☐ Secondary Source

Title: ______________________ Author: ______________

Publication Information: ______________________

Page(s): ______________________

Main Idea: ______________________

____

Quotation or Paraphrase: ______________________

____

Source Information Check one: ☐ Primary Source ☐ Secondary Source

Title: ______________________ Author: ______________

Publication Information: ______________________

Page(s): ______________________

Main Idea: ______________________

____

Quotation or Paraphrase: ______________________

____

Name ______________________________ Date ______________

"The Return of the Multi-Generational Family Household" by Pew Research Center

Take Notes for Writing to Sources

Planning Your Argument: Before you begin drafting your **argumentative essay,** use the chart below to organize your ideas. Follow the directions at the top of each section of the chart.

1. Statement of your claim:
2. Reasons to support your claim with details that support each reason:
3. Counterclaims and your refutations of those claims:
4. Notes for your conclusion:

Name ______________________________ Date ______________

Unit 4: Drama
Big Question Vocabulary—1

The Big Question: Is it our differences or our similarities that matter most?

Thematic Vocabulary

assumption: *n.* the act of supposing that something is true, without seeking proof; other form: *assume*

class: *n.* a group in society, separate from others, often based on jobs, income, or level of education; other forms: *classify, classification*

distinguish: *v.* to separate or classify according to special features or differences

represent: *v.* to personify a special quality or value; other forms: *representative, representation*

sympathy: *n.* a feeling of sorrow for someone who is in a bad situation; other forms: *sympathize, sympathetic*

A. DIRECTIONS: *Write the Thematic Vocabulary word that best completes each sentence.*

1. Because Carlos is very tall, I made the ________________ that he was a basketball player.
2. How will the judges ________________ between the very talented and the less talented singers?
3. John and Ramon ________________ the highest level of academic achievement.
4. I felt a great deal of ________________ for the player who was hurt during the game.
5. Members of each social ________________ should have equal opportunities for quality education.

B. DIRECTIONS: *Write the Thematic Vocabulary word that best completes each group of related words.*

1. compassion, support, ________________
2. group, division, ________________
3. exemplify, embody, ________________
4. divide, judge, ________________
5. guess, idea, ________________

Name ______________________ Date ______________

Unit 4: Drama
Big Question Vocabulary—2

The Big Question: Is it our differences or our similarities that matter most?

Thematic Vocabulary

common: *adj.* shared with others, such as mutual ideas or interests; other form: *commonly*

discriminate: *v.* to treat someone differently and unfairly; other forms: *discrimination, discriminated*

divide: *v.* to separate objects or people into groups; other forms: *division, divided, divisive*

generalization: *n.* a statement that may be true sometimes but not always; other form: *generalize*

superficial: *adj.* uninterested in important matters; shallow; other form: *superficially*

DIRECTIONS: *Read the passage, and then answer the question below. Use the vocabulary words in parentheses for your responses.*

"I don't want to be on a study committee with Grace," Peg said to her friend Ilene. "She's too quiet, and you know that people who are quiet tend to be sneaky and mean. If you're my friend, Ilene, you'll refuse to work with her, too." Ilene wasn't sure what to say. Should she go along with her friend or stand up for Grace, whom she hardly knew? What was Ilene thinking?

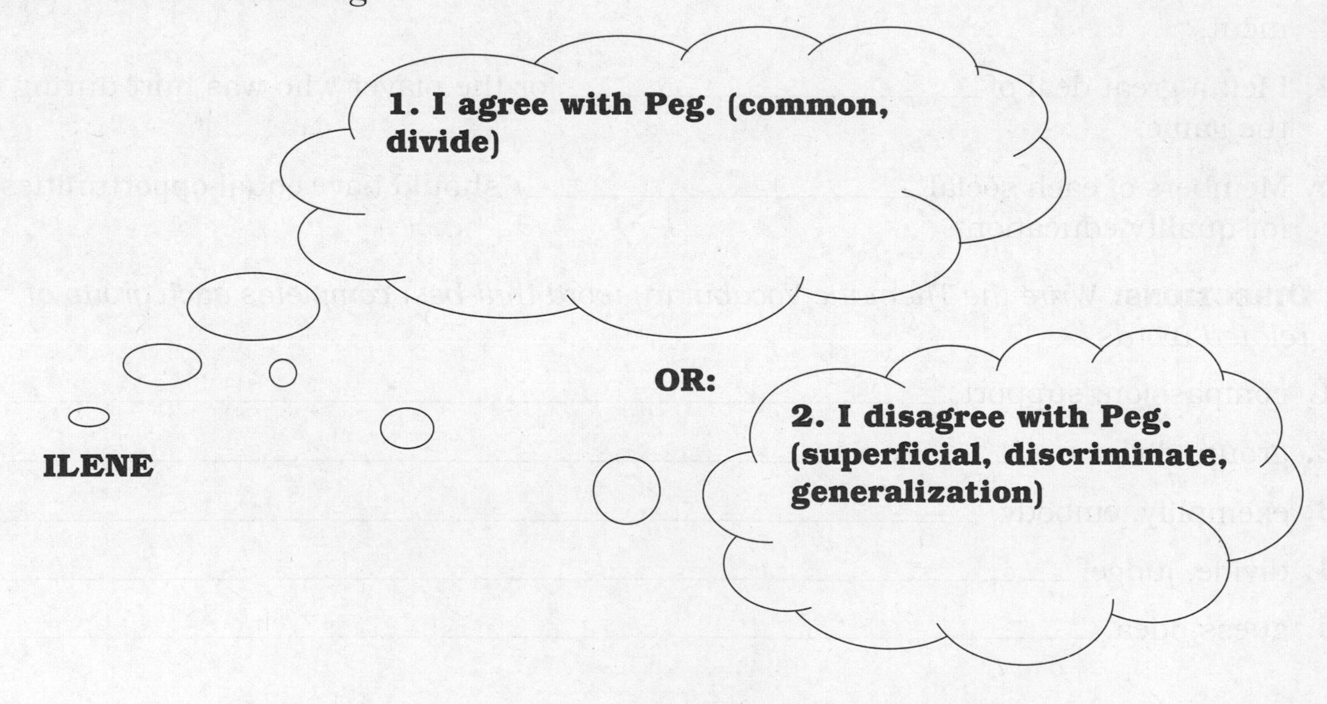

Name ______________________ Date ______________

Unit 4: Drama
Big Question Vocabulary—3

The Big Question: Is it our differences or our similarities that matter most?

Thematic Vocabulary

identify: *v.* to recognize or call out as being something; other forms: *identifying, identified, identification*

judge: *v.* to have or express a strong opinion as to the value of something; other forms: *judgment, judging*

separate: *v.* to move apart or divide two or more things into different groups
adj. different or apart from something else; other form: *separation*

tolerance: *n.* a willingness to accept and respect others, despite differences; other forms: *tolerate, tolerant*

unify: *v.* to bring things or people together into a workable group; other forms: *unity, union*

DIRECTIONS: *Answer each question. Use the word or words in parentheses.*

1. What are the most important aspects of friendship? **(judge, identify)**

____

____

____

____

2. If you were the President of the United States, what would you do to encourage different groups of people to work together? **(unify, separate)**

____

____

____

____

3. Why is it important to teach children the importance of respecting and accepting others, regardless of differences? **(tolerance)**

____

____

____

____

Name ______________________________ Date ________________

Unit 4: Drama
Applying the Big Question

Is it our differences or our similarities that matter most?

DIRECTIONS: *Complete the chart below to apply what you have learned about differences and similarities, and which matter most. One row has been completed for you.*

Example	Type of difference or similarity	How did it matter?	Effect on the people involved	What I learned
From Literature	Working-class governess feels inferior to upper-class employer in "The Governess"	Governess would not stand up for herself and allowed employer to walk all over her	Employer was using the situation to instruct the governess about asserting herself, and so treated her fairly	It is possible to recognize and overcome class differences.
From Literature				
From Science				
From Social Studies				
From Real Life				

Name ______________________________ Date ______________

The Diary of Anne Frank, *Act I*, by Frances Goodrich and Albert Hackett

Writing About the Big Question

Is it our differences or our similarities that matter most?

Big Question Vocabulary

assumption	class	common	discriminate	distinguish
divide	generalization	identify	judge	represent
separate	superficial	sympathy	tolerance	unify

A. *Use one or more words from the list above to complete each sentence.*

1. Their shared feelings of support for a local sports team helped ______________________ the people of the town.
2. The color of a person's hair is an example of a ______________ characteristic.
3. Someone who claims that all kids hate vegetables is making a ______________________.

B. *Use complete sentences to respond to each of the items below.*

1. Describe a time when you witnessed or experienced an act of **discrimination.**
____
____
____
2. How did this experience make you feel?
____
____
____

C. *Use the sentence starter below as the lead-in to a paragraph that deals with the Big Question.*

When people must face danger together, it tends to make them focus on ______________
____
____
____
____
____
____

Name ______________________________ Date ______________

The Diary of Anne Frank, *Act I,* by Frances Goodrich and Albert Hackett

Reading: Use Background Information to Link Historical Causes With Effects

A **cause** is an event, action, or feeling that produces a result, or an **effect.** When you read a work that is set in a particular time and place, you can **use background information to link historical causes with effects.** This background information includes the following:

- the introduction to a literary work
- information provided in footnotes
- facts you learned in other classes
- information you already know about the topic

In *The Diary of Anne Frank*, Act I, Anne states the following in her diary:

As my family is Jewish, we emigrated to Holland when Hitler came to power.

You already know that Adolph Hitler was a German dictator who persecuted the Jews of Europe. The effect of his persecution on Anne and her family was their forced immigration to Holland and then more than two years in a hideout—the attic rooms where the play is set.

Directions: *In the right column of the chart, write the effects on Anne Frank and the others of each historical cause noted in the play.*

Historical Cause	Effect on Anne and Others
1. Jews were treated badly in Holland when the Germans took over.	
2. Jews had to hide if they were to survive.	
3. Goods were rationed in wartime.	
4. Some people escaped to Switzerland.	

Name ______________________________ Date ______________

The Diary of Anne Frank, ***Act I,*** by Frances Goodrich and Albert Hackett

Literary Analysis: Dialogue

Dialogue is a conversation between or among characters. In the *script*, or text, of a play, lines of dialogue follow the name of the speaker who delivers them. Dialogue can reveal character traits. It also advances the plot, and it shows conflict between characters or against outside forces.

DIRECTIONS: *Explain what each example of dialogue from the play reveals about the characters and events.*

1. **MR. KRALER.** I never thought I'd live to see the day when a man like Mr. Frank would have to go into hiding. When you think—

____

____

____

2. **MR. FRANK.** It'll be hard, I know. But always remember this, Anneke. There are no walls, there are no bolts, no locks that anyone can put on your mind. Miep will bring us books. We will read history, poetry, mythology.

____

____

____

3. **MR. VAN DAAN.** [*restraining himself with difficulty*] Why aren't you nice and quiet like your sister Margot? Why do you have to show off all the time? Let me give you a little advice, young lady. Men don't like that kind of thing in a girl. You know that? A man likes a girl who'll listen to him once in a while . . . a domestic girl, who'll keep her house shining for her husband . . . who loves to cook and sew and . . .
ANNE. I'd cut my throat first! I'd open my veins! I'm going to be remarkable! I'm going to Paris . . .

____

____

____

4. **ANNE.** Things have changed. People aren't like that any more. "Yes, Mother." "No, Mother." "Anything you say, Mother." I've got to fight things out for myself! Make something of myself!

____

____

____

Name ______________________________ Date ______________

The Diary of Anne Frank, *Act I,* by Frances Goodrich and Albert Hackett

Vocabulary Builder

Word List

bewildered conspicuous fatalist insufferable resent tension

A. Directions: *Use the underlined word in your answer to each question. Your answer should show you know the meaning of the word.*

1. Would a fatalist believe that good acts can change a person's fate?

____

2. How would you react if a friend's behavior were insufferable?

____

3. If you have a conspicuous rip in your jacket, can others see it?

____

4. Would you be likely to resent someone who was constantly bragging about how much bigger his house is than yours?

____

5. If the owner's manual of your new DVD player left you bewildered, would you be likely to have an easy time setting up the machine?

____

6. If there were a lot of tension at a business meeting, would the participants probably be agreeing or disagreeing on most points?

____

B. Word Study: The **suffix *-ist*** means "one who performs, makes, practices, is skilled in, or believes in." Think about the meaning of *-ist* in each italicized word. On the line before each sentence, write *T* if the statement is true and *F* if the statement is false. Then, explain your answer.

1. ______________ A *soloist* is someone who plays an equal role with other musicians in a band.

____

2. ______________ A *pharmacist* can help you fill a prescription for medicine from your doctor.

____

3. ______________ A *finalist* is someone who is eliminated in the first round of a competition.

____

Name ______________________________ Date ______________

The Diary of Anne Frank, *Act I,* by Frances Goodrich and Albert Hackett

Conventions: Prepositions and Prepositional Phrases

A **preposition** is a word that relates a noun or pronoun to another word in the sentence. The noun or pronoun is called the **object of the preposition**. A **prepositional phrase** consists of a preposition, its object, and any words that modify the object. The entire phrase serves as an adjective or an adverb. Study this example:

The boy *with Mary* danced *around the empty room.*

The first preposition, *with,* relates its object, the noun *Mary,* to another word in the sentence, *boy.* The preposition and its object form the prepositional phrase *with Mary.* The phrase serves as an adjective, describing the noun *boy*—it tells you *which* boy. The second preposition, *around,* relates its object, the noun *room,* to another word in the sentence, *danced.* The preposition, its object, and the words *the* and *empty,* which modify the object, form the prepositional phrase *around the empty room.* The phrase serves as an adverb, describing the verb *danced*—it tells you *where* the boy danced.

The chart shows some words that are often used as prepositions.

Sequence	Location		Direction		Other Relationships	
after before during until	above below behind between	in on near under	across around down from	into through toward up	about against at by	for of with without

A. Practice: *Circle the prepositional phrase in each sentence, labeling the preposition* P *and its object* OP. *Draw an arrow to the word that the phrase modifies. On the line before the sentence, indicate whether the phrase serves as an* adjective *or an* adverb.

__________ 1. Anne Frank lived during World War II.

__________ 2. She kept a diary about her experiences.

__________ 3. After the war, many people read it.

__________ 4. It became the basis of a famous play.

__________ 5. We are studying the play in English class.

B. Writing Application: *Expand each sentence by adding a prepositional phrase to describe the underlined word. Write the new sentence on the line.*

1. The <u>dog</u> barked all night. ______________________________
2. The moonlight <u>streamed</u>. ______________________________
3. We <u>sat</u> together. ______________________________

Name ______________________ Date ______________

The Diary of Anne Frank, ***Act I,*** by Frances Goodrich and Albert Hackett

Support for Writing to Sources: Diary Entries

To prepare for writing diary entries from the points of view of two other characters, choose the event you will write about and the two characters besides Anne. Enter this information on the lines below. Then, write details about the scene as each character you have chosen might experience or see them.

Event: ______________________

Details as Experienced or Seen by Characters Besides Anne	
Character 1: ______________	Character 2: ______________

Now, use the details you have gathered to write your diary entries.

Name ______________________________ Date ______________

The Diary of Anne Frank, ***Act I,*** by Frances Goodrich and Albert Hackett

Support for Speaking and Listening: Guided Tour

To prepare for your guided tour, fill in the T-chart below with details about the Secret Annex from the play and from other sources, such as Anne's real diary and the Web site of the Anne Frank House.

Details From the Play	Details From Other Sources

Now, write up the text for your guided tour.

Name ______________________________ Date ______________

The Diary of Anne Frank, *Act II,* by Frances Goodrich and Albert Hackett

Writing About the Big Question

THE BIG ?

Is it our differences or our similarities that matter most?

Big Question Vocabulary

assumption	class	common	discriminate	distinguish
divide	generalization	identify	judge	represent
separate	superficial	sympathy	tolerance	unify

A. *Circle the more appropriate word from each pair listed to complete each sentence.*

1. My friend Etta and I get along well because we have many common/separate interests.
2. Having different political views is an example of something that might divide/unify people.
3. The people of our town elected a new official to represent/judge us in Congress.

B. *Respond to the following item, using full sentences.*

Describe a situation in which you might have to show **tolerance.**

____

____

____

____

C. *Use the sentence starter below as the lead-in to a paragraph that deals with the Big Question.*

People who face persecution can maintain their humanity and dignity by __________

____

____

____

____

____

____

____

____

____

Name ______________________ Date ______________

The Diary of Anne Frank, *Act II,* by Frances Goodrich and Albert Hackett

Reading: Ask Questions to Analyze Cause-and-Effect Relationships

Cause-and-effect relationships explain the connection between events, but they do not always follow the simple pattern of a single cause producing a single effect. Sometimes, a single cause produces multiple effects. Alternatively, multiple causes can produce a single effect. A chain of causes and effects, in which one cause triggers an effect that becomes the cause of another effect, also is common. **Ask questions to analyze cause-and-effect relationships** in a literary work. Here are examples:

- What are all the possible causes that might have triggered this event?
- What are the various effects that might result from this cause?
- Are these events really related in a cause-and-effect way? Just because two events occur in chronological, or time, order does not mean they are a cause and an effect. They may be coincidental or random occurrences.

Directions: *Fill in the diagrams with the answers to these questions.*

1. What are all the possible causes that might have triggered the effect shown?

Cause 1: ______________________

Cause 2: ______________________

Cause 3: ______________________

Effect: The tension in the attic grows in Act II, Scene 4.

2. What are the various effects that result from the cause shown?

Cause: News comes of the invasion of Normandy

Effect 1: ______________________

Effect 2: ______________________

Effect 3: ______________________

Name ______________________________ Date ______________

The Diary of Anne Frank, ***Act II,*** by Frances Goodrich and Albert Hackett

Literary Analysis: Character Motivation

A **character's motivation** is the reason he or she takes a particular action. Motivation may be internal, external, or a combination of both.

- **Internal** motivations are based on emotions, such as loneliness or jealousy.
- **External** motivations are sparked by events or situations, such as a fire or poverty.

In *The Diary of Anne Frank*, Act II, Peter Van Daan kisses Anne on the cheek. His internal motivation is a strong feeling of affection for her. His external motivation is his mother's disapproval of his feelings and of Anne.

DIRECTIONS: *Fill in the chart with examples of internal and external motivations for each character's actions.*

Character's Action	Internal Motivation	External Motivation
1. Miep helps the families in the attic.		
2. Margot wishes for the end to come (Act II, Scene 1).		
3. Mr. Van Daan steals food (Act II, Scene 3).		
4. Anne confides in Peter (Act II, Scenes 1 and 2).		

Name ______________________________ Date ______________

The Diary of Anne Frank, *Act II,* by Frances Goodrich and Albert Hackett

Vocabulary Builder

Word List

apprehension blackmail forlorn inarticulate ineffectually intuition

A. Directions: *Circle* T *if the statement is true or* F *if the statement is false. Then, explain your answer.*

1. If you *blackmail* another person, you are showing kindness and generosity.
   T / F ______________________________
2. A violinist who practices *ineffectually* will become a much better player.
   T / F ______________________________
3. If you have a strong *intuition*, you can sense something that has happened or will happen.
   T / F ______________________________
4. If your friend looks *forlorn*, she has probably just done unexpectedly well on an exam.
   T / F ______________________________
5. When you feel *apprehension* about a test, you are fearful about it.
   T / F ______________________________
6. An *inarticulate* speaker can easily move or persuade an audience.
   T / F ______________________________

B. Word Study: The prefix *in-* can mean "into" or "within." Think about the meaning of *in-* in each italicized word. On the line before each sentence, write *T* if the statement is true and *F* if the statement is false. Then, explain your answer.

1. ________ An *injection* involves taking blood from the body. ______________________________
2. ________ The *infield* is the part of the baseball field that is closest to the batter. ______________________________
3. ________ If you were *inflating* a tire, you would be taking air out of it. ______________________________

Name ______________________________ Date ______________

The Diary of Anne Frank, *Act II* by Frances Goodrich and Albert Hackett

Conventions: Participial and Infinitive Phrases

A **participle** is a verb used as an adjective to modify a noun or a pronoun. Most participles end in *-ing* or *-ed*, but some are irregular: *swaying* trees, *tired* runner, *broken* wing. A **participial phrase** is a participle with modifiers and objects or complements; the entire phrase serves as an adjective.

The dancers, *tired of the slow songs,* requested a mambo. (modifies *dancers*)

Moving her feet expertly, Tina danced to the lively music. (modifies *Tina*)

An **infinitive** is the form of a verb that includes the word *to* and acts as a noun, an adjective, or an adverb. For example, in the sentence *To dance can be hard,* the infinitive *to dance* acts as a noun—the subject of the sentence. An **infinitive phrase** is an infinitive with modifiers, objects, or complements. The entire phrase acts as a single part of speech.

Noun: I would love *to dance well.* (direct object)

Adjective: He made a request *to dance a mambo.* (modifies *request*)

Adverb: I find it easy *to dance to that music.* (modifies *easy*)

A. Practice: *Underline each participial phrase, and circle each infinitive phrase. If the phrase serves as an adjective or as an adverb, write the word that the phrase modifies. If the phrase serves as a noun, write whether it is a* subject *or a* direct object.

1. I like to read poetry aloud. ______________
2. To recite a poem is easiest when the poem has a strong rhythm. ______________
3. We had an assignment to do a poetry reading. ______________
4. Speaking clearly, Andrea recited her favorite poem. ______________
5. The poem, divided into sections, was fairly long. ______________

B. Writing Application: *Complete each sentence by adding the type of phrase requested in parentheses.*

1. I really want (infinitive phrase) ______________
2. It is fun (infinitive phrase) ______________
3. (participial phrase) ______________, my cousin gave me tips.
4. Her advice, (participial phrase) ______________, was very helpful.

Name ______________________________ Date ______________

The Diary of Anne Frank, ***Act II,*** by Frances Goodrich and Albert Hackett

Support for Writing to Sources: Film Review

Use the chart below to help you prepare to write your review of a film adaptation of *The Diary of Anne Frank*. Jot down your answers to the questions, as well as other comments or observations you may have.

Key Scenes: Does the film change or omit any key scenes? If so, what is the effect?
Portrayal of Characters: Assess the work of the actors. Do they live up to your expectations?
Directorial Choices: Do the sets, background music, camera angles, and so on enhance or detract from the story?
Overall Impressions: Is the film faithful to the text? Does it capture the general sense of the play?

Now, use the details you have collected to write your review.

Name ______________________________ Date ______________

The Diary of Anne Frank, *Act II,* by Frances Goodrich and Albert Hackett

Support for Research and Technology: Bulletin Board Display

To streamline your research process, list the sources you will consult to collect documents for your bulletin board display.

Primary Sources:

____

____

____

____

Reference Works:

____

____

____

____

Other Nonfiction Books:

____

____

____

____

Web Sites:

____

____

____

____

Name ______________________ Date ______________

The Governess by Neil Simon

Writing About the Big Question

Is it our differences or our similarities that matter most?

Big Question Vocabulary

assumption	class	common	discriminate	distinguish
divide	generalization	identify	judge	represent
separate	superficial	sympathy	tolerance	unify

A. *Use one or more words from the list above to complete each sentence.*

1. It can be hard to communicate with someone if you don't have ______________ interests.
2. People show ______________ when they accept that other people may not always share their views.
3. It is not fair to ______________ against people just because they are different from you.

B. *Respond to the following item, using full sentences.*

Describe a time when someone showed **sympathy** to you.

____

____

____

____

C. *Complete the sentence below. Then, write a short paragraph in which you connect the completed sentence to the Big Question.*

People sometimes **identify** themselves as part of a group on the basis of ______________

____

____

____

____

____

____

Name ______________________________ Date ________________

The Governess by Neil Simon

Reading: Draw Conclusions

When you **draw conclusions** about something, you reach decisions or opinions after considering facts and details. To draw conclusions from a play, observe what characters say and do.

- Look for statements that reveal underlying ideas and attitudes.
- Analyze interactions that show how characters treat one another.
- Notice actions that create a clear pattern of behavior.

Make connections among these items to learn about the character.

In this excerpt from the play, Julia's actions and words tell you about her.

JULIA. [Lifts her head up] Yes, madame. [But her head has a habit of slowly drifting down again]

Julia's words tell you that Julia is Mistress's inferior; her actions tell you that Julia is either shy or afraid.

Directions: *Fill in the graphic below with examples of Mistress's statements, actions, and treatment of Julia. In the center, write conclusions you can draw about Mistress.*

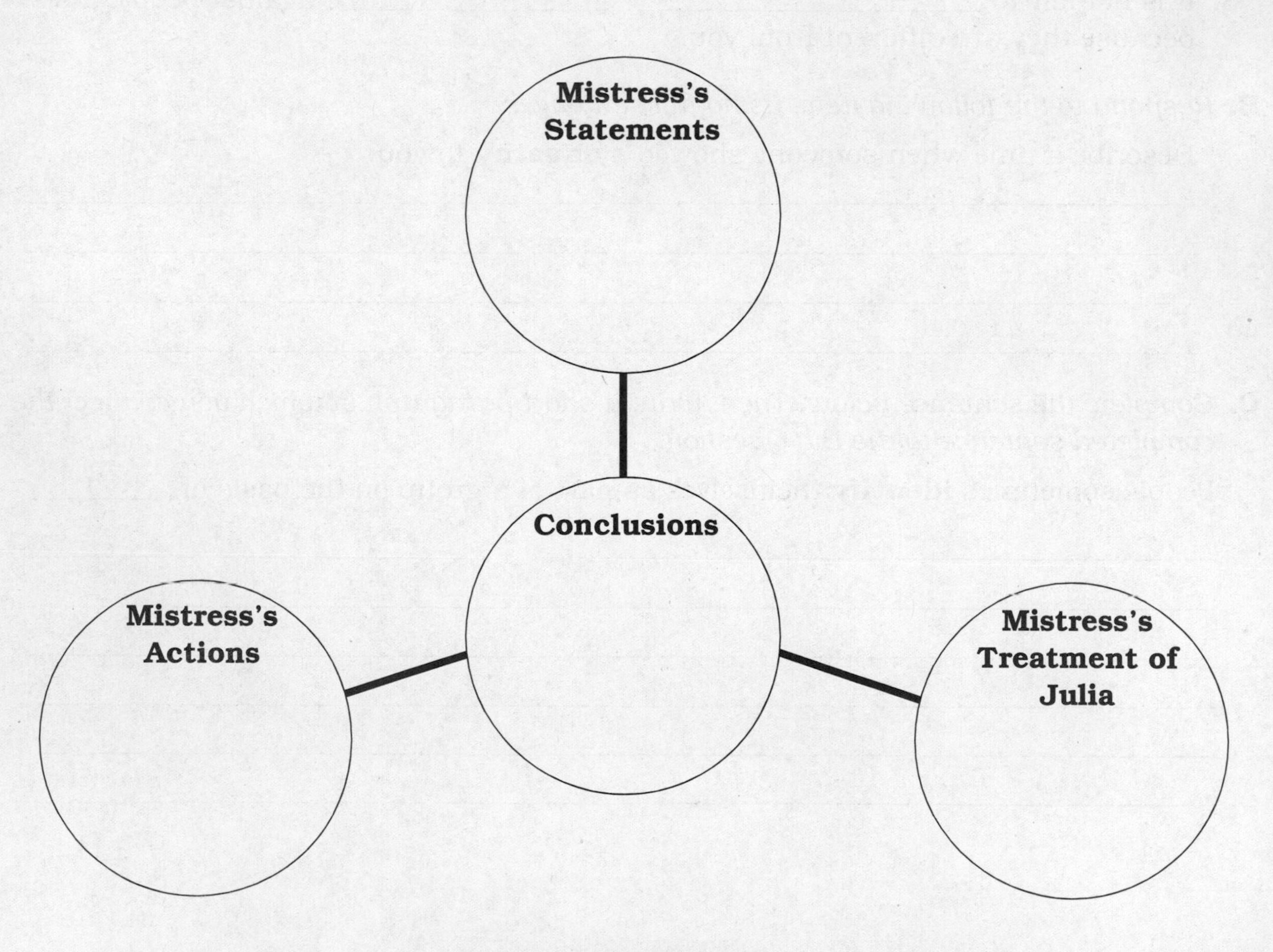

Name ______________________________ Date ______________

The Governess by Neil Simon

Literary Analysis: Setting and Character

Playwrights use dialogue and stage directions to develop **characters** and establish **setting**. **Stage directions** describe the scenery, costumes, lighting, and sound, and tell how the characters feel, move, and speak. Stage directions are usually printed in italics and set in brackets. The following stage directions describe the setting of a play.

[*It is late evening. The stage is dark, except for the glow of a small lamp beside the bed.*]

When you read a play, use the stage directions to create a mental image of how a stage production would look and sound.

DIRECTIONS: *Fill in this chart with the information the stage directions give you. The first entries have been completed for you.*

Stage Direction	What It Describes (scenery, costumes, lighting, sound; characters' feelings, movements, tone of voice)	What It Tells You
1. [*A young governess,* JULIA, *comes rushing in. She stops before the desk and curtsies.*]	Scenery Character's movements	The room probably belongs to someone important. Julia is young, a governess; she is energetic and humble.
2. [*But her head has a habit of slowly drifting down again*]		
3. [*She turns away, softly crying*]		
4. [*She curtsies again and runs off. The* MISTRESS *looks after her a moment, a look of complete bafflement on her face. The lights fade.*]		

Name ______________________ Date ______________

The Governess by Neil Simon

Vocabulary Builder

Word List

discharged   discrepancies   guileless   inferior   lax   satisfactory

A. Directions: *Use the underlined word in your answer to each question. Your answer should show you know the meaning of the word.*

1. If the stories told by two witnesses to a crime have serious discrepancies, what should the investigating officer do?

   ____

2. If you got to work late each day, would it be surprising if your boss discharged you?

   ____

3. Who is more likely to believe a lie, someone who is guileless or someone who is not?

   ____

4. If a supervisor finds a worker's performance satisfactory, is she likely to fire the worker?

   ____

5. Who was considered inferior in a medieval kingdom, the king or his subjects?

   ____

6. If a reporter is lax when she is taking notes, is she likely to record every word spoken during an interview?

   ____

B. Word Study: The **suffix *-ory*** means "of," "relating to," or "characterized by." Think about the meaning of *-ory* in each italicized word. On the line before each sentence, write *T* if the statement is true and *F* if the statement is false. Then, explain your answer. Consult a dictionary if necessary.

1. ____________ A *mandatory* payment is one that you can make or not make according to your preference.

   ____

2. ____________ A *predatory* animal eats only plants.

   ____

3. ____________ Hearing a sound is a form of *sensory* perception.

   ____

Name ______________________________ Date ______________

The Governess by Neil Simon

Conventions: Clauses

A **clause** is a group of words with its own subject and verb. An **independent clause** has a subject and verb and can stand by itself as a sentence. A **subordinate clause** has a subject and verb but cannot stand by itself because it does not express a complete thought. There are three kinds of subordinate clauses. An **adverb clause** acts as an adverb and begins with a subordinating conjunction such as *although, if, when, because,* or *since*. A **relative clause** acts as an adjective and usually begins with a relative pronoun such as *who, whom, whose, which,* or *that*. A **noun clause** acts as a noun and begins with a word such as *what, whatever, when, where, how,* or *why*.

Independent Clause	Because Karen came late, *she missed the start of the movie.*
Adverb Clause	*Because Karen came late,* she missed the start of the movie.
Relative Clause	The movie, *which had won many awards,* was filmed in Finland.
Noun Clause	Karen could not understand *what the actors were saying.*

A. PRACTICE: *Underline the independent clauses once and the subordinate clauses twice. On the lines, write whether the subordinate clauses are* adverb, relative, *or* noun clauses. *If there is no subordinate clause, write* none.

1. Julia, who worked as a governess, was well educated. ______________
2. Because she was poor, she needed the job badly. ______________
3. Julia's employer seemed confused about what she would pay Julia.
4. The employer was just joking about the lower salary. ______________

B. Writing Application: *On the lines, expand these subordinate clauses into sentences that express a complete thought.*

1. which summer job would be better ______________
____
2. that pays a better salary ______________
____
3. because it is closer to home ______________
____

Name ____________________ Date ____________

The Governess by Neil Simon

Support for Writing to Sources: Public Service Announcement

To prepare for writing a **public service announcement** (PSA) on fair treatment of workers, use the graphic organizer below:

Choose a public figure who will be your spokesperson:	Summarize, in one or two sentences, the points you will use to persuade your audience:	List words, phrases, images, sound effects, or symbols you might use in your message:

Write a rough draft or sketch out the main ideas for a radio or television message to be delivered by your spokesperson, using elements from your notes and lists. Use sound effects and images as part of your message. Write or continue your draft on a separate sheet of paper if you wish.

Name ______________________ Date ______________

The Governess by Neil Simon

Support for Speaking and Listening: Debate

An important part of preparing for a **debate** is to anticipate and answer any questions, objections, or points your opponent might make. Use the chart below to help you predict at least four of your opponent's major points and to come up with effective answers for them.

Anticipated Points, Objections, or Questions From Opponent	My Responses to Opponent
Opponent's objection/question 1:	My response:
Opponent's objection/question 2:	My response:
Opponent's objection/question 3:	My response:
Opponent's objection/question 4:	My response:

Incorporate these ideas into your notes for possible use during the debate.

Name ______________________________ Date ______________

The Governess by Neil Simon

The Ninny by Anton Chekhov

Writing About the Big Question

Is it our differences or our similarities that matter most?

Big Question Vocabulary

assumption	class	common	discriminate	distinguish
divide	generalization	identify	judge	represent
separate	superficial	sympathy	tolerance	unify

A. *Circle the more appropriate word from each pair listed to complete each sentence.*

1. You might make a mistaken assumption/class if you do not know all the facts.
2. Miguel felt sympathy/tolerance for his friend when her dog died.
3. It is not always easy to distinguish/represent between facts and opinions.

B. *Use complete sentences to respond to each item.*

1. How would you **identify** yourself when meeting a new neighbor for the first time?

____

____

2. Does this introduction focus more on what you and your neighbor have in **common** or on your differences?

____

____

C. *Complete the sentence below. Then, write a short paragraph in which you connect the completed sentence to the Big Question.*

When people focus only on their differences, ______________________

____

____

____

____

____

____

Name ______________________ Date ______________

The Governess by Neil Simon
The Ninny by Anton Chekhov

Literary Analysis: Compare Adaptations With Originals

A literary **adaptation** is a work that has been changed or adjusted to fit a different form or genre. For example, a novel may be adapted into a play or a movie. Adapting a literary work usually means changing or leaving out some parts of the original to suit the new form. For instance, a play depends almost entirely on dialogue, without the narration or description that is often included in a story. Neil Simon's play *The Governess* is an adaptation of "The Ninny," a short story by the Russian writer Anton Chekhov.

To compare an adaptation with the original work, keep in mind the differences in the two literary forms.

Directions: *Answer the following questions to compare an adaptation with an original.*

1. What form is "The Ninny" written in? What form is *The Governess* written in?

____

____

2. What important information do we learn from both the original and the adaptation?

____

____

____

3. Which details in the original are left out of the adaptation or are changed?

____

____

____

4. What elements has the writer of the adaptation introduced?

____

____

____

5. Are the styles of the two authors similar, or is one style lighter or funnier?

____

____

6. Which form do you find more engaging? Why do you like one better than the other?

____

____

Name ______________________________ Date ______________

The Governess by Neil Simon
The Ninny by Anton Chekhov

Vocabulary Builder

Word List

account   carelessness   spineless   timidly

A. DIRECTIONS: *Revise each sentence so that the underlined vocabulary word is used logically. Be sure not to change the vocabulary word.*

1. The building contractor settled his account with the carpenter but forgot to pay him.

____

____

2. Yulya timidly approached the assembled student body and gave her speech with confidence and ease.

____

____

3. The spineless crowd of people helped to free a man trapped in his car.

____

____

4. The chemist's carelessness about small details is what enabled him to succeed with the complicated experiment.

____

B. DIRECTIONS: *Circle the letter of the word or phrase most opposite in meaning to the word in CAPITAL LETTERS.*

1. SPINELESS
   A. weak   B. ineffectual   C. strong-willed   D. furious

2. CARELESSNESS
   A. foolishness   B. sloppiness   C. inability   D. responsibility

3. TIMIDLY
   A. boldly   B. fearfully   C. wisely   D. firmly

Name ______________________________ Date ______________

The Governess by Neil Simon
The Ninny by Anton Chekhov

Support for Writing to Compare Adaptations With Originals

In addition to a comparison chart, you may find the graphic organizer presented here helpful in gathering your ideas for the writing assignment. For each question on the graphic, place a check in either the column for Chekhov's story "The Ninny" or the column for Simon's play *The Governess.* Then, in the same box, jot down details from the play or story to support your evaluation.

Criteria	The Chekhov Story	The Simon Play
1. Which work tells you more about the setting?		
2. Which work gives you a fuller portrait of the employer?		
3. In which work do you feel more empathy for the governess?		
4. Which work makes you think more as you read and/or as you reflect on the work?		

Now, using your notes from this sheet and from your comparison chart, write an essay in which you compare and contrast the adaptation, *The Governess*, with the original, "The Ninny."

Name ______________________ Date ______________

Writing Process

Cause-and-Effect Essay

Prewriting: Discuss with a Classmate

To find topics that interest you, pair up with a classmate and take turns answering the questions below. Then choose the topics that interest you the most.

What is your favorite book? What natural or historical events are crucial to the story?	
What interesting facts have you learned in science class?	
Which political leader do you admire most? What was happening in the world when he or she was in office?	

Drafting: Organizing Your Ideas

Use the appropriate graphic organizer below to choose which description best fits your topic as well as to organize your causes and effects.

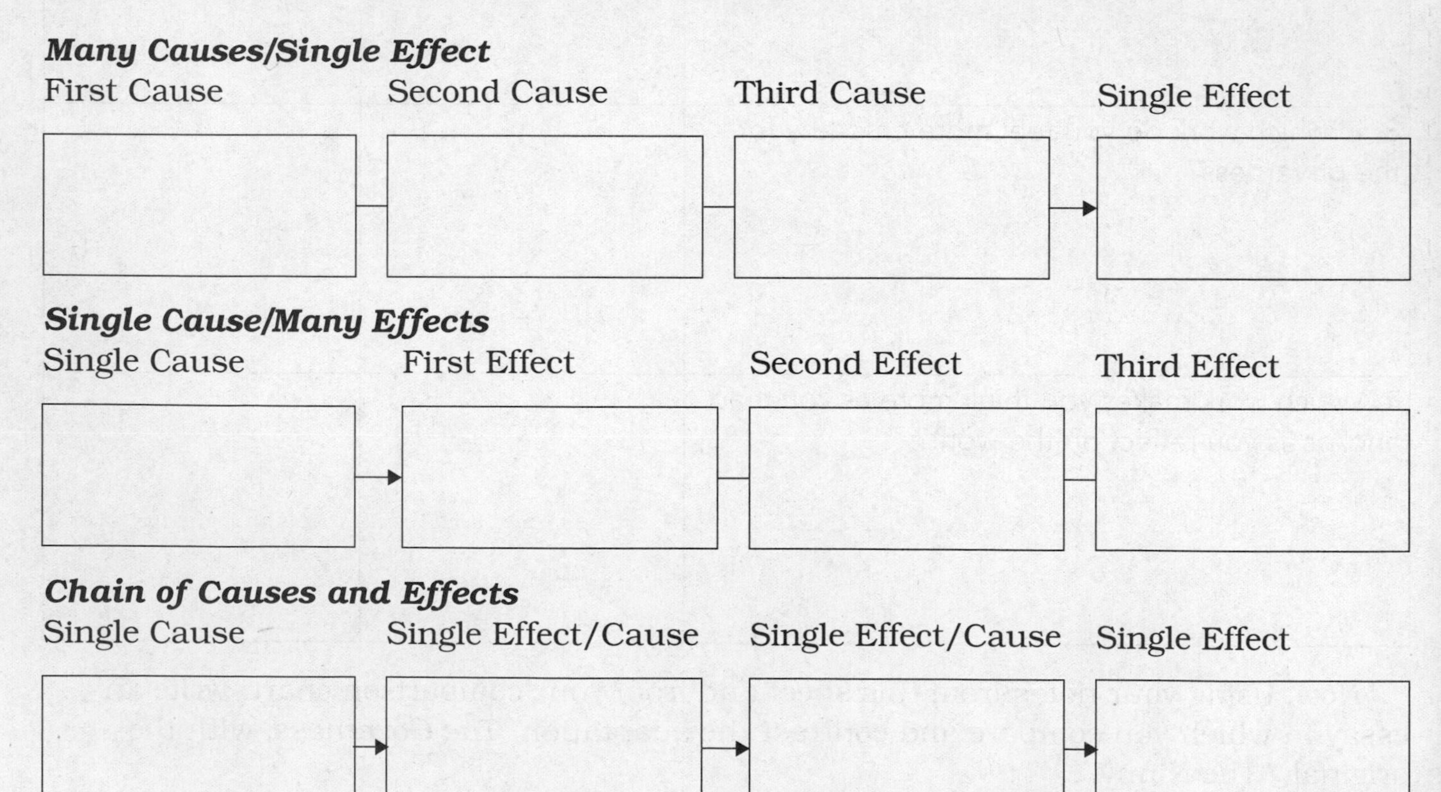

Name ______________________________ Date ______________

Writer's Toolbox

Conventions: Revising to Combine Sentences Using Gerunds and Participles

A **gerund** is a verbal ending in *-ing* that acts as a noun. A **gerund phrase** is a gerund with modifiers, objects, or complements, all acting together as a noun.

Gerund phrase as subject: *Baking cookies* is Heather's hobby.
Gerund as direct object: Lucille enjoys *swimming.*

A **participle** is a verbal that acts as an adjective, modifying a noun or a pronoun. **Present participles** end in *-ing;* **past participles** frequently end in *-ed.* A **participial phrase** is a participle and its modifiers, objects, or complements, all acting together as an adjective.

Present Participle: The *chirping* canary sang sweetly.
Past Participle in Participial Phrase: *Filled with hope,* we entered the race.

Combine choppy or short sentences with gerunds and participles.

Choppy Sentences:	The sisters enjoy music. They like to sing together.
Combined With Gerund:	The sisters enjoy music and *singing together.*
Combined With Participle:	*Singing together,* the sisters enjoy music.

A. Directions: *Write* gerund *or* participle *to identify the word or phrase in italics.*

__________ 1. *Surprised by the results,* I didn't realize we had won.

__________ 2. *Winning the race* is always fun.

__________ 3. Sometimes I learn more by *losing.*

__________ 4. Max is the most *improved* player on the team.

B. Directions: *Combine the two short sentences by using a gerund or a participle.*

1. The twins skate at the ice rink. They enjoy it.

____

2. Aimee races across the ice. She slips and falls.

____

3. Annie skates over to Aimee. She helps Aimee get up.

____

4. People have accidents. They skate too fast.

____

Name ______________________________ Date ______________

from **Kindertransport, Act II** by Diane Samuels

Vocabulary Builder

Selection Vocabulary

callous monumental morbid

A. DIRECTIONS: *From the following lists, select one synonym and one antonym for each of the numbered words in the table below. Write your choices in the appropriate boxes.*

Synonyms	**Antonyms**
overwhelming	cheerful
gloomy	sympathetic
insensitive	trivial

Word	Synonym	Antonym
1. callous		
2. morbid		
3. monumental		

Academic Vocabulary

distinguishes evidence motive

B. DIRECTIONS: *Complete each sentence with a word, phrase, or clause that contains a context clue for the italicized word.*

1. What *distinguishes* this speech from the others is ____.

2. He revealed his *motive* by telling everyone ____.

3. I provided *evidence* for my response by ____.

Name ______________________________ Date ______________________

from **Kindertransport, Act II** by Diane Samuels

Take Notes for Discussion

Before the Group Discussion: Read the following passage from the selection.

> [EVELYN *rips.* LIL *picks up the "Rattenfänger" book and starts to tear out the first page.*]
>
> **EVELYN.** No. Not that.
>
> **LIL.** It's in German. Horrible pictures.
>
> **EVELYN.** You can't damage a book. I'll give it to a secondhand shop.
>
> **LIL.** [*picking up the Haggadah*] What about this?
>
> **EVELYN.** That too.

During the Discussion: As you discuss each question, take notes on how other students' ideas either differ from or build upon your own.

Discussion Questions	Other Ideas Expressed	Comparison to My Own Ideas
1. How are the books different from the photos and papers Evelyn destroys?		
2. In what way does the story in the play resemble the traditional *Rattenfänger* story? In what way does the play make this story new?		
3. What aspects of the past do the two books symbolize?		
4. What do these symbols suggest about Evelyn's decision not to remember? Does she truly have a choice? Explain.		

Name ______________________ Date ______________

from **Kindertransport, Act II** by Diane Samuels

Take Notes for Writing to Sources

Planning Your Argument: Before you begin drafting your **argumentative essay,** use the chart below to organize your ideas. Follow the directions in each section.

1. Write a statement of your claim. You will use your statement in your introduction.
2. List details about the effects of the Kindertransport on the characters.
3. List the points you will make in arguing for your claim. When you finish your list, number them in order of importance.

Name ____ Date ____________________

from **Kindertransport, Act II** by Diane Samuels

Take Notes for Research

As you research **how common or rare it was for a survivor of the Holocaust to reunite with family and what difficulties these reunions may have presented,** use the forms below to take notes from your sources. As necessary, continue your notes on the back of this page, on note cards, or in a word-processing document.

Source Information Check one: ☐ Primary Source ☐ Secondary Source

Title: ______________________________ Author: ____________________

Publication Information: ____

Page(s): ____

Main Idea: ____

____

Quotation or Paraphrase: ____

____

Source Information Check one: ☐ Primary Source ☐ Secondary Source

Title: ______________________________ Author: ____________________

Publication Information: ____

Page(s): ____

Main Idea: ____

____

Quotation or Paraphrase: ____

____

Source Information Check one: ☐ Primary Source ☐ Secondary Source

Title: ______________________________ Author: ____________________

Publication Information: ____

Page(s): ____

Main Idea: ____

____

Quotation or Paraphrase: ____

____

Name ______________________________ Date ______________

from **Anne Frank: Diary of a Young Girl** by Anne Frank

Vocabulary Builder

Selection Vocabulary

enhance   emigrated   evading

A. DIRECTIONS: *Provide an explanation for your answer to each question.*

1. Will bringing the proper equipment *enhance* a person's camping experience?

____

____.

2. If you have *emigrated* somewhere, does that mean you have lived in one place your whole life?

____

____.

3. If someone were *evading* a question, does that mean she was giving truthful answers?

____

____.

Academic Vocabulary

investigate   observations   precise

B. DIRECTIONS: *Write a sentence that demonstrates the meaning of each word. Follow this example:*

imitate: Ava can *imitate* people by copying the way they walk and talk.

1. *observations:* ____

____.

2. *investigate:* ____

____.

3. *precise:* ____

____.

Name ______________________ Date ______________

from **Anne Frank: Diary of a Young Girl** by Anne Frank

Take Notes for Discussion

Before the Partner Discussion: Read the following passage from the selection.

> Yes, there is no doubt that paper is patient and as I don't intend to show this cardboard-covered notebook, bearing the proud name of "diary," to anyone, unless I find a real friend, boy or girl, probably nobody cares. And now I come to the root of the matter, the reason for my starting a diary: it is that I have no such real friend.

During the Discussion: As you discuss each question, take notes on how your partner's ideas either differ from or build upon your own.

Discussion Questions	Other Ideas Expressed	Comparison to My Own Ideas
1. What reason does Anne identify for keeping her diary?		
2. How might learning Anne's thoughts help readers see the injustice of her death?		
3. Why might publishing Anne's private thoughts and feelings be the right thing to do?		

Name ____________________ Date ____________

from **Anne Frank: Diary of a Young Girl** by Anne Frank

Take Notes for Research

As you research **where Anne's diary is read, the number of copies sold, and other works—such as books, movies, and music—that use it as inspiration,** use the chart below to take notes from your sources. As necessary, continue your notes on the back of this page, on note cards, or in a word-processing document.

Anne Frank's Diary	
Main Idea ____________________ ____________________ **Quotation or Paraphrase** ____________________ ____________________ ____________________ ____________________ ____________________ **Source Information** ____________________ ____________________ ____________________ ____________________	**Main Idea** ____________________ ____________________ **Quotation or Paraphrase** ____________________ ____________________ ____________________ ____________________ ____________________ **Source Information** ____________________ ____________________ ____________________ ____________________
Main Idea ____________________ ____________________ **Quotation or Paraphrase** ____________________ ____________________ ____________________ ____________________ ____________________ **Source Information** ____________________ ____________________ ____________________ ____________________	**Main Idea** ____________________ ____________________ **Quotation or Paraphrase** ____________________ ____________________ ____________________ ____________________ ____________________ **Source Information** ____________________ ____________________ ____________________ ____________________

Name ______________________________ Date ______________

from **Anne Frank: Diary of a Young Girl** by Anne Frank

Take Notes for Writing to Sources

Planning Your Narrative: Before you begin drafting your **first-person narrative,** use the chart below to organize your ideas. Follow the directions in each section.

1. Write notes about the situation that forms the foundation for your narrative. Think about the questions *Who? What? When? Where? Why?* and *How?*

2. List details from Anne's diary to include in Dussel's narrative.

3. Write notes for your conclusion. What is Dussel reflecting upon at this time?

Name ______________________________ Date ______________

from **Anne Frank Remembered** by Miep Gies with Alison Leslie Gold

Vocabulary Builder

Selection Vocabulary

chaos refugee succumbed

A. Directions: *Revise each sentence so that the underlined vocabulary word is used logically. Be sure not to change the vocabulary word.*

1. It is easy to adapt to the chaos of wartime. ______________________________
______________________________.
2. The refugee stayed comfortably in his home village. ______________________________
______________________________.
3. She succumbed to his urging her to read the diary and left it unopened.
____
______________________________.

Academic Vocabulary

document perception transfer

B. Directions: *Complete each sentence with a word, phrase, or clause that contains a context clue for the italicized word.*

1. Our *perception* of events can sometimes ______________________________
______________________________.
2. After the *transfer,* the group of new arrivals had to ______________________________
______________________________.
3. Please submit an official *document* or some other ______________________________
______________________________.

Name ______________________________ Date ______________

from **Anne Frank Remembered** by Miep Gies with Alison Leslie Gold

Take Notes for Discussion

Before the Debate: Read the following passage from the selection.

> When I had read the last word, I didn't feel the pain I'd anticipated. I was glad I'd read it at last. The emptiness in my heart was eased. So much had been lost, but now Anne's voice would never be lost. My young friend had left a remarkable legacy to the world.

During the Debate: As you discuss and debate each question, take notes on how other students' ideas either differ from or build upon your own.

Discussion Questions	Other Ideas Expressed	Comparison to My Own Ideas
1. What does Gies see as the value of the diary?		
2. Is the diary a kind of victory over the destruction caused by the Holocaust? Explain.		
3. What functions should a memorial to Holocaust victims fulfill?		

Name ______________________ Date ______________

from **Anne Frank Remembered** by Miep Gies with Alison Leslie Gold

Take Notes for Research

As you research **events related to the Holocaust,** use the forms below to take notes from your sources. As necessary, continue your notes on the back of this page, on note cards, or in a word-processing document.

Source Information Check one: ☐ Primary Source ☐ Secondary Source

Title: ______________________ Author: ______________

Publication Information: ______________________

Page(s): ______________________

Main Idea: ______________________

____

Quotation or Paraphrase: ______________________

____

Source Information Check one: ☐ Primary Source ☐ Secondary Source

Title: ______________________ Author: ______________

Publication Information: ______________________

Page(s): ______________________

Main Idea: ______________________

____

Quotation or Paraphrase: ______________________

____

Source Information Check one: ☐ Primary Source ☐ Secondary Source

Title: ______________________ Author: ______________

Publication Information: ______________________

Page(s): ______________________

Main Idea: ______________________

____

Quotation or Paraphrase: ______________________

____

Name ______________________ Date ______________

from **Anne Frank Remembered** by Miep Gies with Alison Leslie Gold

Take Notes for Writing to Sources

Planning Your Explanatory Text: Before you begin drafting your **analytical essay,** use the chart below to organize your ideas. Follow the directions in each section.

1. Your claim regarding Miep Gies's perspective:
2. Facts, examples, and other details that support your analysis:
3. Notes for your conclusion:

Name ______________________________ Date ______________

***from* Night** by Elie Wiesel, translated by Marion Wiesel

Vocabulary Builder

Selection Vocabulary

delirious protruded vulnerable

A. DIRECTIONS: *Complete each sentence with a word, phrase, or clause that contains a context clue for the italicized word.*

1. The rock that *protruded* from the hillside looked like ______________________________.
2. Megan was *vulnerable* to the flu and colds, so she ______________________________.
3. The actor was *delirious* because ______________________________.

Academic Vocabulary

credible evidence respond

B. DIRECTIONS: *Write the letter of the word or phrase that is the best synonym for the italicized word. Then, use the italicized word in a complete sentence.*

_____ 1. *credible*

A. trustworthy
B. interesting
C. dramatic
D. questionable

____

_____ 2. *respond*

A. answer
B. analyze
C. examine
D. consider

____

_____ 3. *evidence*

A. opinion
B. preference
C. result
D. proof

____

Name ______________________________ Date ______________

***from* Night** by Elie Wiesel, translated by Marion Wiesel

Take Notes for Discussion

Before the Panel Discussion: Read the following passage from the selection.

> No prayers were said over his tomb. No candle lit in his memory. His last word had been my name. He had called out to me and I had not answered.
>
> I did not weep, and it pained me that I could not weep. But I was out of tears. And deep inside me, if I could have searched the recesses of my feeble conscience, I might have found something like: Free at last! . . .

During the Discussion: As the group discusses each question, take notes on how other students' ideas either differ from or build upon your own.

Discussion Questions	Other Ideas Expressed	Comparison to My Own Ideas
1. Is Eliezer right or wrong to feel free? Explain, using details from the text.		
2. What connection can you see between Wiesel's failure to answer his father and his need to write this memoir?		

Name ______________________________ Date ______________

***from* Night** by Elie Wiesel, translated by Marion Wiesel

Take Notes for Research

As you research **resistance in the camps and in the ghettos,** you can use the organizer below to take notes from your sources. As necessary, continue your notes on the back of this page, on note cards, or in a word-processing document.

Resistance in the Camps and Ghettos	
Main Idea ______________	Main Idea ______________
Quotation or Paraphrase ______________	Quotation or Paraphrase ______________
Source Information ______________	Source Information ______________
Main Idea ______________	Main Idea ______________
Quotation or Paraphrase ______________	Quotation or Paraphrase ______________
Source Information ______________	Source Information ______________

Name ______________________ Date ____________

from **Night** by Elie Wiesel, translated by Marion Wiesel

Take Notes for Writing to Sources

Planning Your Informational Text: Before you begin drafting your **informational essay,** use the chart below to organize your ideas. Follow the directions in each section.

1. Notes for your introduction:
2. Events and situations:
3. Evidence and other details that explain and describe the situation at Buchenwald:

Name ______________________ Date ______________

"Remarks on a Visit to Buchenwald" by Elie Wiesel

Vocabulary Builder

Selection Vocabulary

aspirations denigrate invoke

A. DIRECTIONS: *Write a response to each question. Make sure to use the italicized word at least once in your response.*

1. What is a reasonable *aspiration* for middle school students? ______________________________.
2. Why might you feel unhappy if someone were to *denigrate* you? ______________________________.
3. Why might a speaker *invoke* the name of a famous and respected leader? ______________________________.

Academic Vocabulary

condition opinion support

B. DIRECTIONS: *Complete each sentence with a word, phrase, or clause that contains a context clue for the italicized word.*

1. I chose this evidence to *support* my claim because ______________________________.
2. That may be your *opinion*, but ______________________________.
3. Improving the human *condition* requires ______________________________.

Name ______________________________ Date ______________

"Remarks on a Visit to Buchenwald" by Elie Wiesel

Take Notes for Discussion

Before the Small Group Discussion: Read the following passage from the selection.

> Memory must bring people together rather than set them apart. Memory's here not to sow anger in our hearts, but on the contrary, a sense of solidarity with all those who need us. What else can we do except invoke that memory so that people everywhere will say the 21st century is a century of new beginnings, filled with promise and infinite hope, and at times profound gratitude to all those who believe in our task, which is to improve the human condition.

During the Discussion: As you discuss each question, take notes on how other students' ideas either differ from or build upon your own.

Discussion Questions	Other Ideas Expressed	Comparison to My Own Ideas
1. Do you agree that memory should bring people together? Explain, citing the text.		
2. Why does Wiesel put such emphasis on memory? What else might he call on?		

Name ______________________ Date ______________

"Remarks on a Visit to Buchenwald" by Elie Wiesel

Take Notes for Research

As you research **who was at Buchenwald and for what reasons,** use the forms below to take notes from your sources. As necessary, continue your notes on the back of this page, on note cards, or in a word-processing document.

Source Information Check one: ☐ Primary Source ☐ Secondary Source

Title: ______________________ Author: ______________

Publication Information: ______________________

Page(s): ______________________

Main Idea: ______________________

____

Quotation or Paraphrase: ______________________

____

Source Information Check one: ☐ Primary Source ☐ Secondary Source

Title: ______________________ Author: ______________

Publication Information: ______________________

Page(s): ______________________

Main Idea: ______________________

____

Quotation or Paraphrase: ______________________

____

Source Information Check one: ☐ Primary Source ☐ Secondary Source

Title: ______________________ Author: ______________

Publication Information: ______________________

Page(s): ______________________

Main Idea: ______________________

____

Quotation or Paraphrase: ______________________

____

Name ______________________ Date ______________

"Remarks on a Visit to Buchenwald" by Elie Wiesel

Take Notes for Writing to Sources

Planning Your Argument: Before you begin drafting your **letter to the editor,** use the chart below to organize your ideas. Follow the directions at the top of each section of the chart.

1. Statement of your opinion:
2. Details of the points you want to make:
3. Counterclaims and your refutations:

Name ______________________________ Date ______________

"Local Holocaust Survivors and Liberators Attend Opening Event for Exhibition"
from the Florida Holocaust Museum

Vocabulary Builder

Selection Vocabulary

genocides liberators testimonies

A. DIRECTIONS: *Complete each sentence with a word, phrase, or clause that contains a context clue for the italicized word.*

1. The *liberators* arrived and ______________________________
______________________________.
2. The *testimonies* of survivors ______________________________
______________________________.
3. In the *genocides* during World War II, ______________________________
______________________________.

Academic Vocabulary

argument contrast primary sources

B. DIRECTIONS: *Write a sentence that demonstrates the meaning of each word. Follow this example:*

reason: The author's *reason* for writing is evident in the first paragraph, where she states her purpose.

1. *argument:* ______________________________
______________________________.
2. *contrast:* ______________________________
______________________________.
3. *primary sources:* ______________________________
______________________________.

Name ______________________________ Date ________________

"Local Holocaust Survivors and Liberators Attend Opening Event for Exhibition"
from the Florida Holocaust Museum

Take Notes for Discussion

Before the Quick Write and Discuss: Read the following passage from the selection.

> *Liberators: Unexpected Outcomes* features 18 photographs of local U.S. troops who, as first responders and liberators at the end of WWII, witnessed the horrors behind camp gates. Without preparation or warning, these men happened upon unexpected and unimaginable scenes during regular military operations. Their stories are featured in photography by Coe Arthur Younger, as well as in an accompanying video that highlights the testimonies of several local liberators and survivors.

During the Discussion: As you discuss each question, take notes on how your partner's ideas either differ from or build upon your own.

Discussion Questions	Other Ideas Expressed	Comparison to My Own Ideas
1. How might the sights of a concentration camp make liberators feel? What responsibility might they feel they have, given what they have witnessed?		
2. What special bond might survivors and liberators feel?		

Name ______________________________ Date ______________

"Local Holocaust Survivors and Liberators Attend Opening Event for Exhibition"
from the Florida Holocaust Museum

Take Notes for Research

As you research **to find out more about the experience of the liberators,** use the forms below to take notes from your sources. As necessary, continue your notes on the back of this page, on note cards, or in a word-processing document.

Source Information Check one: ☐ Primary Source ☐ Secondary Source

Title: ______________________ Author: ______________________

Publication Information: ______________________

Page(s): ______________________

Main Idea: ______________________

____

Quotation or Paraphrase: ______________________

____

Source Information Check one: ☐ Primary Source ☐ Secondary Source

Title: ______________________ Author: ______________________

Publication Information: ______________________

Page(s): ______________________

Main Idea: ______________________

____

Quotation or Paraphrase: ______________________

____

Source Information Check one: ☐ Primary Source ☐ Secondary Source

Title: ______________________ Author: ______________________

Publication Information: ______________________

Page(s): ______________________

Main Idea: ______________________

____

Quotation or Paraphrase: ______________________

____

Name ______________________________ Date ______________

"Local Holocaust Survivors and Liberators Attend Opening Event for Exhibition"
from the Florida Holocaust Museum

Take Notes for Writing to Sources

Planning Your Narrative: Before you begin drafting your **imaginary interview,** use the chart below to organize your ideas. Follow the directions at the top of each section of the chart.

1. Notes on the exhibitions and museum:
2. Questions for the interview:
3. Answers to the interview questions:

Name ______________________ Date ______________

Unit 5: Themes in American Stories
Big Question Vocabulary—1

The Big Question: Are yesterday's heroes important today?

Thematic Vocabulary

admirably: *adv.* in a way that earns respect and high praise; other forms: *admire, admiration*

bravery: *n.* courage and confidence in the face of danger; other form: *brave*

emphasize: *v.* to stress or show that something is very important; other forms: *emphasis, emphasizing*

endure: *v.* to continue to exist for a long time; other forms: *endurance, endurable, enduring*

outdated: *adj.* not useful or valuable anymore

A. Directions: *From the words in the box, choose the correct synonym and antonym for each Thematic Vocabulary word. You will not use every word in the box.*

old-fashioned	strong	survive	heavily	excellently	fearlessness	downplay
poorly	die	modern	cowardice	pride	pretend	highlight

1. admirably **Synonym:** ______ **Antonym:** ______
2. bravery **Synonym:** ______ **Antonym:** ______
3. emphasize **Synonym:** ______ **Antonym:** ______
4. endure **Synonym:** ______ **Antonym:** ______
5. outdated **Synonym:** ______ **Antonym:** ______

B. Directions: *Complete each sentence by writing the correct Thematic Vocabulary word on the line.*

1. The soldier received a medal for his outstanding ______________.
2. Use an exclamation point to ______________ your character's strong feelings.
3. My love for the beauty of this island will ______________ for the rest of my life.
4. Even though he lost the contest, he performed ______________.
5. Grandma writes letters on a computer, but Grandpa still uses his ______________ typewriter.

Name ______________________ Date ______________

Unit 5: Themes in American Stories
Big Question Vocabulary—2

The Big Question: Are yesterday's heroes important today?

Thematic Vocabulary

accomplishments: *n.* successful or impressive achievements; other form: *accomplish*

aspects: *n.* parts of a situation, idea, or plan; other form: *aspect*

courage: *n.* bravery; other form: *courageous*

exaggerate: *v.* to make something seem better, larger, or worse than it actually is; other forms: *exaggeration, exaggerating*

imitate: *v.* to copy or duplicate another's actions; other forms: *imitation, imitating, imitated*

DIRECTIONS: *Respond to each of the items below.*

1. Rewrite this sentence so that it *exaggerates* the situation described: *He has a huge dog.*

____

2. Name a historical figure who you feel exhibited great *courage*. Explain your choice.

____

____

3. List the *aspects* of the task of making a sandwich.

____

____

4. What steps would you follow to *imitate* a robot?

____

____

5. What do you consider to be one of your greatest *accomplishments*? Explain your choice.

____

____

Name ______________________________ Date ______________

Unit 5: Themes in American Stories
Big Question Vocabulary—3

The Big Question: Are yesterday's heroes important today?

Thematic Vocabulary

cultural: *adj.* belonging or relating to a particular society and its way of life; other form: *culture*

influence: *v.* to have an effect on the thinking or behavior of another person; other forms: *influential, influencing*

overcome: *v.* to successfully control or do away with a harmful feeling or problem; other form: *overcame*

suffering: *v.* having serious mental or physical pain; other forms: *suffer, suffered*

symbolize: *v.* to represent something large or intangible; other forms: *symbol, symbolized*

A. DIRECTIONS: *Write the Thematic Vocabulary word that best completes each sentence.*

1. The people of many different societies use a dove to ______________ peace.
2. If you want to be a successful actor, you will have to ______________ your stage fright.
3. My kindergarten teacher worked hard to ______________ us to have a lifelong love of reading.
4. In Great Britain, the queen's birthday is a widely celebrated ______________ holiday.
5. Many students in our school are ______________ from colds this winter.

B. DIRECTIONS: *Answer each question.*

1. Which animal would you choose to *symbolize* strength and courage? Explain.

   ____

2. If a friend were *suffering* from a lack of confidence, what would you do to help him or her *overcome* this problem? ______________________

   ____

3. What is your favorite holiday, and what *cultural* tradition makes it so special?

   ____

4. What family member, famous person, or historical figure has *influenced* your thinking or values? Explain. ______________________

   ____

Name ______________________________ Date ______________

Unit 5: Themes in American Stories
Applying the Big Question

Are yesterday's heroes important today?

DIRECTIONS: *Complete the chart below to apply what you have learned about yesterday's heroes and their importance today. One row has been completed for you.*

Example	Hero's action	Cause of hero's action	Effect of hero's action	What I Learned
From Literature	Daddy in "Out of the Dust" continues to work and hope while other families leave.	Dust storms ravage the land, but he is a farmer and chooses to be true to his work.	Narrator's family stays behind while others flee to faraway places.	The odds against success may be high, but perseverance may lead to triumph.
From Literature				
From Science				
From Social Studies				
From Real Life				

Name ______________________________ Date ______________

"Coyote Steals the Sun and Moon" retold by Richard Erdoes and Alfonso Ortiz

Writing About the Big Question

THE BIG ?

Are yesterday's heroes important today?

Big Question Vocabulary

accomplishments	admirably	aspects	bravery	courage
cultural	emphasize	endure	exaggerate	imitate
influence	outdated	overcome	suffering	symbolize

A. *Use a word or words from the list above to answer each question.*

1. Myths from different countries differ because they emphasize what kinds of values?
____
2. If a mythical hero faces a challenge, what does the hero always do?
____
3. To create a hero of myth, what would a storyteller do to the hero's personality traits? ______________________________

B. *Write two or three sentences in response to each item below.*

1. List your ideas about why myths explain **aspects** of nature and **emphasize courage.**
____
____
____
2. Explain why you believe myths are **outdated** or whether mythical heroes can still **influence** people.
____
____
____

C. *Complete the sentence below. Then, write a short paragraph in which you connect this answer to the Big Question.*

Myths have endured throughout the ages because they ______________________________
____
____

Name ______________________________ Date ______________

"Coyote Steals the Sun and Moon" retold by Richard Erdoes and Alfonso Ortiz

Reading: Create a Summary

A **summary** is a short statement that presents the main points in a piece of writing. Summarizing helps you focus on the most important information and remember it better. You also may need to summarize a work as part of your discussion of it.

Follow this strategy when you summarize a work that tells a story:

- Reread the work to identify the main events.
- Restate these events in complete sentences.
- Put the sentences in chronological order.
- Cross out any minor details that do not seem important enough to include.
- Be sure that your sentences mention all the major points, including the main characters and settings.
- Revise your sentences so that they use as few words as possible.

A. DIRECTIONS: *Answer the questions about a summary of "Coyote Steals the Sun and Moon."*

1. Which two characters would be most important to mention in your summary?

______________________ ______________________

2. What are three settings that should be mentioned in your summary?

______________ ______________ ______________

3. Restate two things a character says that should be included in your summary.

____

____

4. List two things the characters do that should be included in your summary.

____

____

B. DIRECTIONS: *Based on the guidelines and your answers to items 1–4 above, write a summary of "Coyote Steals the Sun and Moon." Use the space below or a separate sheet of paper.*

____

____

____

____

____

____

Name ______________________________ Date ______________

"Coyote Steals the Sun and Moon" retold by Richard Erdoes and Alfonso Ortiz

Literary Analysis: Myth

In ancient times, people wondered about the world, just as people do today. Sometimes they told stories to try to explain it. These stories are called myths. A **myth** is an ancient tale that presents the beliefs or customs of a culture. Most myths try to explain an aspect of nature, history, or human behavior. They usually feature supernatural creatures and often contain animals or forces of nature that display human qualities.

You can usually understand a myth better if you know something about the culture that produced it. For example, when you read the Zuni myth "Coyote Steals the Sun and Moon," it helps to know that the Zuni are a Native American people from the American Southwest. The myth itself also reveals information about the culture or landscape in which it is set.

DIRECTIONS: *Use this chart to show what "Coyote Steals the Sun and Moon" tells you about Native American people like the Zuni and their life in the Southwest. For each detail in the left column, list at least one insight it gives you into the culture or setting. The insight from the first detail has been given as an example.*

Detail	Insight
1. Coyote and Eagle hunt rabbits.	• Coyotes and eagles are found in the Southwest. • Southwestern tribes sometimes hunted.
2. Coyote and Eagle come to a village called a pueblo.	
3. The people in the pueblo watch Kachinas do a sacred dance.	
4. Coyote says to Eagle, "You're my chief."	
5. Eagle gives Coyote the box because "if someone asks four times, you'd better give him what he wants."	
6. Peaches, squashes, and melons shrivel up with the cold.	

Name ______________________ Date ______________

"Coyote Steals the Sun and Moon" retold by Richard Erdoes and Alfonso Ortiz

Vocabulary Builder

Word List

curiosity lagged pestering pursuit sacred shriveled

A. Directions: *Answer the questions with complete sentences, using each World List word only once and underlining it.*

1. What small, wrinkled fruit is made by drying grapes in the sun?
____
2. What does a police car do when chasing a criminal?
____
3. How do most people react to being annoyed constantly?
____
4. What is something about which people have lots of questions?
____
5. How might someone react after trailing behind everyone else in a race?
____
6. What is one book that many people consider holy?
____

B. Word Study: *The word root* -sacre- *means "sacred" or "holy." Use what you know about* -sacre- *to answer the questions.*

1. Do all religions have the same *sacred* book?
____
2. In what kind of building will you find a room called a *sacristy*, which holds sacred items?
____
3. What do *sacraments* such as baptism and communion have in common?
____

Name ______________________________ Date ______________

"Coyote Steals the Sun and Moon" retold by Richard Erdoes and Alfonso Ortiz

Conventions: Basic Sentence Structures

A **clause** is a group of words with at least one subject and one verb. An **independent clause** can stand on its own as a sentence; a **subordinate clause** cannot.

Sentences are sometimes classified by their clauses. A **simple sentence** includes one independent clause.

The school bell rang. The boys and girls shouted and cheered.

A **compound sentence** has two or more independent clauses joined by a comma (or commas) and a coordinating conjunction (*and, or, but, so, nor, for,* or *yet*) or by a semicolon. In these examples, each independent clause is underlined.

The school bell rang, *but* class continued. The school bell rang; class continued.

A **complex sentence** has one independent clause (indicated here by one underline) and one or more subordinate clauses (indicated by a double underline).

When the school bell rang, the children raced to the bus that stood by the curb.

A **compound-complex** sentence has at least two independent clauses and at least one subordinate clause.

When the clock chimed three, the school bell rang, and the children raced to the bus.

A. Practice: *Underline each independent clause once and each subordinate clause twice. Label the sentence* simple, compound, complex, or compound-complex.

__________ 1. The Northwest is damp and rainy, but the Southwest is dry.

__________ 2. When it rains, many desert flowers bloom.

__________ 3. Desert plants store water, for they need it until more rain falls.

__________ 4. The spines on cactuses stop water loss through evaporation.

__________ 5. An inland sea once covered the area; today, little water remains.

B. Writing Application: *Rewrite the sentences as instructed.*

1. The beach traffic is usually heavy in summer. This weekend was an exception. (Combine into a compound sentence.) ______________________________

____

2. I stood on the beach. The waves rushed to shore. The seagulls flew overhead. (Combine into a compound-complex sentence.) ______________________________

____

Name ______________________________ Date ______________

"Coyote Steals the Sun and Moon" retold by Richard Erdoes and Alfonso Ortiz

Support for Writing to Sources: Myth

Use the chart below to help you gather details for the myth you will create. For statements by the characters, use dialect, idioms, and humor. They will make the myth seem authentic.

Subject (Natural Feature or Event to Be Explained)	
Main Characters	
Setting (Time and Place)	
Main Events of the Myth	
Statements by Characters (include Dialect, Idioms, and Humor)	

Name ______________________ Date ____________

"Coyote Steals the Sun and Moon" retold by Richard Erdoes and Alfonso Ortiz

Support for Speaking and Listening: Oral Presentation

Use this chart to record details about cultural traditions of the Zuni and the influence of other cultures on the Zuni. You can investigate such Zuni traditions as the Snake Dance or the use of the ceremonial space known as the kiva.

Traditional Zuni beliefs	
Traditional influences on the Zuni today	

Name ______________________ Date ______________

"Chicoria" adapted by José Griego y Maestas, retold by Rudolfo A. Anaya
***from* The People, Yes** by Carl Sandburg

Writing About the Big Question

Are yesterday's heroes important today?

Big Question Vocabulary

accomplishments	admirably	aspects	bravery	courage
cultural	emphasize	endure	exaggerate	imitate
influence	outdated	overcome	suffering	symbolize

A. *Write the word from the list above that best completes each sentence.*

1. Tall tales always ______________ the hero's actions.
2. In tall tales, the ______________ of the hero are generally outrageous.
3. Tall tales reveal the ______________ background of the people they come from.
4. Heroes in tall tales ______________ unbelievable difficulties.

B. *Write two or three sentence answers to each of the following questions.*

1. What aspects of a hero's character might the teller of a tall tale exaggerate? Why?

____

____

____

2. What would a writer have to do to **imitate** the style of a tall tale?

____

____

____

C. *Complete the sentence below. Then, write a short paragraph in which you connect this answer to the Big Question.*

In today's stories, qualities such as ______________ are still admired in a heroic character. ______________

____

____

Name ______________________________ Date ______________

"Chicoria" adapted by José Griego y Maestas, retold by Rudolfo A. Anaya
***from* The People, Yes** by Carl Sandburg

Reading: Use a Graphic to Summarize Literature

A **summary** is a short statement that presents the main points of a piece of writing. Since a summary leaves out the less important details, it provides a quick way to preview or review a much longer work and focus on what is most important in it. You also will use a summary of a work as part of your discussion of the work.

In the passage from "The People, Yes," Carl Sandburg presents summaries of more than twenty American folk tales, which he calls "yarns." Each summary can complete his opening statement, "They have yarns. . . ." For example, lines 1–7 can read as "They have yarns of a skyscraper. . . . They have yarns of one corn crop. . . . They have yarns of pancakes so thin. . . ."

DIRECTIONS: *Write a summary of "Chicoria" that could have appeared as an item in "The People, Yes." Before you write the summary, determine which events or ideas from "Chicoria" are important enough to include. Use a graphic aid such as a cluster diagram or a timeline to organize the important events or ideas.*

Graphic Aid

Summary

They have yarns ______________________________

____

____

____

____

____

Name ______________________________ Date ______________

"Chicoria" adapted by José Griego y Maestas, retold by Rudolfo A. Anaya
***from* The People, Yes** by Carl Sandburg

Literary Analysis: Oral Tradition

Although "The People, Yes" is a piece of written literature, it pulls together many stories from the American **oral tradition,** which is the body of stories, poems, and songs passed down by word of mouth from one generation to the next. The yarns and legends of oral tradition often contain exaggeration, references to magic, and other invented details that do not reflect reality. At the same time, they often have some basis in actual fact. Consider, for example, Sandburg's summary of a yarn about a corn crop:

> They have yarns . . .
> Of one corn crop in Missouri when the roots
> Went so deep and drew off so much water
> The Mississippi riverbed that year was dry. . . .

Although no corn crop could cause the Mississippi riverbed to go dry, it is a fact that corn was grown in Missouri along the Mississippi River, and the yarn probably had its origins in a time when a Mississippi drought followed a good corn crop.

DIRECTIONS: *Identify another yarn that Sandburg summarizes in "The People, Yes." Then, from the summary, list one exaggerated detail and one factual detail.*

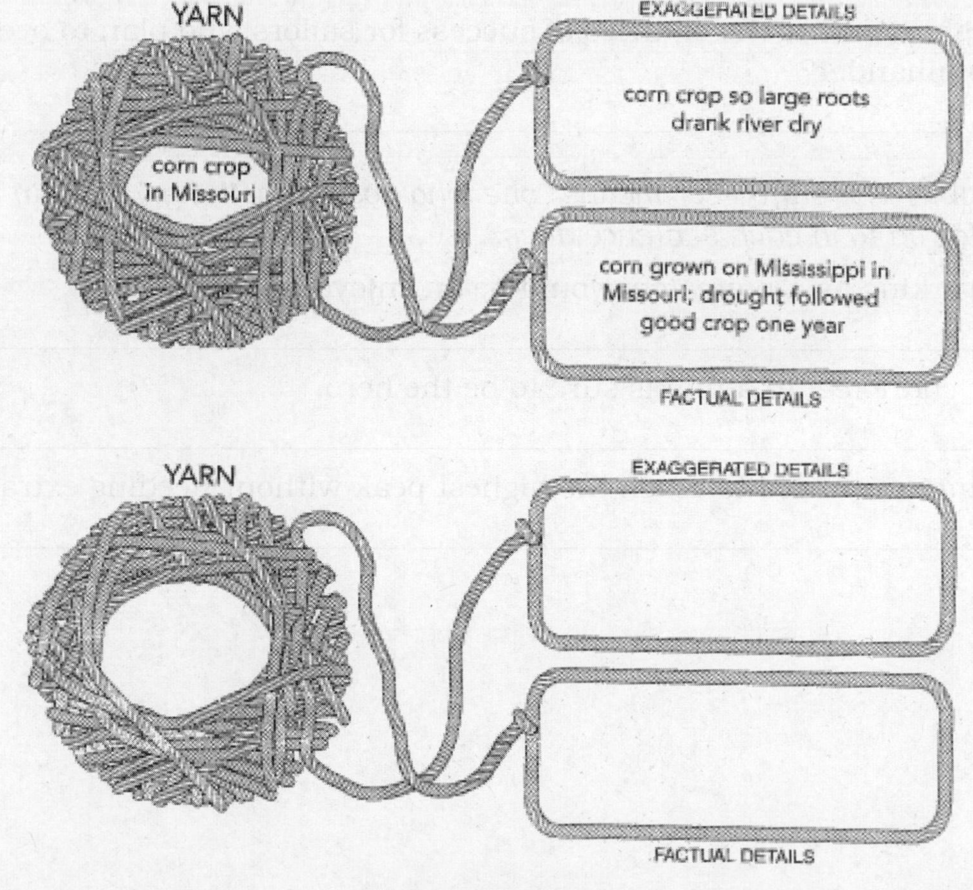

Name ______________________________ Date ______________

"Chicoria" adapted by José Griego y Maestas, retold by Rudolfo A. Anaya
***from* The People, Yes** by Carl Sandburg

Vocabulary Builder

Word List

cordially   cyclone   haughty   mutineers   self-confident   straddling

A. Directions: *Answer the questions with complete sentences, using each Word List word only once.*

1. Could a rotating windstorm destroy a farmer's crops?

___

2. Does a good receptionist usually greet visitors in a friendly way?

___

3. When might you be standing over your bicycle with your legs wide apart?

___

4. Can people who have too strong a belief in their own abilities and judgment ever have problems as a result?

___

5. In some fairy tales, is the queen proud and superior?

___

6. What might increase the chances of success for sailors who plan to overthrow their ship's commander?

___

B. Word Study: *The suffix* -eer *means "one who does something." Explain what the person referred to in each sentence does.*

1. I think working as a *puppeteer* would be an enjoyable job.

___

2. The best *charioteer* in a film is sure to be the hero.

___

3. The *mountaineer* tried to reach the highest peak without needing extra oxygen.

___

Name ______________________________ Date ______________

"Chicoria" adapted by José Griego y Maestas, retold by Rudolfo A. Anaya
***from* The People, Yes** by Carl Sandburg

Conventions: Commas and Semicolons

Use a **comma** in the following situations:

- before a conjunction that separates two independent clauses:
  Cats are my favorite pet, but my sister prefers dogs.
- between items in a series:
  We own a cat, a dog, and a hamster.
- after introductory words, phrases, or clauses:
  Yes, our cat is very shy and quiet.
  Walking on her soft paws, she rarely makes a sound.
- to set off nonrestrictive, or nonessential, phrases or clauses:
  Bobo, our dog, is friendly.
  Bobo, welcoming us home, always expects a pat.

Use a **semicolon** in the following situations:

- to join independent clauses not joined by the conjunctions *and, but, or, nor, for, so,* or *yet:*
  Some police dogs sniff out bombs; others help rescue trapped victims.
- to separate independent clauses joined by adverbs such as *however* and *therefore* or by phrases such as *on the other hand*:
  Cats can be unfriendly; on the other hand, some dogs are too friendly.

A. Practice: *Insert any missing commas and semicolons in these sentences.*

1. When I read I prefer humorous tales Heidi prefers detective stories.
2. Annie Oakley a famous sharpshooter appeared in one tale that I read.
3. Yes Gracia was a fine poet however Chicoria was even better.

B. Writing Application: *Expand each sentence according to the instructions in parentheses. Use commas where necessary.*

1. People enjoy all kinds of music. (Add an independent clause.) ______________

____

2. I like the singers Nanci Griffith and Natalie Merchant. (Add another singer.) ______

____

3. I met a famous singer. (Add an introductory clause and an appositive.) __________

____

Name ______________________ Date ______________

"Chicoria" adapted by José Griego y Maestas, retold by Rudolfo A. Anaya
***from* The People, Yes** by Carl Sandburg

Support for Writing to Sources: Critical Analysis

Use this chart to gather examples you plan to discuss in your **critical analysis**.

Type	Example	Work and Location	Effect on Tone, Mood, or Meaning
Hyperbole or Other Comic Technique	skyscraper so tall top two stories have hinges to let moon go by (hyperbole)	The People, Yes, lines 1–2	adds to humorous mood and tone and stresses idea of creativity in folk traditions
Idiom			
Analogy			
Metaphor or Simile			

Name ______________________________ Date ____________________

"Chicoria" adapted by José Griego y Maestas, retold by Rudolfo A. Anaya
***from* The People, Yes** by Carl Sandburg

Support for Speaking and Listening: Storytelling Workshop

Complete this tip sheet with specific advice for storytellers.

Tip Sheet for Storytellers			
How to Find a Story to Tell	**What Kind of Eye Contact to Make**	**How to Use Voice and Body**	**How to Add Humor to Storytelling**

Name ____________________ Date ____________

from **Out of the Dust** by Karen Hesse

Writing About the Big Question

Are yesterday's heroes important today?

Big Question Vocabulary

accomplishments	admirably	aspects	bravery	courage
cultural	emphasize	endure	exaggerate	imitate
influence	outdated	overcome	suffering	symbolize

A. *Use a word or words from the list above to answer each question.*

1. What qualities did Dust Bowl farmers of the 1930s often display?
   ______________ ______________

2. What did some farm families do when a dust storm hit? ______________

3. What caused some Dust Bowl farm families to move west? ______________

B. *Write two sentences in response to each item below. Use at least two Big Question vocabulary words in your sentences.*

1. Who reacted more heroically—the Dust Bowl farm families of the 1930s that stayed on their farms or the ones that left? Explain.

   ____

   ____

   ____

2. What importance do stories of heroic farm families of the Dust Bowl era hold for us today?

   ____

   ____

   ____

C. *Complete the sentence below. Then, write a short paragraph in which you connect this answer to the Big Question.*

The ability to endure tough challenges shows that ______________.

____

____

Name ______________________________ Date ______________

from **Out of the Dust** by Karen Hesse

Reading: Ask Questions to Set a Purpose for Reading

Setting a purpose for reading helps you focus your attention as you read a literary work. One way to set a purpose is to **ask questions** about the topic of the work, questions that you can answer as you read. Use a K-W-L chart to ask questions, and then answer them. See the example below, using material from *Out of the Dust.*

"K" (What I already know about the topic): I know that the Dust Bowl during the Great Depression made farming life on the Great Plains almost impossible.	**"W" (What I want to know):** How did people keep going when their crops were so often destroyed in the Dust Bowl?	**"L" (What I learned):** I will answer this question after I have read the selection.

DIRECTIONS: *Read each passage from* Out of the Dust, *and then answer each question.*

Debts
Daddy is thinking
of taking a loan from Mr. Roosevelt and his men,
to get some new wheat planted
where the winter crop has spindled out and died.
Mr. Roosevelt promises
Daddy won't have to pay a dime
till the crop comes in.

1. What is one solution the Roosevelt administration set up to help farmers?

____

Migrants
We'll be back when the rain comes,
they say,
pulling away with all they own,
straining the springs of their motor cars.
Don't forget us.

And so they go,
fleeing the blowing dust . . .

2. What did some Dust Bowl farmers do instead of trying to grow another wheat crop?

____

Name ______________________________ Date ______________

***from* Out of the Dust** by Karen Hesse

Literary Analysis: Cultural Context

The **cultural context** of a literary work is the social and historical environment in which the characters live. Major historical events can shape people's lives in important ways. Consider this passage from *Out of the Dust:* "While Ma and Daddy slept, / the dust came, / tearing up fields where the winter wheat, / set for harvest in June, / stood helpless. / I watched the plants, / surviving after so much drought and so much wind, / I watched them fry . . ."

This passage describes the onset of a dust storm, narrated by a character who lived in the Dust Bowl in the 1930s. The Dust Bowl era, in which failed crops led to poverty and hunger, is the historical context of the passage.

DIRECTIONS: *Read this example from* Out of the Dust, *and answer the questions.*

Daddy says, / "I can turn the fields over, / start again. / It's sure to rain soon. / Wheat's sure to grow."

Ma says, "Bay, / it hasn't rained enough to grow wheat in / three years."

I ask Ma / How, / After all this time, / Daddy still believes in rain.

"Well, it rains enough," Ma says, / "now and again, / to keep a person hoping. / But even if it didn't / your daddy would have to believe. / It's coming on spring, / And he's a farmer."

1. How do the father and mother respond to the event that rules their lives?

____

____

____

____

2. According to the mother, why does the father continue to hope for rain?

____

____

____

____

Name ______________________________ Date ______________

from **Out of the Dust** by Karen Hesse

Vocabulary Builder

Word List

drought feuding grateful rickety sparse spindly

A. DIRECTIONS: *For each item below, think about the meaning of the italicized Word List word, and then answer the question.*

1. Would you expect a pair of *feuding* brothers to live together? Why or why not?

____

____

2. Does a hippopotamus or a rhinoceros have *spindly* legs? Explain.

____

____

3. Is a *drought* a good period in which to plant vegetables and flowers? Why or why not?

____

____

4. Would you expect the hair on a newborn baby to be *sparse*? Explain.

____

____

5. Is a *rickety* stepladder one that needs repair before you use it? Explain.

____

____

6. Is a *grateful* person more likely to be happy or unhappy? Explain.

____

____

B. WORD STUDY: *The Latin root* -grat- *means "thankful" or "pleased." Use the meaning of* -grat- *to help you answer the following questions.*

1. Would you express *gratitude* by thanking someone or by complaining?

____

2. What are some occasions for which *congratulations* are expected?

____

3. Who might accept a *gratuity*, and why?

____

Name ______________________________ Date ______________

from **Out of the Dust** by Karen Hesse

Conventions: Ellipses and Dashes

Use **ellipses (. . .)** in the following situations:

- to show that you have omitted text from a quotation:
  According to Karen Hesse, the dust was "tearing up . . . the winter wheat."
- to indicate a pause or an interruption in speech:
  "The dust! It's . . . it's terrible," the farmer stammered.

Use a **dash (—)** in the following situations:

- to show a strong, sudden break in thought or speech:
  "We're leaving the farm for—don't be surprised—California."
- in place of *in other words, namely,* or *that is* before an explanation:
  Some farmers had just one way to survive—leave their farms and head west.
- to set off nonrestrictive elements (modifiers or other elements that are not essential to the meaning of the sentence):
  In the 1930s—the time of the Great Depression—farmers were especially hard hit.

A. Practice: *On the lines provided, correctly rewrite each sentence by supplying the dash or dashes that are missing. If a sentence is correct as is, write* correct.

1. Woody Guthrie became the model for a typical folk singer someone who travels the country and sings about people's problems.

   ____

2. Many of the songs he wrote are about hard times in his native Oklahoma.

   ____

3. The Dust Bowl the great drought in Oklahoma affected him deeply.

   ____

4. His most famous song just about everyone knows it is "This Land Is Your Land."

   ____

B. Writing Application: *Use ellipses to rewrite these quotations with portions omitted. You may omit details, but do not change the basic meaning of the original quotation.*

1. Daddy is thinking of taking a loan from Mr. Roosevelt and his men to get some new wheat planted.

   ____

2. "Bay, it hasn't rained enough to grow wheat in three years."

   ____

3. Ma sank down into a chair at the kitchen table and covered her face.

   ____

Name ______________________________ Date ______________

from **Out of the Dust** by Karen Hesse

Support for Writing to Sources: Research Proposal

To prepare a **research proposal** for a report on how farmers in the 1930s were affected by the Dust Bowl, use the Internet and library resources, and enter data into the chart below.

Research Proposal	
Three questions about the topic	
Three sources that contain information to answer questions	
Points to make in proposal	

On a separate page, write a draft of your research proposal. Include a description of the sources you found, and explain why they will be useful.

Name ______________________ Date ______________

from **Out of the Dust** by Karen Hesse

Support for Research and Technology: Letter

As you gather information for the speaker's **letter** to a friend, enter important experiences, images, emotions, and other details in the chart below.

Information for Letter from the Speaker's Point of View	
Experiences	
Images (sight, sound, touch, etc.)	
Emotional response	

Name ______________________________ Date ______________

"**An Episode of War**" by Stephen Crane

Writing About the Big Question

Are yesterday's heroes important today?

Big Question Vocabulary

accomplishments	admirably	aspects	bravery	courage
cultural	emphasize	endure	exaggerate	imitate
influence	outdated	overcome	suffering	symbolize

A. *Use a word or words from the list above to complete each sentence.*

1. Many people believe that soldiers' ______________ will never be ______________.
2. Their commanders ______________ the way soldiers respond to war.
3. Soldiers hope to ______________ the enemy.
4. There are many ______________ of war that soldiers do not like to discuss.

B. *Follow the directions in responding to each item.*

1. Do you think a heroic Civil War soldier would make a good soldier today? In two or three sentences, explain why or why not. Use at least one Big Question vocabulary word in your sentences.

____

____.

2. Write two or three sentences in which you describe an important way that warfare is different today from long ago. Use at least one Big Question vocabulary word in your sentences.

____

____.

C. *Complete the sentence below. Then, write a short paragraph in which you connect this answer to the Big Question.*

The experience of suffering is ______________________________.

____

____

Name ______________________________ Date ______________

"An Episode of War" by Stephen Crane

Reading: Set a Purpose for Reading and Adjust Your Reading Rate

When you **set a purpose for reading,** you determine your focus before reading a written work. Once you have set a purpose, **adjust your reading rate** according to that goal. You might read fiction for both entertainment and information. Entertainment does not always mean amusement or enjoyment. It can also mean that you learn about characters and why they act as they do. When you read fiction that is written more formally than today's writing, read slowly and carefully. Reread long sentences, or material with unfamiliar facts and content. When you read modern fiction, you can usually read faster. Nonfiction, both older and modern, needs careful reading and rereading so that you can understand important information.

DIRECTIONS: *Answer the questions about setting purpose and adjusting reading rate.*

1. What purpose might you set for reading Stephen Crane's famous novel of the Civil War, *The Red Badge of Courage,* published in 1895?

____

____

2. What reading rate might you set for reading this novel?

____

____

3. What purpose might you set for reading nonfiction accounts of Civil War battles?

____

____

4. What reading rate might you set for reading about Civil War battles?

____

____

5. What purpose might you set for reading a short story about the Vietnam War?

____

____

6. What reading rate might you use for reading this story?

____

____

7. What purpose might you set for reading a modern novel about war?

____

____

8. What reading rate might you use for reading a modern novel about war?

____

____

Name ______________________________ Date ______________________

"**An Episode of War**" by Stephen Crane

Literary Analysis: Author's Influences

An **author's influences** are the cultural and historical factors that affect his or her writing. These factors may include the time and place of an author's birth and life, the author's cultural background, or world events that happened during the author's lifetime. Read the following facts about the Civil War and Stephen Crane.

A. Civil War field hospitals were unclean and crowded with wounded soldiers.

B. Medical practices included cutting off injured limbs to keep soldiers from dying from infection.

C. Crane was fascinated by war. He interviewed Civil War veterans, and studied battlefield maps and accounts of the fighting.

DIRECTIONS: *Read each passage from "An Episode of War." Decide which of the historical and cultural factors above is reflected in the passage. Write the correct letter or letters in the blank.*

1. __________ As the wounded officer passed from the line of battle, he was enabled to see many things which as a participant in the fight were unknown to him.
2. __________ An interminable [unending] crowd of bandaged men were coming and going. Great numbers sat under the trees nursing heads or arms or legs.
3. __________ "Nonsense, man! Nonsense! Nonsense!" cried the doctor. "Come along, now. I won't amputate it. Come along. Don't be a baby."

   "Let go of me," said the lieutenant, holding back wrathfully, his glance fixed upon the door of the old schoolhouse, as sinister to him as the portals of death.
4. __________ A battery, a tumultuous and shining mass, was swirling toward the right. The wild thud of hoofs, the cries of the riders shouting blame and praise, menace and encouragement, and last, the roar of the wheels, the slant of the glistening guns, brought the lieutenant to an intent pause.

Name ______________________________ Date ______________

"An Episode of War" by Stephen Crane

Vocabulary Builder

Word List

audible compelled contempt disdainfully tumultuous winced

A. Directions: *For each item below, think about the meaning of the italicized Word List word, and then answer the question.*

1. How would you feel if a friend *compelled* you to go to a party you didn't want to attend?

   ____

2. How would someone in the grip of *tumultuous* emotions handle a surprise event? Explain.

   ____

3. What kind of behavior would cause you to have *contempt* for a person?

   ____

4. If someone *winced*, what sort of thing happened to him or her?

   ____

5. How would you feel if you were treated *disdainfully*?

   ____

6. What might you do if the music on the radio were barely *audible*?

   ____

B. Word Study: *The Latin root* -aud- *means "to hear." Use the meaning of the root* -aud- *to help you complete the following sentences.*

1. Use the *audio* control to ______________________________

   ____

2. We should hold the concert in an *auditorium* because ______________________________

   ____

3. I want to *audition* for ______________________________

Name ______________________________ Date ____________________

"An Episode of War" by Stephen Crane

Conventions: Capitalization

Use a capital letter at the beginning of a sentence and for the pronoun *I*. Also use a capital for the first letter of every main word in a proper noun or proper adjective and for titles before names.

Stephen **C**rane is a well-known **A**merican short-story writer.

My **E**nglish teacher, **M**rs. **A**vi, praised his writing about the **C**ivil **W**ar.

A. DIRECTIONS: *Rewrite each sentence below. Substitute capital letters or lowercase letters where they belong.*

1. my neighbor, mrs. gold, deeply admired dr. martin luther king, jr.

   ____

2. she loved to hear him preach at ebenezer baptist church.

   ____

3. at the time She was studying american history at the university of georgia.

   ____

4. when she talks about those days, i love to listen.

   ____

B. DIRECTIONS: *Write a short paragraph about a person, a place, or an event that has affected you. Be sure to use correct capitalization.*

____

____

____

____

____

____

____

____

____

____

Name ______________________________ Date ______________

"An Episode of War" by Stephen Crane

Support for Writing to Sources: Persuasive Speech

To prepare to write a **persuasive speech** in favor of building a memorial in honor of soldiers of the Civil War, enter important information into the chart below.

The Common Soldier: Courage and Determination	
Details from "An Episode of War" about hardships of war on soldiers	
Why Civil War soldiers deserve to be remembered and honored	
Vivid words and phrases	

On a separate page, write a draft of your speech.

Name ______________________________ Date ______________________

"An Episode of War" by Stephen Crane

Support for Research and Technology: Research Article

Enter information for your **research article** in the chart below.

Research Question:

Historical Facts	**Crane's Details**	**Comments on Crane's Accuracy**

Name ______________________________ Date ______________

"Davy Crockett's Dream" by Davy Crockett
"Paul Bunyan of the North Woods" by Carl Sandburg
"Invocation" ***from*** **John Brown's Body** by Stephen Vincent Benét

Writing About the Big Question

THE BIG ?

Are yesterday's heroes important today?

Big Question Vocabulary

accomplishments	admirably	aspects	bravery	courage
cultural	emphasize	endure	exaggerate	imitate
influence	outdated	overcome	suffering	symbolize

A. *Use a word or words from the list above to complete each sentence.*

1. The pioneers behaved ______________________ as they traveled west.
2. But no pioneer could match the ______________________ of folk tale heroes.
3. However, a pioneer could ______________ ______________ of the traits of those heroes, such as courage and grit.

B. *Follow the directions in responding to the items below.*

1. Write a two-sentence comparison of the tales about Davy Crockett and Paul Bunyan. Use at least two Big Question vocabulary words in your comparison.

____

____

____

2. In two sentences, explain why you think Davy Crockett and Paul Bunyan were such appealing folk heroes to the pioneers. Use at least two Big Question vocabulary words.

____

____

____

C. *In different ways, these selections look back to the heroes of an earlier America. Complete the sentence below. Then, write a short paragraph in which you connect this sentence to the Big Question.*

To be a hero today, a person can win admiration through such actions as ______________ and ______________________.

____

____

____

Name ______________________________ Date ______________

"Davy Crockett's Dream" by Davy Crockett
"Paul Bunyan of the North Woods" by Carl Sandburg
"Invocation" *from* **John Brown's Body** by Stephen Vincent Benét

Literary Analysis: Comparing Heroic Characters

Heroic characters are men and women who show great courage and overcome difficult challenges. A heroic character can be fictional or real. Often, the hero in a tall tale or legend is a combination of both—a real historical figure whose actions have become so exaggerated over time that he or she becomes a legend.

Many American legends and stories focus on the pioneers of the western frontier. Because survival in such a harsh setting depended on skill and strength, many tall tales and legends exaggerate these admirable qualities.

DIRECTIONS: *Answer the questions about each heroic character in the following chart.*

Questions	Davy Crockett	Paul Bunyan
1. In what ways did the hero(es) show great courage?		
2. Did these characters overcome difficult challenges? How?		
3. What actions, if any, by the character(s) are exaggerated?		
4. Label the characters with one of these three phrases: real historical figure, fictional legend, or combination of both.		

Name ______________________________ Date ______________

"Davy Crockett's Dream" by Davy Crockett
"Paul Bunyan of the North Woods" by Carl Sandburg
"Invocation" ***from*** **John Brown's Body** by Stephen Vincent Benét

Vocabulary Builder

Word List

arrogant commotion kindled shanties subdued

A. Directions: *Write a sentence to answer each question. Your answer must show that you know the meaning of the italicized word.*

1. Would a camper want to have a fire *kindled* just before he or she packs up and leaves a campsite?

 ____

2. Would young business executives like to live in *shanties*?

 ____

3. During a movie, would you prefer for the people sitting in front of you to create a *commotion* or sit still?

 ____

4. Would someone feel *subdued* after winning a contest?

 ____

5. Why might an *arrogant* person be difficult to live with?

 ____

B. Directions: *For each related pair of words in CAPITAL LETTERS, circle the lettered pair that best expresses a similar relationship.*

1. SHANTIES : MANSIONS ::
 A. fire : cook
 B. glass : diamonds
 C. flower : spring
 D. construction : building

2. ARROGANT : PROUD ::
 A. child : adult
 B. pleasant : nasty
 C. voter : election
 D. ecstatic : happy

Name ______________________________ Date ______________

"Davy Crockett's Dream" by Davy Crockett
"Paul Bunyan of the North Woods" by Carl Sandburg
"Invocation" ***from*** **John Brown's Body** by Stephen Vincent Benét

Support for Writing to Sources: Compare-and-Contrast Essay

Before you write your essay that compares and contrasts the way in which "Davy Crockett's Dream" and "Paul Bunyan of the North Woods" present heroic characters, use the graphic organizer below to list ideas about each character.

	David Crockett	Paul Bunyan
How does each writer use exaggeration? What is the effect?		
How important is humor in each selection?		
What do these selections show about the American character and what we admire in our heroes?		

Now, use your notes to write an essay comparing the presentations of the two heroic characters.

Name ______________________________ Date ______________

Writing Process

Problem-and-Solution Essay

Prewriting: Finding a Topic

Think about the following sentence starters to help you brainstorm for problems to solve.

Our community should fix . . .
I really wish people would . . .
Our school would be better if . . .
I get so annoyed when . . .

Then use this cluster diagram to help you brainstorm for topics. Write your favorite sentence starter in the center circle. Write your endings for that sentence starter in the circles around it. Finally, draw a box around the ending you like best.

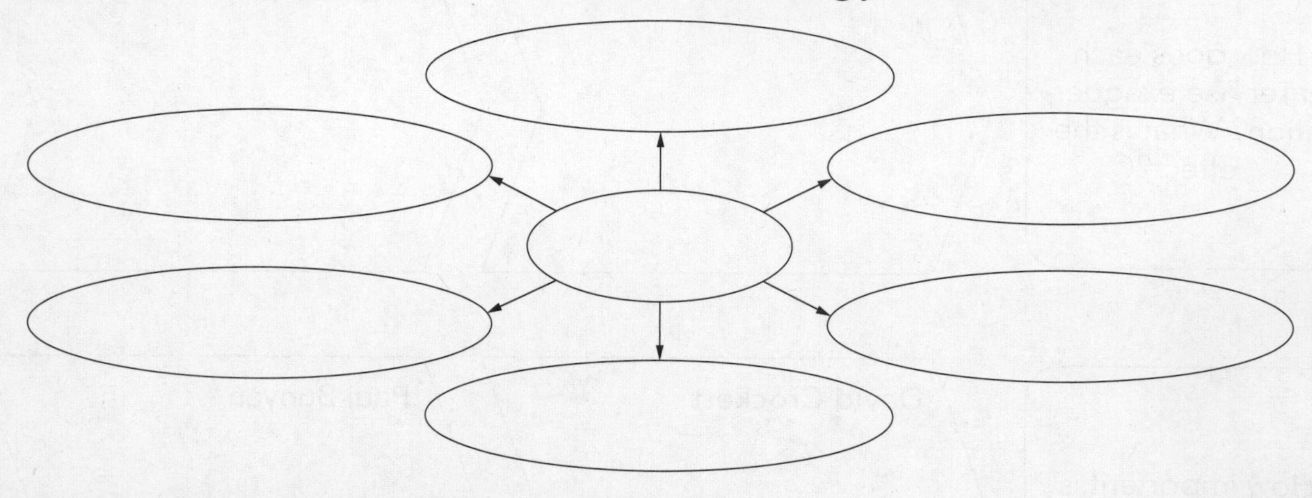

Drafting: Organizing and Supporting Your Ideas

To develop your problem-and-solution essay, fill in the boxes below.

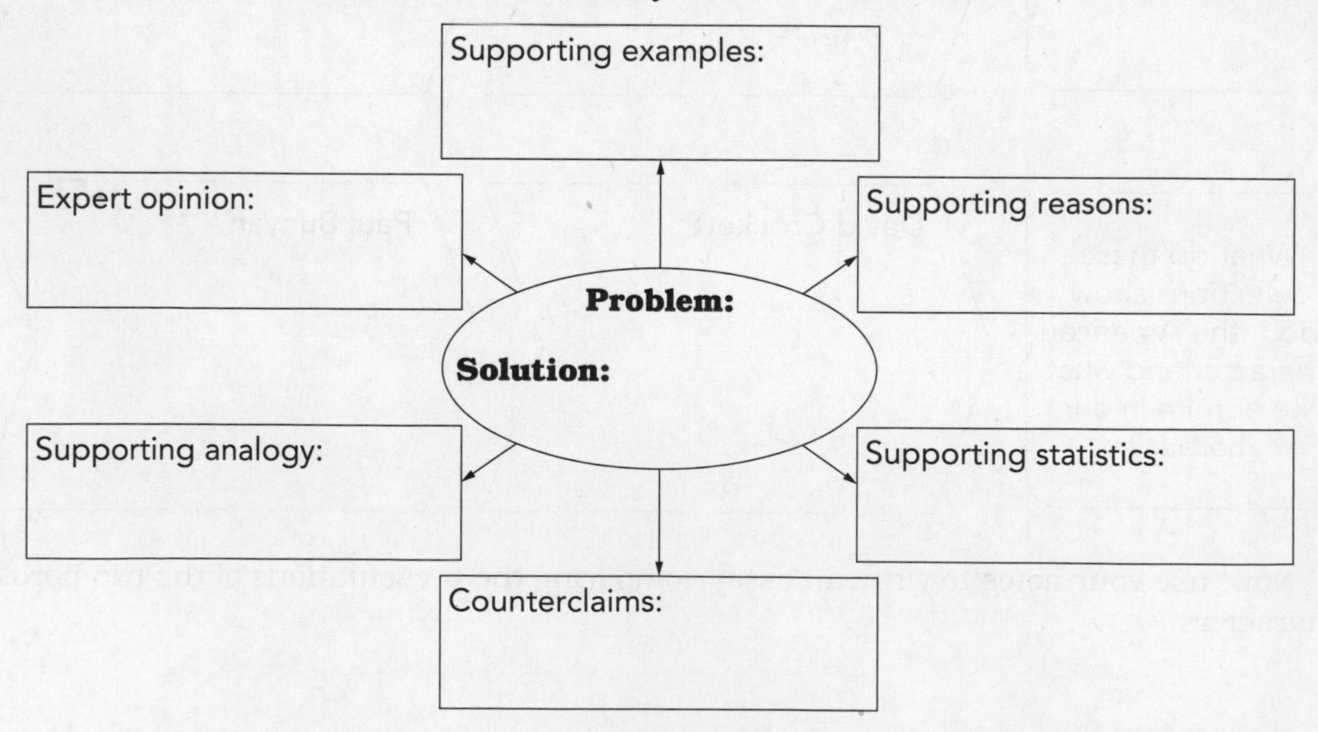

Name ______________________ Date ____________

Writer's Toolbox

Conventions: Revising to Correct Comparative and Superlative Forms

The **comparative form** is used to compare two items. The **superlative form** is used to compare three or more items. The most common way to form these degrees is by adding *-er* or *-est* to words with one or two syllables. *More, most, less,* and *least* are used with longer modifiers and most adverbs ending in *-ly.*

Positive	Comparative	Superlative
high	higher	highest
heavy	heavier	heaviest
exciting	more exciting	most exciting
nutritious	less nutritious	least nutritious

The patterns of irregular adjectives and adverbs must be memorized.

Positive	Comparative	Superlative
bad or badly	worse	worst
good or well	better	best
many or much	more	most
far (distance)	farther	farthest
far (extent)	further	furthest

A. Directions: *Underline the correct word for each set of choices in the sentences.*

1. Of my three sisters, Ginny is *(close, closer, closest)* to me in age.
2. Jason is a *(good, better, best)* friend than Paul.
3. Toby writes well, but Mickey writes *(well, better, best).*
4. My two-year-old brother speaks *(clearer, more clearly, most clearly)* than this child.

B. Directions: *On the lines provided, rewrite these sentences using the correct comparative or superlative form.*

1. Fries and a soda make one of the less nutritious lunches of all.

____

2. For a healthiest lunch than fries and a soda, try a salad.

____

3. Of all these desserts, carrot cake has the more calories.

____

4. To lose weight, you must exercise most seriously than you do now.

____

Name ________________________________ Date ________________

"The American Dream" by Martin Luther King, Jr.

Vocabulary Builder

Selection Vocabulary

devoid paradoxes perish

A. DIRECTIONS: *Write the letter of the word or phrase that is the best synonym for the italicized word. Then, use the italicized word in a complete sentence.*

____ 1. *paradoxes*

A. certainties C. questions

B. contradictions D. realities

____

____ 2. *devoid*

A. complete C. revised

B. full D. empty

____

____ 3. *perish*

A. renew C. revise

B. die D. create

____

Academic Vocabulary

observation distinguish evidence

B. DIRECTIONS: *Complete each sentence with a word, phrase, or clause that contains a context clue for the italicized word.*

1. An *observation* of the night sky ____
____.

2. To *distinguish* between two ideas, ____
____.

3. The jury was instructed to listen carefully to the *evidence* and to ____________
____.

Name ______________________ Date ______________

"The American Dream" by Martin Luther King, Jr.

Take Notes for Discussion

Before the Partner Discussion: Read the following passage from the selection.

The price America must pay for the continued exploitation of the Negro and other minority groups is the price of its own destruction. The hour is late; the clock of destiny is ticking out. It is trite, but urgently true, that if America is to remain a first-class nation she can no longer have second-class citizens.

During the Discussion: As you discuss each question, take notes on how your partner's ideas either differ from or build upon your own.

Discussion Questions	Other Ideas Expressed	Comparison to My Own Ideas
1. What link does King make between the ideas of exploitation and destruction?		
2. What argument is King making about the importance of freedom for all?		

Name ______________________ Date ______________

"The American Dream" by Martin Luther King, Jr.

Take Notes for Writing to Sources

Planning Your Informative Text: Before you begin drafting your **informative essay,** use the chart below to organize your ideas. Follow the directions in each section.

1. Statement of main idea:
2. Examples and supporting details:
3. Notes for your conclusion:

Name ______________________________ Date ______________

"The American Dream" by Martin Luther King, Jr.

Take Notes for Research

As you research **another civil rights leader of your choice,** use the forms below to take notes from your sources. As necessary, continue your notes on the back of this page, on note cards, or in a word-processing document.

Source Information Check one: ☐ Primary Source ☐ Secondary Source

Title: ______________________ Author: ______________

Publication Information: ______________________

Page(s): ______________________

Main Idea: ______________________

____

Quotation or Paraphrase: ______________________

____

Source Information Check one: ☐ Primary Source ☐ Secondary Source

Title: ______________________ Author: ______________

Publication Information: ______________________

Page(s): ______________________

Main Idea: ______________________

____

Quotation or Paraphrase: ______________________

____

Source Information Check one: ☐ Primary Source ☐ Secondary Source

Title: ______________________ Author: ______________

Publication Information: ______________________

Page(s): ______________________

Main Idea: ______________________

____

Quotation or Paraphrase: ______________________

____

Name ______________________________ Date ______________

"Runagate Runagate" by Robert Hayden

Vocabulary Builder

Selection Vocabulary

anguish beckoning shackles

A. DIRECTIONS: *Provide an explanation for your answer to each question.*

1. If someone is *beckoning* to you, will you probably walk away?

____

____.

2. When a man is wearing *shackles*, will he be able to go far?

____

____.

3. How might you tell if someone were in *anguish*?

____

____.

Academic Vocabulary

elements intensify objective

B. DIRECTIONS: *Write a sentence that demonstrates the meaning of each word. Follow this example:*

evidence: The man's fingerprints and other evidence put him at the scene of the crime.

1. *objective:* ____

____.

2. *intensify:* ____

____.

3. *elements:* ____

____.

Name ______________________ Date ______________

"Runagate Runagate" by Robert Hayden

Take Notes for Discussion

Before the Panel Discussion: Read the following passage from the selection.

> And fear starts a-murbling. Never make it,
> we'll never make it. *Hush that now,*
> and she's turned upon us, leveled pistol
> glinting in the moonlight:
> Dead folks can't jaybird-talk, she says;
> You keep on going now or die, she says.

During the Discussion: As you discuss each question, take notes on how other students' ideas either differ from or build upon your own.

Discussion Questions	Other Ideas Expressed	Comparison to My Own Ideas
1. What is happening in these lines? What do the italicized words indicate?		
2. Why does Tubman take an angry tone with the slaves?		
3. What does this passage reveal about the risks associated with seeking freedom?		

Name ______________________________ Date ______________

"Runagate Runagate" by Robert Hayden

Take Notes for Research

As you research **the Underground Railroad and its role in the antislavery movement,** use the chart below to take notes from your sources. As necessary, continue your notes on the back of this page, on note cards, or in a word-processing document.

The Underground Railroad	
Main Idea ______________________ ______________________ **Quotation or Paraphrase** ______________________ ______________________ ______________________ ______________________ ______________________ **Source Information** ______________________ ______________________ ______________________ ______________________	**Main Idea** ______________________ ______________________ **Quotation or Paraphrase** ______________________ ______________________ ______________________ ______________________ ______________________ **Source Information** ______________________ ______________________ ______________________ ______________________
Main Idea ______________________ ______________________ **Quotation or Paraphrase** ______________________ ______________________ ______________________ ______________________ ______________________ **Source Information** ______________________ ______________________ ______________________ ______________________	**Main Idea** ______________________ ______________________ **Quotation or Paraphrase** ______________________ ______________________ ______________________ ______________________ ______________________ **Source Information** ______________________ ______________________ ______________________ ______________________

Name ______________________ Date ____________

"Runagate Runagate" by Robert Hayden

Take Notes for Writing to Sources

Planning Your Narrative: Before you begin drafting your **narrative,** use the chart below to organize your ideas. Follow the directions in each section.

1. Details about your character:
2. The internal and external conflicts faced by your character:
3. Sequence of events, including the climax:
4. Resolution of the issues:

Name ______________________________ Date ______________

"Emancipation" *from* Lincoln: A Photobiography by Russell Freedman

Vocabulary Builder

Selection Vocabulary

alienate compensate humiliating

A. Directions: *From the following lists, select one synonym and one antonym for each of the numbered words in the table below. Write your choices in the appropriate boxes.*

Synonyms
repay
turn against
embarrassing

Antonyms
win over
satisfying
deprive

Word	Synonym	Antonym
1. alienate		
2. compensate		
3. humiliating		

Academic Vocabulary

citing contribute develop

B. Directions: *Read each sentence. If the italicized word is used correctly, write* Correct *on the line. If it is not used correctly, rewrite the sentence to correct it.*

1. They remained silent as they began to *contribute* ideas to the discussion.

   ____.

2. His *citing* of his sources didn't allow us to judge his research.

   ____.

3. You *develop* a plot by adding events and situations.

   ____.

Name ______________________________ Date ______________

"**Emancipation**" *from* **Lincoln: A Photobiography** by Russell Freedman

Take Notes for Discussion

Before the Class Discussion: Read the following passage from the selection.

> Besides, enslaved blacks were eager to throw off their shackles and fight for their own freedom. Thousands of slaves had already escaped from behind Southern lines. Thousands more were ready to enlist in the Union armies. "You need more men," Senator Charles Sumner told Lincoln, "not only at the North, but at the South, in the rear of the rebels. You need the slaves."

During the Discussion: As you discuss each question, take notes on how other students' ideas either differ from or build upon your own.

Discussion Questions	Other Ideas Expressed	Comparison to My Own Ideas
1. Even prior to the Emancipation Proclamation, blacks were ready to fight for the Union. What does this detail reveal about their situation?		
2. In what ways does Sumner's military strategy also serve to promote freedom?		

Name ______________________________ Date ______________

"Emancipation" *from* Lincoln: A Photobiography by Russell Freedman

Take Notes for Research

As you research **an abolitionist of your choice,** use the forms below to take notes from your sources. As necessary, continue your notes on the back of this page, on note cards, or in a word-processing document.

Source Information Check one: ☐ Primary Source ☐ Secondary Source

Title: ______________________ Author: ______________

Publication Information: ______________________

Page(s): ______________________

Main Idea: ______________________

____

Quotation or Paraphrase: ______________________

____

Source Information Check one: ☐ Primary Source ☐ Secondary Source

Title: ______________________ Author: ______________

Publication Information: ______________________

Page(s): ______________________

Main Idea: ______________________

____

Quotation or Paraphrase: ______________________

____

Source Information Check one: ☐ Primary Source ☐ Secondary Source

Title: ______________________ Author: ______________

Publication Information: ______________________

Page(s): ______________________

Main Idea: ______________________

____

Quotation or Paraphrase: ______________________

____

Name ______________________ Date ______________

"Emancipation" *from* Lincoln: A Photobiography by Russell Freedman

Take Notes for Writing to Sources

Planning Your Explanatory Text: Before you begin drafting your **analysis,** use the chart below to organize your ideas.

1. Summary of Russell Freedman's point of view:
2. Summary of William H. Seward's point of view:
3. Points of agreement and disagreement:
4. Notes for your conclusion:

Name ______________________________ Date ______________

"**Harriet Beecher Stowe**" by Paul Laurence Dunbar

Vocabulary Builder

Selection Vocabulary

complacent transfigured

A. DIRECTIONS: *Write a response to each question. Make sure to use the italicized word at least once in your response.*

1. What might cause a good student to become *complacent*? Explain.

____

____

2. In fiction, if an angry, unpleasant character becomes gentle and kind, has he or she been *transfigured*? Explain.

____

____

Academic Vocabulary

overall response result

B. DIRECTIONS: *Write the letter of the word or phrase that is the best synonym for the italicized word. Then, use the italicized word in a complete sentence.*

____ 1. *result*

A. explanation
B. argument
C. event
D. outcome

____

____ 2. *response*

A. answer
B. agreement
C. concern
D. analysis

____

____ 3. *overall*

A. specific
B. general
C. controversial
D. initial

____

Name ______________________ Date ______________

"Harriet Beecher Stowe" by Paul Laurence Dunbar

Take Notes for Writing to Sources

Planning Your Informative Text: Before you begin drafting your **essay,** use the chart below to organize your ideas. Follow the directions in each section.

1. Statement of your claim:

2. Reasons for your claim and support for each reason:

3. Notes for your conclusion:

Name ______________________________ Date ______________

"Brown vs. Board of Education" by Walter Dean Myers

Vocabulary Builder

Selection Vocabulary

deliberating oppressed predominantly

A. Directions: *Write a complete sentence to answer each question. In each sentence, use a vocabulary word from the above list in place of the underlined word(s) with similar meanings.*

1. In a courthouse, what group of people might you find thinking and considering something carefully and fully?

____

2. Are there mainly people under the age of twenty-one living in your neighborhood?

____

3. What group of people did plantation owners keep down by cruel and unjust power?

____

Academic Vocabulary

advocate elements revealed

B. Directions: *Decide whether each statement below is true or false. On the line before each item, write* TRUE *or* FALSE*. Then, explain your answers.*

________ 1. An *advocate* for a position is someone who agrees with that position.

____.

________ 2. An author's style includes *elements* such as word choice and sentence structure.

____.

________ 3. What is *revealed* in a text will be of no help to an analysis of the text.

____.

Name ______________________________ Date ______________

"Brown vs. Board of Education" by Walter Dean Myers

Take Notes for Discussion

Before the Group Discussion: Read the following passage from the selection.

> There was a time when the meaning of freedom was easily understood. For an African crouched in the darkness of a tossing ship, wrists chained, men with guns standing on the decks above him, freedom was a physical thing. . . .
>
> Slowly, surely, the meaning of freedom changed to an elusive thing that even the strongest people could not hold in their hands. There were no chains on black wrists, but there were shadows of chains. . . .

During the Discussion: As you discuss each question, take notes on how other students' ideas either differ from or build upon your own.

Discussion Questions	Other Ideas Expressed	Comparison to My Own Ideas
1. What two aspects of freedom are explored in this passage?		
2. Which type of freedom do you think is harder to attain? Explain.		

Name ______________________________ Date ______________

"Brown vs. Board of Education" by Walter Dean Myers

Take Notes for Research

As you research **a specific contribution to the civil rights movement made by Thurgood Marshall,** use the forms below to take notes from your sources. As necessary, continue your notes on the back of this page, on note cards, or in a word-processing document.

Source Information Check one: ☐ Primary Source ☐ Secondary Source

Title: ______________________________ Author: ______________

Publication Information: ______________________________

Page(s): ______________________________

Main Idea: ______________________________

____

Quotation or Paraphrase: ______________________________

____

Source Information Check one: ☐ Primary Source ☐ Secondary Source

Title: ______________________________ Author: ______________

Publication Information: ______________________________

Page(s): ______________________________

Main Idea: ______________________________

____

Quotation or Paraphrase: ______________________________

____

Source Information Check one: ☐ Primary Source ☐ Secondary Source

Title: ______________________________ Author: ______________

Publication Information: ______________________________

Page(s): ______________________________

Main Idea: ______________________________

____

Quotation or Paraphrase: ______________________________

____

Name ______________________________ Date ______________________

"**Brown vs. Board of Education**" by Walter Dean Myers

Take Notes for Writing to Sources

Planning Your Narrative: Before you begin drafting your **narrative,** use the chart below to organize your ideas. First, identify the character who will be the subject of your narrative. Then, follow the directions at the top of each section of the chart.

Character: ______________________________

1. Notes on the character's personality, background, and purpose in coming to America:
2. Plot events:
3. Notes for your conclusion:

Name ______________________________ Date ______________

"On Woman's Right to Suffrage" by Susan B. Anthony

Vocabulary Builder

Selection Vocabulary

derived mockery rebellion

A. Directions: *Write the letter of the word or phrase that is the best synonym for the italicized word. Then, use the italicized word in a complete sentence.*

_____ 1. *derived*

A. opposed
B. forgotten
C. obtained
D. increased

____

_____ 2. *mockery*

A. compliment
B. admiration
C. humor
D. ridicule

____

_____ 3. *rebellion*

A. retraining
B. revision
C. remarking
D. resistance

____

Academic Vocabulary

discriminate emphasizing granted

B. Directions: *Complete each sentence with a word, phrase, or clause that contains a context clue for the italicized word.*

1. Women's right to vote was fully *granted* after _______________
____.
2. To ensure that it does not *discriminate,* the company hires _______________
____.
3. The theme park brochure attracts visitors by *emphasizing* _______________
____.

Name ______________________ Date ______________

"On Woman's Right to Suffrage" by Susan B. Anthony

Take Notes for Discussion

Before the Panel Discussion: Read the following passage from the selection.

It was we, the people; not we, the white male citizens; nor yet we, the male citizens; but we, the whole people, who formed the Union. And we formed it, not to give the blessings of liberty, but to secure them; not to the half of ourselves and the half of our posterity, but to the whole people—women as well as men.

During the Discussion: As you discuss each question, take notes on how other students' ideas either differ from or build upon your own.

Discussion Questions	Other Ideas Expressed	Comparison to My Own Ideas
1. According to Anthony, who formed the Union, and why did they form it?		
2. Identify three contrasts Anthony makes. What point is she making with each?		
3. In what way is Anthony a freedom fighter?		

Name ______________________ Date ______________

"On Woman's Right to Suffrage" by Susan B. Anthony

Take Notes for Research

As you research **the movement for women's suffrage and arguments made against it,** use the forms below to take notes from your sources. As necessary, continue your notes on the back of this page, on note cards, or in a word-processing document.

Source Information Check one: ☐ Primary Source ☐ Secondary Source

Title: ______________________ Author: ______________

Publication Information: ______________________

Page(s): ______________________

Main Idea: ______________________

____

Quotation or Paraphrase: ______________________

____

Source Information Check one: ☐ Primary Source ☐ Secondary Source

Title: ______________________ Author: ______________

Publication Information: ______________________

Page(s): ______________________

Main Idea: ______________________

____

Quotation or Paraphrase: ______________________

____

Source Information Check one: ☐ Primary Source ☐ Secondary Source

Title: ______________________ Author: ______________

Publication Information: ______________________

Page(s): ______________________

Main Idea: ______________________

____

Quotation or Paraphrase: ______________________

____

Name ______________________________ Date ______________

"On Woman's Right to Suffrage" by Susan B. Anthony

Take Notes for Writing to Sources

Planning Your Argument: Before you begin drafting your **argument**, use the chart below to organize your ideas. Follow the directions at the top of each section of the chart.

1. Clear statement of your claim:
2. Relevant details to support your claim:
3. Notes for your conclusion:

Name ______________________________ Date ______________

from **Address to the Commonwealth Club of San Francisco** by Cesar Chavez

Vocabulary Builder

Selection Vocabulary

exploit implements infamy

A. Directions: *Write one example of people or things that demonstrates the meaning of each word. Follow this example:*

INJUSTICE: an unfair treatment, as when a worker is not paid a fair wage

1. IMPLEMENTS: ______________________________
2. EXPLOIT: ______________________________
3. INFAMY: ______________________________

Academic Vocabulary

expert investigate promote

B. Directions: *Write a response to each question. Make sure to use the italicized word at least once in your response.*

1. Why does *expert* testimony support a claim?

____

____

2. What would you do to *promote* something you believed in?

____

____

3. Why is the Internet helpful when someone must *investigate* a topic?

____

____

Name ______________________________ Date ______________

from **Address to the Commonwealth Club of San Francisco** by Cesar Chavez

Take Notes for Discussion

Before the Partner Discussion: Read the following passage from the selection.

> We attacked that injustice not by complaining; not by seeking handouts; not by becoming soldiers in the War on Poverty.
>
> We organized!
>
> Farm workers acknowledged we had allowed ourselves to become victims in a democratic society—a society where majority rule and collective bargaining are supposed to be more than academic theories or political rhetoric.
>
> And by addressing this historical problem, we created confidence in an entire people's ability to create the future.

During the Discussion: As you discuss each question, take notes on how your partner's ideas either differ from or build upon your own.

Discussion Questions	Other Ideas Expressed	Comparison to My Own Ideas
1. What strategy did the farm workers put into place to combat injustice?		
2. Do you agree that the workers had allowed themselves "to become victims"?		
3. How did Chavez's movement help "an entire [people]" win freedom?		

Name ______________________ Date ______________

from **Address to the Commonwealth Club of San Francisco** by Cesar Chavez

Take Notes for Research

As you research **Chavez's campaign for fair treatment of grape workers,** use the organizer below to take notes from your sources. As necessary, continue your notes on the back of this page, on note cards, or in a word-processing document.

Chavez's Campaign for Fair Treatment for Grape Workers	
Main Idea ______	**Main Idea** ______
Quotation or Paraphrase ______	**Quotation or Paraphrase** ______
Source Information ______	**Source Information** ______
Main Idea ______	**Main Idea** ______
Quotation or Paraphrase ______	**Quotation or Paraphrase** ______
Source Information ______	**Source Information** ______

Name ______________________ Date ______________

from **Address to the Commonwealth Club of San Francisco** by Cesar Chavez

Take Notes for Writing to Sources

Planning Your Poem: Before you begin drafting your **poem,** use the chart below to organize your ideas. Follow the directions at the top of each section.

1. Vivid descriptions from Chavez's speech:
2. Possible words, phrases, and images to use in the poem:
3. Possible rhymes and ideas for rhythm:

Name ______________________ Date ______________

Media: Nonviolence Tree

Vocabulary Builder and Take Notes for Research

Academic Vocabulary

civil convey valid

DIRECTIONS: *Choose the synonym, or word closest in meaning to the vocabulary word.*

		A.	B.	C.
______	1. *civil*	A. private	B. intense	C. public
______	2. *convey*	A. communicate	B. create	C. contradict
______	3. *valid*	A. descriptive	B. trustworthy	C. modern

Take Notes for Research

As you research **Henry David Thoreau and his philosophies,** use the forms below to take notes from your sources. As necessary, continue your notes on the back of this page, on note cards, or in a word-processing document.

Source Information Check one: ☐ Primary Source ☐ Secondary Source

Title: ______________________ Author: ______________

Publication Information: ______________________

Page(s): ______________________

Main Idea: ______________________

____

Quotation or Paraphrase: ______________________

____

Source Information Check one: ☐ Primary Source ☐ Secondary Source

Title: ______________________ Author: ______________

Publication Information: ______________________

Page(s): ______________________

Main Idea: ______________________

____

Quotation or Paraphrase: ______________________

____